Fort Ticonderoga, The Last Campaigns

A View of TICONDEROGA, *from a Point on the North Shore of Lake Champlain.*

Mark Edward Lender

FORT TICONDEROGA,

The Last Campaigns

The War in the North, 1777–1783

WESTHOLME
Yardley

Facing title page: "A View of TICONDEROGA from a Point on the North Shore of Lake Champlain." James Hunter, 1777. (*British Museum/Alamy*)

© 2022 Mark Edward Lender

Westholme Publishing, LLC
904 Edgewood Road
Yardley, Pennsylvania 19067
Visit our Web site at www.westholmepublishing.com

ISBN: 978-1-59416-383-8
Also available as an eBook.

Printed in the United States of America.

For
Aunt Dee and Uncle Ray

CONTENTS

Illustrations

MAPS AND PLANS

ILLUSTRATIONS

PREFACE

ANY REAL ESTATE AGENT will tell you: location is everything. So will a lot of generals. In war, location, if not *everything*, means a great deal. Location can be the key to holding a position or controlling access to some vital terrain or communications route. And it was location that lent Fort Ticonderoga an almost unparalleled importance in the early military history of North America. This book is the story of the fort—and its location—in the later years of the War for American Independence.

Long before even rudimentary roads offered Europeans ready access to the North American interior, water transport was the only practical entrée. This point is central to this narrative. As various colonists settled (and contested) the North, for over a century—from the mid-1600s to the late 1700s—water provided the best means of travel between Canada and New York City. The route led out of Quebec province up the Richelieu River to Lake Champlain and thence to a short portage to Lake George. From the top of Lake George, travel moved overland less than twenty miles to the Hudson River and then south on the river to New York. Parties headed north reversed the route. Travel in either direction, however, had to take Ticonderoga into account.

The Ticonderoga peninsula lay on the southern shore of Lake Champlain virtually at the junction with Lake George. Moreover, it was a geographical choke point. Champlain was only a quarter-mile wide at Ticonderoga, and the fort that rose on its western shore became the gatekeeper to travel and communications up and down the northern waterways. All shipping, from canoes to men-of-war, had to pass below Ticonderoga's threatening guns—guns that dominated the water. As historian Edward P. Hamilton has put it, Fort Ticonderoga was the "Key to a Continent."[1] Location mattered, and it is hardly novel to point out that people have fought over things that matter. Indeed, throughout its history, Ticonderoga would be no stranger to conflict. During the turmoil of the American Revolution, no single fortification in North America was the focus of more military concern; no other military post loomed so large in the public imagination.

Fort Ticonderoga, The Last Campaigns: The War in the North, 1777–1783 concerns the fort's involvement in the final campaigns—both large and small—in the northern theater of the struggle for independence. Some of these operations are well known. In fact, the literature on the 1777 campaign in particular is quite deep.[2] But it has been some time since anyone has devoted a book specifically to Ticonderoga's role in these final campaigns. The story is significant and sometimes dramatic. In 1777, Ticonderoga was a primary target in British Lieutenant General John Burgoyne's effort to crush American resistance in the North and end the rebellion in a decisive stroke. But Burgoyne's eventual defeat at Saratoga brought no final peace to the northern theater, and Ticonderoga would be central to military and political maneuverings—many of them little known but to specialist historians—that would keep the region on edge until the end of the war in 1783.

Having noted what this book is, a word is in order on what it is not. As a military narrative, the history of operations and attendant political implications will take center stage. But the sources invite scholarship into areas only touched on in this book. The British and American garrisons at Ticonderoga included families of enlisted men and officers; there also were civilian laborers, sutlers, teamsters, artisans, and other contractors. They are here only to a limited extent and are largely beyond the ken of my narrative. They deserve a more thorough exploration, and in fact, Ticonderoga's sources hold promise of a local variant of Holly Mayer's classic study of the army's camp followers.[3] There is much more to say on the roles of the American Indians, although I have discussed only the military aspects of their efforts to preserve their homelands. They deserve a fuller treatment in relation to the fort, as their agendas—including their alliances, generally with the British and loyalists—were complex and politically sophisticated, and they left an indelible mark on the northern theater.[4] Ticonderoga was also witness to the Tory diaspora during the war's later years. Again, my narrative touches on but does not delve deeply into these areas. I could go on: Ticonderoga is a fascinating place, and its history leads in many directions I have not pursued. If *Fort Ticonderoga, The Last Campaigns* leads others to follow these paths, well and good.

Chapter 1

A Crossroads of War

L AKE CHAMPLAIN is one of the most beautiful bodies of water in North America. Champlain is also large. Its waters extend north and south for some 120 miles, lapping the shores of the modern states of New York and Vermont and reaching over the Canadian border into the province of Quebec. The lake drains north into the Richelieu River, then on into the St. Lawrence and ultimately to the Atlantic. To Champlain's immediate south is the equally scenic Lake George, itself over thirty miles long. George discharges into Champlain through the short (about three and a half miles) but swift and turbulent La Chute River. The lakes and their related rivers lie in a long and relatively narrow valley system. That geographical pathway, albeit with portages around rapids, falls, and stretches of terra firma, linked the Hudson River with the St. Lawrence; thus the Champlain-Hudson Valley system formed a natural north-south communications corridor.

That corridor was well traveled. American Indians had traversed the long valley along well-established trails and its two large lakes since time immemorial. In their comings and goings, they crossed a prominent and still picturesque point of land on Champlain's western bank at the mouth of the La Chute. The peninsula afforded a relatively manageable mile-and-a-half-long portage to and from Lake George. The Iroquois aptly called the place *tekontaró:ken*, meaning roughly "it is at the junction of two waterways." And from this Iroquois origin, the British would call the site "Ticonderoga."[1]

The Ticonderoga region (and we will use the British place name from now on), like the lakes that flank it, is stunningly beautiful. The Adirondack Mountains lie to the immediate west, and across Champlain, the Green Mountains of Vermont rise in the distance. Today the local towns are mostly small and often quaint, as is the modern village of Ticonderoga. In spring and summer, the high peaks and lakes draw thousands of hikers and campers, and the hundreds of smaller lakes and streams lure legions of boaters and anglers. In the autumn, the mountains blaze with color, and the winters, which can be severe, nevertheless are alive with the full run of winter sports. Vacation homes dot the lake shores and scenic valleys, and tourism is the lifeblood of the regional economy. Few who visit the area ever forget it.

If a lively region today, through the mid-eighteenth century, the Ticonderoga area was sparsely settled. Yet the Ticonderoga name was familiar to thousands of colonial Americans who never set foot there. They knew it not so much as a vital carrying place between Lakes Champlain and George, although they certainly knew it as such. Rather, it was memorable as a seat of war.

The location of Ticonderoga mattered even before European exploration and colonization of North America. The extensive Champlain-Hudson Valley system (a subsystem of the larger Appalachian Valley) was part of "the Great Indian Warpath," a network of long-established Indian foot trails that stretched throughout the Appalachian Mountains chain from upper New York State to modern Alabama. Later branches of the warpath wound their ways well into the Trans-Appalachian West. Any number of tribes used the path to trade, but also to raid, sometimes over considerable distances. In fact, the precolonial Ticonderoga area was far from a peaceful place.[2]

The French were the first Europeans to see Lake Champlain, and they quickly discovered they had walked into a hostile environment. On July 30, 1609, on his first exploration of the lake that bears his name, Samuel de Champlain and a few other Frenchmen, as auxiliaries, joined a war party of Huron, Algonquin, and Montagnais Indians. The Indians were looking for trouble, and they found it when they came upon a Mohawk compound on the Ticonderoga peninsula very near the site of the eventual fort. The Mohawks were one of the region's dominant tribes, and it was a foolish party indeed that took to the Great Warpath in Mohawk territory without a prior understanding with the tribe. Champlain and his party had no such understanding, and the Indians the French accompanied had come uninvited as well. When combat ensued, Champlain and the Frenchmen became involved. To the astonishment of the more-numerous Mohawks, who had no knowledge of gunpowder or firearms, the French quickly shot and killed several Indians. This initial meeting did nothing for long-term Mohawk relations with the French.[3] Only briefly chastened, the Mohawks remained jealous of their local preeminence and hostile to French intruders. In 1666, however, the French, once again traversing the Ticonderoga area, struck the Mohawks twice in retaliation for Mohawk raids on the Hurons and other French-allied tribes. (The French operations represented the first use of regular troops in North America.) The Mohawks and the French were never fully reconciled, although the Mohawks came to terms in 1667, and in 1701, a broader treaty with many tribes negotiated in Montreal (the Peace of Montreal) brought peace for a couple of decades.[4] Even so, travel on the warpath near Ticonderoga proceeded with a regard for the Mohawk presence.

As European settlement began in earnest in the late seventeenth and early eighteenth centuries, violence assumed an extensive and much grimmer dimension. Contests between the French and Indians blended with European imperial rivalries. The long Champlain-Hudson Valley corridor became a military thoroughfare as the French and British used it to press their territorial claims. The French, who certainly had penetrated the northern lakes region well before other Europeans, asserted ownership based on discovery; their claims encompassed all territory in which waters flowed north to the St. Lawrence. The French also took the first steps toward actual settlement of the Ticonderoga peninsula.

From time to time, various Frenchmen tried their hands at fur trading at the site. Chief among these was a somewhat shady lieutenant in a French regiment, Philippe de Carrion, sieur du Fresnoy. Carrion established a fur trading post on the peninsula sometime in the late 1600s. Knowing that trade moved up and down the two lakes, Carrion obviously had an eye for prime commercial real estate. According to some accounts, roving hunters, fur trappers, and some rather disreputable characters used Carrion's post as a source of temporary refuge, trade, and supplies. The post was something akin, as historian Michael O. Lugusz has rather prosaically put it, to "a modern-day truck stop and shopping center located at a critical junction." Carrion also carried on a brisk and illegal trade in brandy with the Indians. For years, travelers supposedly referred to the locale as "Carrion's trading post."[5] Whatever contemporaries called the place, eventually France would have to fight to make good its claim to it.

The British, having conquered the Dutch colony of New Netherlands, of which Albany sat on the northern frontier (some 222 miles south of French Montreal), rejected French pretensions. They probed north with desultory fighting erupting in the late 1600s, and Ticonderoga quickly became part of the military narrative. In July 1691, Peter Schuyler, the sometime mayor of Albany and occasional acting governor of New York province, marched a force north, reacting to intelligence that the French were pressing south against Albany. Schuyler used Ticonderoga as a rendezvous with Mohawk allies before moving farther north.[6] His mission resulted in some stiff fighting, although it settled nothing. It was, however, a prelude to Ticonderoga's role in the deadly serious warfare to come. (Not incidentally, Peter Schuyler was great-uncle to Continental Major General Philip Schuyler, who will figure prominently later in this narrative.)[7]

Fighting between Britain and France was periodic over the late seventeenth and first half of the eighteenth centuries. Beginning with King William's War in 1688 (the American phase of what Europeans called the Nine Years' War or the War of the Grand Alliance), the imperial powers waged four major conflicts in North America. The first three of these began in Europe and spread to America, which the European antagonists generally considered a secondary theater. During King William's War (1689–97), Queen Anne's War (1702–13), and King George's War (1744–48), Britain and France usually restricted their regular forces to European operations; thus the militia and irregular forces of the British colonies and of New France, plus their respective Indian allies, carried the burdens of combat. There were episodes of vicious fighting in these earlier conflicts, but without a major commitment of regular forces to North America neither side had the strength to drive its opponent from the continent. The conflicts ended with territorial adjustments or a return to status quo ante.[8] And except for Peter Schuyler's brief sojourn in the area, none of these struggles involved significant operations in the Champlain Valley region, let alone at Ticonderoga.

This relative calm ended in 1754 with the outbreak of the Seven Years' War—or, as Americans have been wont to call it, the French and Indian War. Formal declarations of war followed in 1755. The conflict had American origins as French and Indian forces clashed with Virginian, and soon British, troops over access to the Ohio River Valley. Now the European powers committed their regular armies to a showdown fight; British war aims envisioned the conquest of New France and the end of the French colonial empire in North America. With the British seeking the most direct route to Quebec, the heart of New France, the war quickly moved into the Lake Champlain-Lake George corridor.

Major combat in the region began in 1755. In August, Sir William Johnson, leading a mixed force of colonial troops and Mohawk allies, moved north intending to assault the French bastion of Fort St. Frédéric at Crown Point on Lake Champlain. Learning of Johnson's advance, the French sallied from St. Frédéric, built and garrisoned an entrenched camp at Ticonderoga, and then the greater part of the force moved south toward Lake George. The armies met on September 8, and after the bruising and drawn-out Battle of Lake George, the colonials and Mohawks defeated the French, capturing their badly wounded general, Jean Erdman (or Jean-Armand), the Baron Dieskau.[9] But the French army got away, and that army proved nothing if not resilient.

The defeat at Lake George forced the French to rethink their defenses. With the British now in possession of Lake George—and building Fort William Henry to make good their occupation—control of the lakes corridor was more important than ever for New France. Fort St. Frédéric was too far from the junction of the lakes to offer the best defense against a further British push north. Besides, St. Frédéric was twenty years old and not designed to withstand heavy artillery fire. That being the case, the Ticonderoga peninsula, some thirteen miles below Crown Point and at the immediate choke point between the lakes, seemed a better location for a defensive work. A fort there could block British efforts to move across the short portage from Lake George and, at the same time, serve as a staging point for French operations to the south. The French decided to build.

The governor of New France, Pierre de Rigaud de Vaudreuil de Cavagnial (the marquis de Vaudreuil),[10] gave the construction contract to his cousin, the French-Canadian military engineer Michel Chartier de Lotbinière. Lotbinière planned a fort designed on the lines of the great French engineer Sébastien Le Prestre de Vauban, the preeminent European military architect of the era. The design called for a "star fort," with pointed bastions projecting from the four corners of an inner square. The square would contain a central parade surrounded by barracks, storage buildings, stables, and other support structures. A dry moat and a series of outer works would add to the fort's defenses. Lotbinière initially called his project Fort Vaudreuil after his governor cousin, but the name quickly became Fort Carillon (as Vaudreuil already had ordered), almost certainly an echo of Philippe de Carrion, who had settled on the site in the late seventeenth century.[11]

Lotbinière built in stages. French troops constructed the central fort of dressed timber with earth fill between the timbers; at about the same time, labor began on an earthwork to cover approaches from the La Chute River. Work commenced on the four bastions in late 1755 and continued through February 1756. Troops intended to dress the walls—some fourteen feet thick—with stone quarried from a site conveniently located only a mile from the fort. But the French never completed the stone facing. They eventually did underpin some sections of the walls with supporting masonry, but except for the demilune (a strong work mounting artillery and projecting west from the main wall of the fort) and counterscarps (the outer walls of protective ditches around the fort), Carillon's walls remained timbered and earthen. This was no real demerit, as the softer walls could absorb the shock from all but the heaviest artillery of the day. The barracks and most inner structures, however, were of stone, and the builders had most of them completed by 1758. Other outworks protected approaches from the land side (the northwest), the most likely direction of any attack. Finally, the garrison mounted artillery shipped from Montreal and St. Frédéric on the bastions and in the various outworks.

The fort wasn't perfect: some officers thought that the fort was too small, that the barracks were too high and too nice a target for enemy artillery, that the main fortification was too far from Lake Champlain, that some of the masonry was of poor quality, that the powder magazine—carved out of solid rock beneath one of the bastions—leaked, and that too much high ground overlooked the fort. It was enough for many to question Lotbinière's competence.[12] Still, whatever its faults, Fort Carillon was a formidable post, and the British took notice.

The war did not wait for the French to finish the fort. In 1757, General Louis-Joseph de Montcalm took the war to the enemy. His regulars and Indian allies sortied from Carillon and famously took Fort William Henry. It was the first in a string of French victories in the North that shocked Britain and its colonies. Determined to right their foundering ship, the following year the British sent Major General James Abercrombie with some fifteen thousand or sixteen thousand (accounts vary) regulars and provincials to take Carillon preparatory to an advance on Montreal. Montcalm had fewer than four thousand troops to defend Carillon, but he intended to fight. And unfortunately for Abercrombie, the outnumbered but determined Frenchmen came up with an ingenious defense.

As Abercrombie closed in, Montcalm's men feverishly constructed a timber breastwork line along a low ridge about three-quarters of a mile northwest of the fort. They placed an abatis—a line of cut branches with sharpened ends pointing out—in front of the timber breastworks. The work was completed in two frantic days. These were the "French Lines," so called by the British, and later by the Americans, who would use them during their own occupations of Ticonderoga. On July 8, Abercrombie, advised that the French Lines were vulnerable, launched a frontal assault. It was a disaster. The British suffered some two thousand casualties and beat a hasty retreat up Lake George. Carillon had weathered its first real storm.

It did not weather a second. The British came back in 1759, and they came back smarter. In July, Jeffery Amherst, the new British commander in chief, advanced on Ticonderoga with some eleven thousand men, and he mounted artillery on nearby high ground. On July 23, Amherst, with no thoughts of any suicidal frontal assault, prepared for a siege. It was hardly necessary. In Carillon, Brigadier General François-Charles de Bourlamaque was badly outnumbered,[13] and obeying orders from Montcalm (then in Canada), on July 26 he set a fuse to blow up as much of the fort as he could—an attempt only partially successful—and then got his men away. The British moved in and renamed the post Fort Ticonderoga.

Amherst took the bulk of his army north to winter at Crown Point, leaving only a skeleton garrison at Ticonderoga. Over the rest of the year, these lonely men largely repaired the damaged fort, which had become a backwater as the war closed in on Canada. The days of New France were numbered, the outcome all but sealed with the fall of Quebec later in the year. The war ended formally in 1763, and the British saw no reason to pay further attention to the Key to the Continent, for which so much British blood had been shed. Ticonderoga's garrison generally numbered merely a few dozen enlisted men and a couple of officers who functioned more as caretakers than as soldiers. Over the following decade, the fort served only as a depot, and during the years of neglect, its walls fell into disrepair and the outer works deteriorated. By spring 1775, the garrison comprised only a weak detachment of the 26th Regiment of Foot—forty-two men and a lieutenant under Captain William Delaplace.[14] And Delaplace could be excused for thinking the rest of the world had forgotten about the crumbling stronghold he commanded.

In fact, events overtook Delaplace before he learned that the British government had new plans for his post. A fire had badly damaged Crown Point in 1773, and royal authorities considered repairs

Opposite: "A Plan of the Town and Fort of Carillon at Ticonderoga," engraved and published by Thomas Jefferys in 1758. This plan shows the British formation to the left, followed by the French postitions along the Height of Carillon toward the center, and the fort and town to the right. The battle here on July 8, 1758, was a stunning defeat for the British and American colonial troops under James Abercrombie. Against relatively light losses the heavily out-numbered French, led by Louis-Joseph de Montcalm, inflicted some 1,980 casualties, including at least 547 killed in action. In early 1777, Anthony Wayne reported some of his Ticonderoga garrison were using the bones of Abercrombie's men as tent pegs. (*Norman B. Leventhal Map & Education Center, Boston Public Library*)

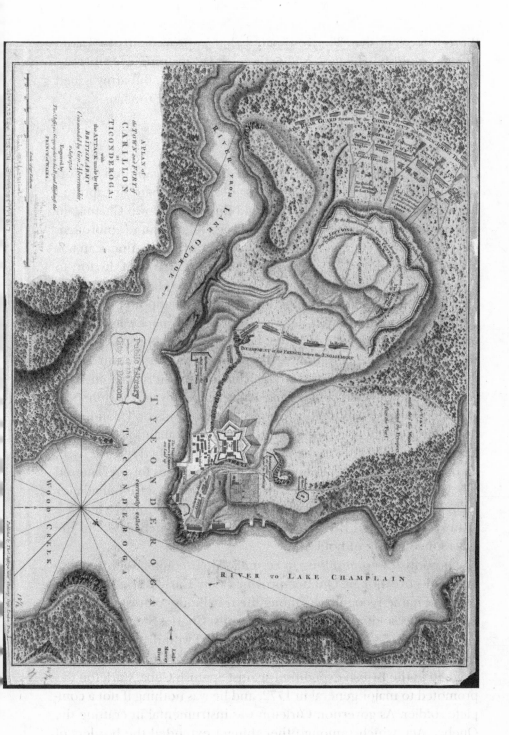

there too expensive. They estimated that improvements to Ticonderoga would be cheaper, and with concerns growing over increasingly strained relations with the American colonies, the army issued orders to refortify Ticonderoga. But the orders were too late.

On May 10, 1775, Ethan Allen and Benedict Arnold captured the fort in a bloodless coup de main. Then Arnold, using whatever captured British boats and other vessels he could find, swept down Champlain and made it an American lake. Ticonderoga then became embroiled, directly and indirectly, in the fortunes of the unfolding American war effort. In December 1775, Colonel Henry Knox arrived at the fort to collect guns for the rebel army besieging Boston. He found the necessary ordnance, but he complained that the manpower at Ticonderoga was so limited that he was barely able to pack the guns for transport. Yet in the dead of winter, he organized an epic trek to Cambridge, Massachusetts, with artillery gathered not only from Ticonderoga, but also from Fort George (on the southern end of Lake George), Crown Point, and as far north as Chambly and St. John's in Quebec province. Mounted above Boston, the guns of Ticonderoga then played a vital role in the British decision to abandon the city in March 1776.[15] Still later in the year, the war approached the fort itself. Ticonderoga and Crown Point became rallying points for the battered rebel army pulling back from its disastrous effort to seize Canada for the revolution. Americans looked to the northern bastion as a bulwark against an expected British counterthrust from Quebec. Could the Key to the Continent hold?

The British were not long in coming. Their commander was general and governor of Quebec province Guy Carleton, a man with plenty of name recognition among the rebellious colonists. Carleton was a veteran soldier who had fought against Charles Stuart—"Bonnie Prince Charlie"—at Culloden; he then served with distinction in the European theater of the Seven Years' War, and in 1762, he even campaigned in the British expedition against Spanish Cuba. Carleton was promoted to major general in 1772, and he was nothing if not a complete soldier. As governor, Carleton was instrumental in crafting the Quebec Act, which (among other things) extended the borders of

Guy Carleton (1724-1808). General and governor of Quebec province, Carleton orchestrated the British campaign that drove the Americans out of Canada in 1776. His
decision not to assault Ticonderoga in October—the fort and its related positions appeared too strong—allowed the rebels invaluable time to stabilize the northern theater. He resigned in some pique when John Burgoyne was assigned to command the
1777 campaign; but before his departure for Britain, Carleton nevertheless did his
best to marshal resources for Burgoyne's army. (*New York Public Library*)

Quebec to include much of Trans-Appalachia, and granted religious
freedom to Catholic Canadians—provisions that enraged many American colonials.[16] Having withstood Arnold's siege of Quebec over the
1775–76 winter, Carleton led the offensive that drove the Americans
from Canada in spring 1776. In the summer he moved south, up the
Richelieu, headed for Lake Champlain and Ticonderoga. His second-
in-command was another major general, one John Burgoyne, of
whom we will learn much more—but later.

At Ticonderoga, the Americans waited under Major General Horatio Gates. History has taken a dim view of Gates; later during the war
he was involved in political machinations against George Washington's
position as commander in chief and, in 1780, he saw his military reputation virtually destroyed in his catastrophic defeat at Camden, South
Carolina. Yet he was a British veteran of long service. He had seen
combat in America during the Seven Years' War and had learned the

intricacies of army administration. The postwar British army offered few prospects for a military career, and in 1769, Gates sold his commission and immigrated to Virginia. As the imperial crisis deepened, he became an ardent patriot, and when war erupted he offered his services to the rebel cause. Commissioned a brigadier general, Gates brought much-needed administrative talent to the fledgling American military. Prior to reporting to Ticonderoga, he had capably served as Washington's adjutant general. He was no military lightweight.

In fact, at Ticonderoga in June 1776, Gates was the right man in the right place at the right time. Promoted to major general, he energetically directed the reorganization of the rebels' battered Northern Army. As units came south from Canada and reported from other locations as reinforcements, he saw to recruiting, supply, and myriad administrative tasks. There is no question that Gates's efficient performance bolstered sagging American morale. By July he commanded some twelve thousand men and had them hard at work improving Ticonderoga's defenses, including the old French Lines. Gates also supported Benedict Arnold as Arnold frantically labored to create a rebel fleet capable of fending off Carleton, who had stopped at St. John's to assemble a British fleet. Gates, whatever misfortunes lay ahead in his career, was preparing to fight in summer 1776.[17]

But he didn't have to. As events developed, Arnold did the fighting in a naval slugfest. On October 11, he engaged Carleton's flotilla at Valcour Island, some sixty-eight miles above Ticonderoga. Outnumbered and outgunned, Arnold fought the British to a standstill and then led a daring after-dark withdrawal up the lake toward the fort. Only four of his gunboats survived the ordeal, but many of his crews escaped to Ticonderoga, while Arnold himself finally reached safety at Crown Point. Arnold, aware of Carleton's pursuit and of the vulnerability of the position at Crown Point, destroyed the works there and pulled back to Ticonderoga.[18] He would fight another day.

Although a tactical defeat, Valcour Island proved a strategic victory. Even in defeat, Arnold's gritty performance had impressed the British. In fact, the British were more impressed than were some Americans who saw only Arnold's loss of the patriot vessels. New Jersey's brigadier, William Maxwell, who didn't like Arnold anyway, caustically dismissed Arnold's fight as "a pretty piece of admiralty." Absent Maxwell's sar-

Horatio Gates (1727-1806). Based at Fort Ticonderoga, Gates admirably reorganized the northern American army after its 1776 retreat from Canada. In 1777 he heatedly disputed the northern command with Philip Schuyler, finally replacing him after British General John Burgoyne took the fort and popular opinion turned against Schuyler. Gates went on to defeat Burgoyne at Saratoga in October. In 1780 he was disastrously defeated at the Battle of Camden in South Carolina, and his military reputation never recovered. Portrait by Gilbert Stuart, c. 1794. (*Metropolitan Museum of Art*)

casm, other patriots were just as critical.[19] But Lieutenant James Hadden, a Royal Artillery officer who served on one of Carleton's gunboats during the action, thought otherwise. He willingly conceded that Arnold's skillful nighttime retreat especially "did great honor to *Gen'l Arnold*, who Acted as Admiral to the Rebel Fleet."[20] Clearly the Americans, if as determined as Arnold's crews at Valcour Island, were not to be taken lightly.

Moreover, intelligence indicated the rebels at Ticonderoga were numerous and well prepared. At the ruins of Crown Point, which the British occupied after Valcour Island, Carleton initially decided to rebuild the partially destroyed barracks and defensive works. The post would serve as a support base for further operations to the south or as winter quarters. But the redcoat commander took pause when he received reports estimating the Ticonderoga garrison at twelve thousand to fourteen thousand men (a high but fairly accurate approximation). A few half-hearted probes of the patriots' outer lines seemed to confirm American strength. Sailing up the lake, Carleton personally inspected Ticonderoga's works from the water, finding them to all appearances quite strong. Second thoughts about continuing the campaign hardened to genuine doubt, and Carleton soon concluded it simply was too late in the season to tackle so strong and well prepared an enemy. Thus, in mid-November, he halted work at Crown Point and began leading his men back to Canada for the winter.[21] Carleton fully intended to come back. He was still convinced a drive through Ticonderoga to Albany, cutting New England off from colonies to the south, was the key to victory. But for the present, the northern campaign was over, and for the time being, Ticonderoga and the northern front was safe. The Key to the Continent remained locked.

Chapter 2

Winter to Spring 1776–1777: Anthony Wayne and the Challenge of Command

WITH CARLETON'S DEPARTURE, there was no reason to maintain a large garrison at Ticonderoga. Accordingly, Gates prepared to move the bulk of his troops south to reinforce the main rebel army under Washington. The regiments began their march over the last days of November, and all of the troops were en route by the first days of December. As far as Washington was concerned, Gates could not march fast enough. Indeed, the American commander in chief was in desperate straits. Even as Carleton withdrew to Canada, the British were on the move in the middle theater; they had forced Washington through New Jersey and across the Delaware River into Pennsylvania. But Gates brought his men safely to Washington's camp on December 22, and many of the Ticonderoga veterans saw action in the astonishing December 26 raid on Trenton.[1] It was a measure of payback for their tribulations in the North.

As Washington counterattacked in New Jersey, the war in the North entered something of a hiatus. On November 18, as Gates prepared his departure, Colonel Anthony Wayne assumed command at Ticonderoga. There was every expectation that the British would be back in 1777, and Wayne had long been of the opinion that Howe would move up the Hudson to meet redcoats advancing out of Canada. In that case, Ticonderoga again would be the critical post if patriots were to prevent the juncture of the British armies.[2] But the new post commandant had inherited a token force of only some 1,400 effective men, including troops on Mount Independence. How was he to hold Ticonderoga and its associated posts, let alone improve their defenses, with such a paltry garrison? His struggle to do so was the story of the fort's winter and spring 1776-1777.

Ticonderoga was Anthony Wayne's first independent command, and he had earned the responsibility. Wayne hailed from Chester County, Pennsylvania, the son of a prosperous tanner of considerable local social standing. Educated at a private academy and then at the College of Philadelphia (today's University of Pennsylvania), Wayne subsequently worked in his father's tannery and as a surveyor. He prospered, and a political ascent followed economic success. Elected to the Pennsylvania assembly, Wayne declared early for independence, and in 1775, he raised a volunteer militia unit. The following year Congress commissioned him a Continental colonel. Commanding the 4th Pennsylvania Regiment, Wayne marched north to bolster the failing patriot assault on Quebec. The American effort ultimately failed disastrously, but Wayne proved a talented combat officer. After the retreat to Ticonderoga, he worked with Gates to restore the order and morale of the routed patriots. The colonel played a leading role in improving the defenses of the fort and its outer works, and his Pennsylvanians were commonly recognized as among the American army's best.[3] Gates had full confidence in him.

So did Major General Philip Schuyler, the commander of the army's Northern Department. Schuyler was a key individual in the Ticonderoga narrative. Born in 1733 in Albany to a family of wealth, political influence, and a sense of public duty, he was a true colonial patrician. Service in the Seven Years' War taught him invaluable lessons in quartermaster operations. He went on to serve in the New York provincial assembly and, with the coming of the Revolution, in the Continental Congress. As a major general, Schuyler had hoped to lead

Philip Schuyler (1733-1804). Schuyler was an effective army administrator who labored to keep the Northern Department, including the Ticonderoga garrison, supplied. Schuyler dueled with Horatio Gates for command of the department, and in May 1777 Congress (where Schuyler was a member) finally restored him to command. However, Congress relieved him in favor of Gates after Ticonderoga fell to Burgoyne in July. A later court martial found Schuyler blameless in the loss of the fort. Portrait by John Trumbull, 1792. (*Yale University Art Gallery*)

the American invasion of Canada personally. Poor health, however, saw him delegate the task to Richard Montgomery.[4]

Despite the invasion's failure, Schuyler retained Washington's confidence as patriots tried to stabilize the northern front. It was a considerable responsibility. The Northern Department (after a number of boundary adjustments by the Continental Congress) was vast. Schuyler was accountable for operations in the present Vermont (then the New Hampshire Grants, a region contested by New York, New Hampshire, and even Massachusetts), and all of New York State north of the Hudson Highlands.[5] While much of the department saw at least some fighting, the key operational areas were the Ticonderoga region and the river valleys west of Albany all the way to Oswego on Lake Ontario. Canada had been a separate department with Gates in command, and when the American forces there retreated, Gates argued he should still command the units that pulled back to Crown Point and Ticonderoga. Congress decided otherwise, and Gates commanded at Ticonderoga as Schuyler's subordinate.[6] The two major generals were never friends, but they worked together professionally. When Gates left Wayne in command, Schuyler, fully aware of Wayne's record, raised no objection.

As Ticonderoga's new commandant, Wayne depended heavily on his relationship with Schuyler, who proved a sympathetic superior. This was fortunate, for Wayne needed all the help he could get. At peak strength, Gates had well over twelve thousand men. Wayne had nowhere near that number to tackle major construction and engineering projects—much less to defend the region. Moreover, he commanded a garrison that, for the time being, was relatively isolated, fearful of attack, sometimes short of key supplies, and facing serious medical and morale problems. Throughout his command at Ticonderoga, he was multitasking virtually every day, dealing with problems simultaneously—and usually with an eye over his shoulder lest the British try something. The colonel had his work cut out for him.

In fact, Wayne's was not a happy command. The Pennsylvanian was at heart a combat officer with little affinity for garrison duty and administrative tedium. Besides, the colonel simply did not like Ticonderoga. The region's scenic beauty was lost on him, and even before taking command, Wayne had found the place distressing. He had lamented to a friend that Ticonderoga "appears to be the last part of the world that God made & I have some ground to believe it was finished in the dark." He compared the fort to "the ancient Golgotha or place of skulls—they are so plenty here that our people for want of other vessels drink out of them whilst the soldiers make tent pins of the shin and thigh bones of Abercrombies men."[7] Over his months in command, he saw no reason to change his mind. As late as April 1777, shortly before his relief, he wrote a family friend, "My situation as Commandant of this post would subject me to insult and contempt *as a prisoner.*"[8] Anthony Wayne did not mince words.

At least in terms of the post's physical state, Wayne had a great deal to dislike. In fact he had inherited a fort in very poor condition. Gates, good as he was at reorganizing the Northern Army, had neither the time nor the resources to devote to all of the major building initiatives the fort and its surrounding defensive works required. And existing works were problematic. The old French Lines were in poor repair, although since the retreat from Canada, garrison troops had been working to improve them, building new breastworks along the traces of the old lines. The high ground on Mount Hope, west of the lines, at least had a strong redoubt; but a sawmill on the La Chute, critical for supporting new construction, lay unprotected to the south of Mount Hope. An antishipping boom and a flimsy floating walkway across the narrow (about a quarter-mile) section of the lake connected Ticonderoga to the eastern shore. But both needed reinforcement, if not replacement.

The rebels called the high ground immediately behind the eastern shore Mount Independence, named in celebration when the garrison learned Congress had issued the Declaration of Independence in July 1776. Through late 1776, the "mountain" held a number (we don't know how many) of regimental hospitals, but it was only lightly defended.[9] If properly garrisoned, however, Mount Independence had defensive potential. Its summit was relatively flat with room to build, and its slopes would be difficult to attack in the face of determined opposition. Artillery on the summit and in shoreline redoubts would command the lake, and the steep banks of East Creek could impede any attack from the north. Marshy ground to the south offered protection from that direction. In time, rebels would understand that Independence was actually a better position than the old fort itself. Schuyler opined that if the garrison was not strong enough to hold the fort and its outworks, then "Mount Independence and the Naval Forces on Lake George are to claim all our attention."[10] The necessary "attention," however, would require skilled engineering and resources.

To the southwest of the fort, also across a narrow stretch of water, rose a prominent eminence locally known as Sugar Loaf, which the Americans had renamed Mount Defiance—a promontory without any defensive works. Mount Defiance was a special case. It rose about six hundred feet above the lakes, and the crest afforded a magnificent prospect of the region. There were wonderful views of the Green Mountains across Lake Champlain to the east and a vista reaching for miles down Champlain to the north, and the lower sections of Lake George were just visible to the south. There was (and is) a bird's-eye view of the fort below and even of Mount Independence across Champlain—and Mount Defiance was within artillery range of both. The mountain was the very definition of key terrain.

Thus began a debate that reverberated over the better part of a year. During Gates's command in 1776, John Trumbull—the future artist of the Revolution, then deputy adjutant general of the Northern Army[11]—pointed out the dangerous significance of the mountain. He evoked only ridicule, however, from other officers who insisted Defiance posed no threat. Artillery on the mountain, they claimed, would be out of range. Trumbull's answer was to have two shots fired, one from a twelve-pounder on Mount Independence and one from a six-pounder from the fort glacis—and both easily carried to Defiance.

Yet Trumbull's doubters were unimpressed. The mountain's steep grade and rough terrain, they retorted, would prevent any sizable enemy force from reaching the top, much less dragging artillery up there. Undeterred, Trumbull led Wayne, Benedict Arnold, and several other officers on a hike up the mountain. It was steep climb, but they "clambered to the summit in a short time." A group of sightseeing soldiers did the same. Point proven. Based on his findings, Trumbull held that a strong post atop Mount Defiance would not only command Ticonderoga, it also could better protect the critical passage between Lakes Champlain and George. And it could do so at a far cheaper cost than the expense necessary to maintain the extensive works around the fort and a garrison of ten thousand or more. Trumbull drew up a detailed proposal and sent copies to Gates, Schuyler, and Congress. To the young officer's chagrin, no one acted; and Trumbull's ideas left the fort along with him later in 1776.[12]

Despite Trumbull's disappointment, it would be unfair to think the other officers were obtuse. Many of them understood the potential threat of an undefended Defiance, and had resources permitted they might have addressed it. Schuyler, as we will soon see, wanted a blockhouse built on the summit. But there was some thought that defending Defiance was unnecessary. This reasoning held that a strong position on Mount Hope, west of the French Lines, would prevent any significant enemy move around Ticonderoga's left, and thus that any advance to Defiance therefore was unlikely.[13] As long as the patriots held Mount Hope, a garrison on Mount Defiance seemed a waste of manpower at a time Ticonderoga had none to waste. Thus Mount Defiance became a secondary concern—a low priority that would come back to haunt the rebels within months.

All things considered, defending Ticonderoga would be a challenge. With Guy Carleton gone, the rebels knew little about what the British might do next or when they might attempt it. Wayne took standard security precautions, sending out scouts, interrogating the occasional prisoner, and posting sentries. Indeed, he threatened sentries caught sleeping on duty with death.[14] (Wayne had a no-nonsense aspect to his character.) In mid-February the colonel put everyone on alert when he received reports of a British scouting mission approaching the fort. It was a false alarm, but he was taking no chances. In case of an alarm, his standing orders called for troops to report to their assigned posts and to "defend them to the last extremity."[15] And if they did fight to the last, some of them would go down memorably. Thinking that "all action" ultimately would come down to the bayonet, Wayne ordered all regiments to designate a quarter of their men to train with thirteen-foot spears for close-quarter defense. They would confront any British storming party with a "Forest of Spears—whose unexpected appearance must be Dreadful to our Enemies—and add Confidence to our own Troops."[16]

In Schuyler's view, Wayne's vigilance was only prudent. The department commander was unconvinced Carleton was really finished for the winter, and in January he told Washington as much. With Lake Champlain frozen, the New Yorker wrote the commander in chief, he considered a British coup de main over the ice quite likely. In fact, Schuyler's intelligence sources warned (falsely as it turned out) that Ticonderoga could expect an attack as soon as the ice was thick enough to support an expedition. Washington in turn used the possibility of an over-the-ice coup to urge the states to hasten recruiting efforts.[17] It was only in March, with the lake thawed, that Schuyler relaxed his fear. Still, he predicted that even if the British left Ticonderoga alone for the winter, they would come back up Champlain "very early in the Spring."[18] Schuyler never stopped believing the enemy might appear at any moment; but as department commander such worries were part of his job.

Wayne and Schuyler were not the only ones skittish about Ticonderoga's security. Jonathan Trumbull Jr.—paymaster of the Northern

Army, older brother of John, and son of Connecticut Governor Jonathan Trumbull Sr.—delighted in telling his father of an incident, funny by itself, but indicative of the garrison's frayed nerves. In mid-December, he reported "the appearance of a hay boat on the lake, which, to the timid apprehensions of its beholders at *Crown-Point*, was magnified into a large ship of force, with guns, &c, supposed to be the enemy approaching." As the rebels fled to Ticonderoga and alarmed the fort, "all hands" set to work "remounting their cannon, &c, and making every preparation for defence, when the poor harmless boat arrived at the wharf, and relieved their anxious fears. All is now quiet, and will be now, unless the enemy take it in their heads to venture on the ice, which may possibly be. I hope by new-year to leave this place."[19] No doubt Anthony Wayne hoped the same thing.

Even as they looked to the garrison's safety, Wayne and Schuyler labored to provision and shelter the troops and keep them healthy. The fort was small, so its existing barracks could comfortably accommodate fewer than seven hundred troops, and even that would be a squeeze. Senior officers used the barracks for headquarters, and some lived there in relative comfort; but most of the junior officers and rank and file sheltered outside of the fort in tents and in huts (hut construction had begun in the summer), many of them in a major camp at the French Lines. No one enjoyed deluxe accommodations, and adequate shelter would remain a major concern. For the time being, however, the small size of the garrison made the housing issue manageable—if not comfortable.

Yet Ticonderoga was short of more than shelter. Effective troops needed clothing, shoes, blankets, and, of course, adequate rations. Many of these necessities were periodically in short supply. Only days after assuming command, Wayne notified Gates he could keep the garrison going only as long as "we are properly supplied with provisions, clothing, soap, &c, &c, articles which you know are much wanted."[20] The occasional shortages of these "much wanted" articles were more annoying than crippling to the garrison, but some wants were more persistent than others. Over the winter and into the early spring, clothing was a constant concern. Heavy fatigue work regularly wore out garments, and new supplies were in steady demand. Arriving troops often lacked uniforms or clothing to allow outside work in cold weather. Blankets and sometimes tents were in short supply, as were shoes and socks, and the soldiery clamored for them against the cold.[21]

The cold could be real enough. Indeed, winters at the foot of the Adirondack Mountains can be brutal. Average December temperatures for the Ticonderoga area range from 16 to 33 degrees Fahrenheit but have dropped as low as minus 32 degrees. Temperatures below zero are not unusual through March.[22] There were cold snaps at the fort early in 1777, and Wayne kept the soldiery busy cutting firewood.[23] But in general, the rebel garrison was lucky over winter 1776–77. Surgeon's mate James Thacher, who had joined his Massachusetts regiment at Ticonderoga in September 1776, remarked on the relatively "mild and temperate" weather. In December he noted that Lake Champlain was frozen a foot thick and that the ground was snow covered but that the storms had not been severe "and the cold not so intense as might be expected in a northern climate." By late February 1777, Schuyler reported Champlain was open, and in March he agreed with Thacher that the lake was "free from ice in its whole extent."[24]

On the whole, the soldiery coped. Quartermaster and commissary personnel, with Wayne and Schuyler urging them on, managed to get shipments through in time to prevent real difficulties. The garrison never starved. Certainly the officers didn't. The journal of the post engineer, Colonel Jeduthan Baldwin, recorded a steady schedule of socializing among commissioned ranks, with dinners washed down with tea, punch, and wine. Wives attended frequently. The fare may not have been of gourmet caliber, but there is no indication that there was any lack of comestibles.[25]

The enlisted men enjoyed no fine dining, but they were fed. In fact, they were relatively easy to feed because they were so few. Records from late January indicate there were enough stocks of meat and other foodstuffs to sustain the garrison of barely three thousand men and camp followers (including the sick). There were occasional complaints about shortages of salted meat, but rations generally were adequate.[26] A Massachusetts militia officer reported that whatever else the troops lacked, they enjoyed "good" stocks of "meat & Bread & peas." If shipments of food and meat (and "meat" could mean cattle on the hoof) were sometimes late, they got through soon enough to prevent anything remotely akin to periods of acute hunger. Wayne did cut back on rum issues when supplies ran short, which no doubt caused grumbling in the ranks.[27] But grumbling did not constitute a crisis.

The fact is that as difficult as living and working conditions sometimes were at Ticonderoga during winter 1776–77—and there is no denying they frequently were difficult—those complications never approached the later ordeals at Valley Forge (1777–78) and Morristown (1779–80). The troops at Ticonderoga were fortunate in comparison.

The relatively mild winter was a Wayne ally in a drawn-out campaign against disease. In this he faced an uphill battle. In 1776, units returning from Canada were riddled with various illnesses. Smallpox, the malady most feared, was only one of a number of killers. Over the 1776–77 winter, military doctors encountered hundreds of cases of dysentery, malaria, and unidentified fevers that at times laid low entire units and threatened to paralyze the army. Poor camp sanitation and shortages of medical personnel and supplies exacerbated the situation. Of some six thousand troops at Ticonderoga in July 1776, thirty-eight hundred were ill. This was probably an exaggeration, but not by much; other reports also estimated the army's sick as numbering at least three thousand.[28] The situation was a tragic but classic illustration of the fact that camp diseases were a greater scourge of eighteenth-century armies than combat.

Credit Horatio Gates and a dedicated medical staff with meeting the situation head-on. Gates cracked down hard on camp sanitation, and he issued repeated pleas to army and civilian authorities to hasten shipments of medicines, bandages, blankets, and all manner of hospital supplies. In a crucial step, he ordered all smallpox cases transported to a general hospital at Fort George. The suffering at the hospital was severe, but the health of the Ticonderoga garrison, which had to be prepared to fight, simply had to come first. Gates ended smallpox inoculations at the fort. The procedure resulted in a mild case of the pox, which left troops briefly incapacitated at a time the army needed every man. Inoculated troops also could spread smallpox to those not inoculated. He had troops arriving at the fort with recent inoculations quarantined at Skenesborough, some twenty-five miles

The Hon.: ANTHONY WAYNE,Esq

Major General in the American Army

Anthony Wayne (1745-1796). Wayne assumed command at Ticonderoga after Horatio
Gates departed in mid-November 1776, and he remained at the fort until early April
1777. In spite of a paltry garrison and a dearth of supplies, he did what he could to
improve the defenses of the fort and Mount Independence. But Wayne disliked the
Ticonderoga region and was temperamentally unsuited for a garrison command; he
was only too glad to leave for a troop command in Washington's main army. Engraved
by Norman John, c. 1782. (*Library of Congress*)

up the lake. In August, an overly optimistic Gates informed Washington that "the Small-Pox is now perfectly removed from the Army."[29]
This was quite an exaggeration, for periodically smallpox reappeared,
usually among newly arriving reinforcements. However, Ticonderoga's
health certainly had improved, and the number of sick at Fort George
had fallen—but the medial battle was far from won.

Upon taking command, Wayne still had plenty to worry about on
the medical front. On an inspection in December, conditions in a
makeshift hospital left him stunned. The first thing he saw was a "man
laying dead at the door . . . [and] inside two more laying dead, two
living lying between them; the living with the dead had so laid for four
and twenty hours."[30] It was a grim picture, and Wayne acted vigorously
to correct the situation. He continued Gates's sanitary regime and the
practice of sending smallpox cases to the Fort George hospital. Re-
taining another Gates policy, he threatened dire punishment for any

soldiers caught self-inoculating.[31] This they attempted using a pustule of a sick comrade; but without proper medical supervision, a self-inoculated soldier could give himself a full-blown case of smallpox and infect others. Schuyler, concerned with another smallpox outbreak in February, became so angry at the practice that he asked Congress to condone death sentences for anyone self-inoculating or assisting a self-inoculation (Congress declined).[32]

Officers recruiting reinforcements for Ticonderoga did their best to shield the fort from the pox. In Boston, Major General William Heath arranged inoculations for Massachusetts recruits before sending them to Wayne. Washington ordered Major General Joseph Spencer to do the same for enlistees from Rhode Island and Connecticut. Even so, the commander in chief was concerned enough about undermanning at Ticonderoga to order some Massachusetts and New Hampshire regiments directly to Ticonderoga for inoculation there.[33] We can assume Wayne sent these units to Skenesborough or Fort George before incorporating them into the garrison. However Wayne handled the matter, he kept smallpox generally at bay.

These efforts, coupled with the timely arrival of new medicines, steadily yielded results.[34] In late December, surgeon's mate Thacher recorded that most of the soldiers were "comfortably situated," provisions were adequate, and "the troops are quite healthy." There were some cases of "rheumatism and pleurisy," but few deaths. By April 1777, a newly constructed general hospital on Mount Independence held some eighty troops suffering from various maladies, but there was no outbreak of contagion.[35] For its day, the medical turnaround at Ticonderoga was a considerable achievement. The garrison may have been small, but it enjoyed reasonably good health as spring dawned.

The importance of the garrison's health mandated steps beyond the obvious need to combat disease. Fighting meant casualties, and wounds required treatment. And if Ticonderoga was the likely scene of action, then the hospital at Fort George was too far away to care promptly for casualties. This concern, and the better care of the non-contagious sick who did not require isolation, spoke for the need of a local hospital. As early as November 1776, a visiting congressional committee, having met with senior commanders and medical staff, recommended construction of a general hospital on Mount Independence, with a garden to supply fresh vegetables.[36] Anticipating the recommendation, Gates had named Dr. Jonathan Potts, a Pennsylvanian already in Continental service, as head of the new facility. In addition, he asked Potts to establish a field (or temporary) hospital at Wayne's headquarters in the fort itself. Plans called for dressing the wounded at the field hospital and then evacuating them to the new general hospital. Fort George would continue as the hospital for contagious illnesses.[37]

Again, Wayne picked up where Gates left off. As a fellow Pennsylvanian, Potts was well known to Wayne, and the doctor had done yeoman work at Fort George combating the smallpox scourge. As the colonel continued with construction on Mount Independence, he looked to Potts to equip and staff the new facility. He also gave Potts notice of upcoming scouting operations, warning him to expect wounded patients.[38] Schuyler was equally concerned for Potts's success, granting the doctor permission to go anywhere in the Northern Department to get anything he needed. No one was taking Ticonderoga's medical needs lightly. Whatever else he did, and however much he disliked garrison duty, Anthony Wayne fought a largely successful campaign for the health of his command.

Another campaign was less successful, although it was hardly Wayne's fault. This was the effort to increase the size of the Ticonderoga garrison, a concern that would be a source of continuing frustration. Before departing, Gates had thought a garrison of 2,500 was necessary just to maintain Ticonderoga and Mount Independence through the winter.[39] To hold the fort against attack, however, was a far different matter. Schuyler estimated that Ticonderoga would need ten thousand men in 1777 to properly defend the extensive works, including Mount Independence. He wanted another thousand "for the several posts on the Communication," meaning Forts Ann, Edward, and George, and other posts such as Skenesborough on the route south to Albany. (And beyond these numbers, Schuyler, as theater commander, had to find men for the posts in the Mohawk Valley as well.) He was not optimistic about finding the needed manpower, as the troops Gates left behind at Ticonderoga made it clear they would not remain a day beyond their enlistments, and the states had shown little vigor in recruiting the new regiments. [40]

Wayne, of course, found encouragement in none of this. As the reader will recall, the departure of the regiments with Gates left Wayne with a minimal garrison, far fewer than the 2,500 Gates had estimated as a safe minimum. As of November 17, when Wayne took command, the garrison comprised six Continental regiments—three from Pennsylvania and one each from New Jersey, Massachusetts, and Connecticut—for a total of 2,783 of all ranks. Of these, however, only 1,413 were effectives; the rest were sick (1,030), on furlough, or on detached duty away from the fort. [41] On February 1, 1777, a new return listed 1,829 effectives, an improvement to be sure, but one that hardly made a dent in the goal of ten thousand Schuyler considered essential to hold the post. [42]

Patriots hoped the states most concerned with the defense of the North—that is, New York and the New England states, plus the New Hampshire Grants—would provide the lion's share of the necessary manpower. But militia seldom served more than three-month tours, and arriving militia units generally replaced units going home and thus contributed little to garrison numbers. Some militia reported to the fort with the understanding they would be there only until Continental regulars appeared. [43] But the Continentals were part of the same problem. The regulars with Wayne in February were slated to depart within weeks, and any new Continentals would only replace them. Worse, in February and March 1777, the New England states had only begun to recruit new Continentals, and no one was reporting a rush to the colors. In early February, Wayne informed the president of the Massachusetts Council that the state had no Continentals at Ticonderoga and that by mid-March even the two regiments of Massachusetts militia would depart. [44]

Wayne, with a volatile personality that preferred action to stewing over thin muster rolls, was almost in despair. On February 2, 1777, the unhappy colonel reported his manpower problems to Congress, noting that he had urgently requested reinforcements from Schuyler. Without new troops, he warned the delegates, "this garrison will be left very weak indeed." [45] Two days later, he dispatched an even more pointed letter to his old commanding officer and friend, Horatio Gates. He reprised the sorry state of his depleted regiments, and he told Gates that while reinforcements of New England militia were due to arrive, it was all he (Wayne) could do to keep his weakened command functional.[46] To all who would listen, Wayne pointed out that virtually all units, militia and the few Continental regiments, insisted on going home as their enlistments concluded. In January, the arrival of some seven hundred reinforcements did nothing more than allow some Pennsylvania Continentals to depart.[47] Wayne must have winced as his veteran regiments, especially those from his home state, marched away.

The experience of the 3rd New Jersey Regiment typified Wayne's dilemma. The regiment had spent most of 1776 in the Mohawk Valley west of Albany. But on October 19, the regiment received news of Valcour Island. "We are informed," Captain Joseph Bloomfield noted in his diary, "Genl. Arnold our admiral on Lake Champlain has been severely handled by the British fleet & obliged to retreat with great loss, and that our Regt. is ordered immediately to Tyconderoga."[48] The regiment reported to the fort on November 1, where they joined the rest of the New Jersey Brigade, which had retreated from Canada. When Carleton's "hourly expected" assault failed to materialize, the 3rd New Jersey settled into garrison routine, only to watch as, several weeks later, other Continental units began moving south with Gates. No doubt with mixed feelings, Bloomfield saw the rest of the New Jersey Brigade march from Ticonderoga with "Musick playing & Colours flying & with great Credit & honor." Then, on the first of March, with their enlistments up, the 3rd New Jersey decamped as well.[49] More veterans gone.

And the case of the Jerseymen was typical. The 1st Pennsylvania Regiment had marched off with the first of the New Jersey regiments, and another Continental unit simply disappeared. On February 1, the men of Colonel Charles Burrall's Connecticut regiment, their enlistments completed, walked away after dark, abandoning their embarrassed officers. Wayne was anything but amused. In his orderly book he tersely recorded, "Burrells [Burrall's] Regiment stole away last Night Except a few Artificers; leaving All their Officers behind." Wayne had no choice but to tell the officers—"being Deserted by their Men"—to leave as well.[50] Two weeks later, a group of Pennsylvanians threatened to leave no matter what the colonel said. This was near, if not outright, mutiny, and Wayne was having none of it. He confronted the men at pistol point, and only then did they agree to remain until their enlistments were up.[51] No doubt they did so believing Wayne would have pulled the trigger. Wayne waved no pistols in militia faces (that we know of), but he had no better luck persuading them to stay in ranks. Still, the colonel (promoted to brigadier general in February 1777) was in no mood to let anyone leave early. "The Militia are not in much expectation of being dismissed," one soldier wrote, "before our times are out for which we were draughted."[52] It was crystal clear that military duty at Ticonderoga was no one's idea of a good time.

It would be pointless to drag the reader through the extensive correspondence Wayne and Schuyler conducted on what was a genuine manpower crisis, but it is necessary to understand the full nature of the problem. Schuyler, a more subdued individual than Wayne, diplomatically asked for help from the governments of his home state of New York and the New England states. "Every account I receive from Tyconderoga," he told the New York Committee of Safety in December 1776, "confirms me in the belief that not a man will remain there beyond the term of their inlistment." The fort needed men, and fast. A few days later he said much the same in a message to Governor Jonathan Trumbull of Connecticut. He added that the troops at the fort seemed to suffer from "the periodical *American* distemper. . . . As soon as the first cold is felt, we are seized with home-sickness, and it increases with the severity of the weather."[53]

Over the next several months, albeit without the snarky humor, Schuyler sent many such letters, all to little avail. New Hampshire authorities responded that they had no relief to send, Connecticut took no immediate action, and New York sent Schuyler's letter to a committee—the classic ploy of governmental delay—before finally giving the major general authority to call out a fifth of the state militia. It was discouraging. Schuyler rightly feared any reinforcements Ticonderoga received would come too late, and he warned in early February that the count of the fort's rank and file could drop as low as "five hundred and Eighty four."[54] Things were no better a month later, when he told Washington that such new units that were arriving were very thin. One regiment had only fifty men, and others had "too Many Boys." Under the circumstances he again felt compelled to advise Washington that it would be impossible to defend Ticonderoga.[55] It was a familiar and bitter refrain.

All Schuyler could really do was keep Congress and the commander in chief informed. And what could they do? Congressional resolutions, couched in pressing terms and urging support for Ticonderoga, did not produce recruits overnight or make service at the fort any more attractive.[56] Washington had his hands full in New Jersey, but he lent what influence he could. He urged senior officers in New England to hasten recruiting and get new regiments to Ticonderoga as soon as possible.[57] It was all of little use, and the available Ticonderoga troop returns never climbed appreciably.

Even as the states tried to fill their new regiments, Ticonderoga did not immediately, or even in the long run, significantly benefit. Over the winter, Massachusetts and New Hampshire mounted an effort to recruit a combined total of eighteen new Continental regiments, all destined for Wayne's command. Recruiting went slowly, however, and rather than wait until full regiments could march, Washington directed the states to send individual companies as they became available.[58] But many of these reinforcements never reached Ticonderoga. Strategic priorities intervened. Much as the general sympathized with Schuyler and Wayne, in mid-March 1777, the commander in chief decided he had to hedge on deployments.

Washington had his reasons. He pointed out that patriot forces in the Middle Theater were directly confronting the main British army under Sir William Howe, while at the same time Ticonderoga was not under attack. A reinforced Howe, he feared, could take the de facto rebel capital of Philadelphia, inflicting an "irreparable Injury" to the cause—and he needed additional men to prevent such a disaster. And what if the British did not attack Ticonderoga in the spring? What if, instead, they sent a major contingent of their forces out the St. Lawrence and reinforced Howe's army by sea? In that case a large Ticonderoga garrison would serve little purpose. Better, he reasoned, to divert about half of the new Massachusetts troops (seven regiments) to Peekskill, New York; from there they could move north or south at need. A concentration at Peekskill might also compel the British to keep more of their men in New York City, troops that otherwise might be chasing Washington. Besides, he noted, New York State intended to raise two Continental regiments for Ticonderoga.[59]

Schuyler respectfully disagreed. The major general had no intelligence indicating the British might launch a seaborne venture from

Canada, and he feared that in the more likely event of an attack up Lake Champlain, Continentals posted at Peekskill would be too far south to support Ticonderoga. Moreover, Schuyler himself was forced to deploy reinforcements intended for Ticonderoga to the Mohawk Valley.[60] But Washington did not change his mind. By no means did anyone consider the northern fort a backwater or place of secondary importance, but it would have to wait its turn for major Continental deployments. Wayne might reasonably have asked if that turn would ever come. Indeed, asked to defend Ticonderoga with such a paucity of troops, the newly promoted brigadier commandant faced the military equivalent of making bricks without straw.

Yet the bricks had to be made—and lots of them. Ticonderoga's location, as the French had found when they constructed Fort Carillon, had advantages and disadvantages. Yes, the fort certainly dominated communications between Lakes Champlain and George. But as Montcalm complained, nearby high terrain commanded the fort, and enemy artillery mounted on that terrain could make the fort untenable. Thus Ticonderoga's security rested less with the original fort itself than with defensive works constructed on neighboring key terrain—works that would compensate for the fort's size and problematic physical location. That meant a lot of new construction on the fort's various outer works, including Mount Independence, while Ticonderoga's original timber and earthen walls remained largely the same.

As commandant, Wayne was responsible for defensive projects, security concerns, and any new operations. But he was neither a military engineer nor, as we will see, much of a project manager. In any event, he did not have to do the actual planning for the new fortifications. That task fell primarily to Schuyler and his staff, and the theater commander envisioned a major building program for 1777. He intended at least eight key projects at Ticonderoga: fabricating a hundred gun platforms and a thousand wheelbarrows; building gun carriages for new artillery; improving the dock in the lake; constructing blockhouses on Mount Independence, near the fort, and west of the French Lines. Troops would also drive piles through the ice to stabilize the existing boom linking Mount Independence with Ticonderoga.

It was quite a to-do list, and it grew in the spring. Patriots planned a new fort on Mount Independence, with barracks and the attached general hospital; major repairs to the old fort's masonry; further improvements to the French Lines; and a new bridge from the western shore to Mount Independence. There would also be work on gun batteries in the improved outworks and in a series of carefully sited new redoubts. And fatefully, for it was never built, there was thought to a final blockhouse "on the southwest hill across the Lake"—meaning Mount Defiance.[61] It was a considerable agenda, and despite Ticonderoga's thin numbers, Wayne and his officers had no choice but to work with the manpower at hand.

New construction of course meant adequate supplies of construction materials, armaments, and munitions—in fact tons of everything. Good quartermaster that he was, Schuyler arranged for estimates of necessary tools and supplies, grouping literally hundreds of thousands of items into twenty-six broad categories: "2,000 iron shovels," "400,000 feet of inch pine board," "800,000 10^d nails," "300 broadaxes," "60,000 feet of 3-inch oak plank, for [gun] platforms" and so on ad infinitum.[62] Keeping a military bastion functional was no small undertaking, and hammers, picks, and spades were every bit as important as weapons.

Schuyler's lists dealing with artillery and munitions were equally impressive. The major general reckoned that Ticonderoga needed 108 artillery pieces of various sizes ranging from fifteen twenty-four-pounders to ten light three-pounders and nine sizes in between, plus ten howitzers. He wanted ordnance of all kinds and quantities, including one hundred thousand flints, a ton of "slow match," tens of thousands of shot of various weights, sixty "tons of cannon powder," sixty-seven tons of "lead for musket balls," and much, much more down to "fifteen ton of old junk"—old cordage for use as cannon wadding.[63]

Small arms were part of the mix, although they were not on Schuyler's original list. Most militia and some of the Continentals sent to Ticonderoga brought with them state-issued arms. But not always. In March 1777, as Massachusetts set out to recruit its new Continental regiments, the state found it had to send them off without weapons—the state had none—hoping Schuyler could equip them.[64] As late as May, another group of recruits arrived expecting to be armed from the fort's stores. In this they were disappointed: there were no spares. To arm them, Major General Heath had to expedite a shipment of three hundred muskets from the Springfield, Massachusetts, arsenal. And when troops did arrive armed, their weapons were not always the best. Schuyler complained that disbanded troops frequently took issued weapons home with them, leaving behind the subpar arms they had carried to the fort. As a result, he told Washington, many of the small arms at Ticonderoga were "mere Trash mostly unfit for any service." Schuyler did have stores of muskets at Albany, however, and it appears he was able to keep Ticonderoga's garrison equipped.[65] Through June, various shipments departed for the fort almost on a daily basis.

Schuyler also considered the naval dimension of the fort's defenses. In fact, patriots far from Ticonderoga understood the importance of naval superiority on Lake Champlain. In late February, the *Maryland Gazette*, published in Annapolis, printed a letter from Albany stressing the need to rebuild the American fleet. The anonymous writer was confident a strong fleet could stymie a second British invasion. Another correspondent told *Gazette* readers that Ticonderoga would boast a "considerable naval force" by early 1777 and that Carleton would have to fight his way past it to reach Lake George.[66] Schuyler shared no such optimism; but with the rebel's fleet almost wiped out at Valcour Island, he launched a major naval construction program. He ordered men from Wayne's garrison to serve on the lakes, asked the New England states to send experienced ship carpenters, and ordered timber to build new vessels on Lake George and recondition the five surviving ships from Arnold's flotilla (including the four Valcour Island veterans). Additional plans called for the repair of the bateaux on Lake Champlain and for 150 new bateaux for the Hudson and Mohawk Rivers.[67] Thus on land and lake, Schuyler was ordering arms, matériel, supplies, and skilled workers at a furious pace; one can only imagine the blizzard of paperwork.

How much of the contents of Schuyler's "want lists" of artillery, construction materials, naval stores, and ship-building personnel actually arrived at the fort is hard to determine. Most shipments of all types probably arrived as requested, if not *when* requested. Supply reports survive in the National Archives, but the records are incomplete, many of them disappearing in 1777 when Ticonderoga fell to the British.

We do know that as late as the end of May, stores and supplies of all sorts intended for Ticonderoga remained stockpiled at Albany awaiting shipment.[68] But there is no doubt that over the early months of 1777, the guns, stores, related equipment, building supplies, and munitions began arriving in quantity from points east and south. The routes to the fort were hives of activity as Schuyler, his staff officers, and private contractors (who sometimes insisted on military escorts) directed shipments and hauled tons of the sinews of war by wagon, sledge, pack animals, and water. The logistics effort, if not impressive, was at least adequate.

In fact, by April, enough weaponry and matériel had accumulated at the post to raise concerns among some senior rebels. In Boston, William Heath, busily trying to marshal men and supplies for Ticonderoga, expressed fears the fort was getting too much of a good thing. He wrote a worried letter to Washington raising the possibility that the influx of items on Schuyler's list was making Ticonderoga an inviting target, especially considering the fort's isolated location. The commander in chief was indeed concerned about the vulnerability of Continental stores, and he informed Heath he had arranged for authorities at Boston; Portsmouth, New Hampshire; and Providence, Rhode Island, "to remove all the military Stores, Arms &ca in their possession, from those places," to the arsenal at Springfield, Massachusetts. But Ticonderoga? Apparently Washington felt stores there were safe enough, and they remained where they were, which in time would prove a grave mistake—but that is getting ahead of our story.[69]

Beyond the quantity of stores and equipment reaching Ticonderoga, of course, was the question of how much the garrison accomplished with them. What did the troops actually build?

In these matters, much depended on Anthony Wayne's leadership. The commandant was a capable officer and motivator of fighting men, but his inspirational skills flagged when it came to managing an industrial worksite, which is essentially what the Ticonderoga command had become. Given that patriots considered the safety of Ticonderoga critical to their cause, Wayne simply could not understand that troops might not work with a will—which apparently they did not. He was furious. "The haste shown by both officers and men," he complained in general orders, "to quit work almost as soon as they begin, clearly evinces that they have not the proper idea of their work, nor a sense of the Importance of this post." The colonel warned he would "no longer Suffer such conduct to pass with Impunity," and from that point on (February 7), work parties mustered on the fort's "grand parade" under the eyes of senior officers.[70] Of course, threats are motivations of a sort, but there is no indication they appreciably spurred anyone to greater heights of productivity.

What did help was the arrival of a military engineer. In late February 1777, Colonel Jeduthan Baldwin, who had served at Ticonderoga in 1776 after the retreat from Canada, returned to the fort.[71] In addition to an almost unique Christian name, Baldwin brought with him a wealth of experience. A Massachusetts native, he had been an officer in the French and Indian War, and as a Continental captain he had helped design the fortifications around besieged Boston. Promoted to colonel of engineers, in later 1776 he served in operations around New York before arriving at Ticonderoga on February 24, 1777.[72] After touring the post with Wayne, Baldwin set to work prioritizing projects and hiring craftsmen—mostly carpenters, masons, brick-makers, and shingle-makers, and spending plenty of money to do so—to work along with the troops. He briefly enjoyed the assistance of "3 French Engineers" whose exact duties have escaped historical notice, but they "went off" in mid-March, leaving the American colonel on his own.[73]

Baldwin quickly discovered what Wayne already knew too well: the ambitious building program was woefully undermanned. But with the brigadier's support, the engineer did what he could. The garrison continued to improve the French Lines, completed an extensive abatis in front of the breastworks, and then started another on Mount Independence. New redoubts went in, and men began crafting new gun carriages. Baldwin built blockhouses as well, including one to protect the sawmill and bridge on the La Chute. Men not actually building something cut firewood, sawed logs, and milled planks and lumber. Wayne backed Baldwin fully. He saw to it that virtually everyone not engaged in missions outside Ticonderoga's lines worked. Women were told to "work for the Men"—which usually meant washing, nursing, or wood gathering—or be "drumm'd out of the Regt."[74]

Baldwin paid close attention to Mount Independence. He did not have to start from scratch. There were already artillery positions on the mountain, and one of the "French engineers"—a Captain "Marquisie"—had sketched preliminary plans for new works.[75] Following Vauban, the Frenchman envisioned another four-bastion stronghold with a central parade, barracks and support structures, room for the new hospital, and extensive outer works. Artillery would cover all approaches. In many respects, the design of the new fort was a miniature of Ticonderoga. Baldwin saw no reason to drastically alter Marquisie's plans as construction began in earnest, and the colonel became a familiar figure on the mountain and made it a point to get to know everyone involved in constructing the new fort.[76]

Another critical project was the bridge across Lake Champlain. Gates's troops had put a narrow walkway across the water, but it was an insubstantial span, inadequate to the transport of large numbers of men and bulky loads of matériel or artillery—a real concern once major work had begun on Mount Independence. A December storm already had "parted the bridge" and "carried away" the antishipping boom.[77] A temporary pontoon bridge of linked bateaux topped with planks replaced the rickety original span. But this was no long-term solution—it was time to start over. On March 1, just days after reporting to the fort, Baldwin began work on "the Great Bridge." As planned, the new structure would rest on timber cribs weighted down and stabilized by rock ballast. Baldwin wanted the cribs to sit on the lake bottom at fifty-foot intervals, linked by cables and supporting floating logs surfaced by planks twelve feet wide. The new bridge would provide a secure communications link and prevent British ships from sailing past Ticonderoga; it also would parallel an improved boom to the immediate north. Forged of one-inch chain links and resting on tethered logs, the boom was also intended to be an antishipping barrier.[78] The projects would have been ambitious under the best of circumstances, but in the winter they would involve breaking through the ice and working in cold and unsheltered conditions—an engineering challenge indeed.

Again, Wayne backed Baldwin fully. His general order of March 5 was a virtual pep talk: The bridge project, it read, was "a matter of the first moment." The brigadier "flatters himself" that officers and men would give the work all they had with "the Greatest Cheerfulness." But again, Wayne was not much of a cheerleader. Only days later he was complaining of "a great supinness" in the work, and he ordered men who were off duty to put in extra time on the bridge project. Worse, Wayne found that troops on Mount Independence had, "in a Most Villainous manner," destroyed some of the fortifications and old huts.[79] The men probably had torn up part of the abatis and timber from the huts for firewood. All Wayne could do was threaten dire consequences for those responsible. But there is no evidence anyone was caught—or that the work went any faster.

These work-related incidents reflected an unrelenting morale problem. It was not surprising. As we have seen, a posting to Ticonderoga was no cushy assignment, and duty on the northern frontier led to feelings of isolation. Spirits rose and fell according to events. Rebel confidence had soared in late 1776 after it became clear that Carleton was not going to assault Ticonderoga's lines. But news from other fronts occasioned growing alarm. Over late fall and early winter 1776, word of the loss of Newport, Rhode Island; Washington's retreat across New Jersey; the capture of Major General Charles Lee; and the flight of Congress to Baltimore successively filtered north. Hundreds of miles from the action to the south, the view from Ticonderoga was grim. "Such is now the gloomy aspect of our affairs," surgeon's mate Thacher recorded in late December, "that the whole country has taken alarm."[80]

The garrison would grasp at any glimmer of good news from elsewhere. In mid-December, two weeks before the Battle of Trenton, word came north of a "glorious Victory gained by Genl Washington over the enemy." Wayne ordered a "Feu de Joy" followed by a celebratory issue of rum. It was fun while it lasted, but word quickly arrived to inform Ticonderoga that news of the "glorious Victory" was mistaken.[81] The garrison's outlook did brighten, however, when the troops learned of Washington's stunning success at Trenton on the twenty-sixth. Yet even with good news there were feelings of remoteness among men, far from home, who could only watch and wait on developments.[82]

As best he could, Wayne kept the troops busy; but men in close proximity under challenging conditions don't always get along. Thus, garrison routine included dealing with recurring disciplinary infractions, most of which were run-of-the-mill matters for bored and lonely troops. The colonel responded variously with the lash, fines, and prison sentences. There were incidents of brawling, petty theft, and insubordination. In mid-March, Wayne court-martialed three soldiers for disobedience and "defamation of the Congress and all the Continental Officers and friends to Congress."[83] There was at least one incident of threatened violence among officers. Sparked by some now-hazy affront (we don't know what triggered the matter), Lieutenant Colonel Anthony Walton White of the 3rd New Jersey considered himself ill-used by Captain Richard Varick, deputy muster-master of the Northern Army. White drew his sword on Varick and threatened to shoot an officer sent to arrest him. Gates and Wayne interceded to calm matters, and White pledged his good behavior to avoid discipline. The army then reassigned White as quickly as possible and got him out of Ticonderoga (White went on to a distinguished career as a Continental dragoon).[84]

There were desertions. These also were no surprise, as desertion was a constant plague of eighteenth-century armies. But personnel returns indicate it was a trickle at Ticonderoga, not a major hemorrhage, and one suspects the relative isolation of the post discouraged men from slipping away in large numbers.[85] Not that Wayne didn't worry about it. In March 1777, a militia lieutenant faced a court of inquiry for "encouraging or advising his men to desert." The lieutenant, Nicholas Van Alstine of Tryon County, New York, apparently convinced the inquiry of his innocence, as he went on to file a postwar pension application based on his military service.[86] Still, whatever Van Alstine did was enough to raise eyebrows, and his case illustrated Wayne's concern to keep his garrison intact.

Sectional tensions, if not outright animosities, also sapped morale. For many soldiers at Ticonderoga, duty with the Northern Army marked their first encounters with anyone from another state. Relations were not always cordial. In particular, some troops (at least some officers) from states south of New England looked askance at the more egalitarian New Englanders, who were more casual in relations between officers and enlisted men.[87] Diarist James Thacher, still a private soldier before his promotion to surgeon's mate, spotted the problem almost as soon as his Massachusetts regiment met Pennsylvanians in late 1776. "A strong prejudice has assumed its unhappy influence," he recorded. Many southern officers—for so the New Englander considered the Pennsylvanians—were "gentlemen of education, and unaccustomed to the equality which prevails in New England: and however desirable, it could scarcely be expected that people from distant colonies, differing in manners and prejudices, could at once harmonize in friendly intercourse. Hence we too frequently hear the burlesque epithet of *Yankee* from one party, and that of *Buckskin* [for the Pennsylvanians], by way of retort, from the other." Schuyler fully reflected this prejudice. He wanted troops from as many states as possible at the fort, especially southern states. Southerners, he explained to Washington, "who have a greater Spirit of Discipline and Subordination will by degrees influence the Eastern people who without such a mixture will never acquire it.[88] So much for Ticonderoga as a version of the American ethnic "melting pot."

Such sectional feelings probably—"probably" because in this case copious amounts of alcohol seemed as much at the root of the matter as anything else—led to a truly disgraceful incident. On Christmas night 1776, a number of Pennsylvania officers took umbrage when Colonel Asa Whitcomb of the 6th Continental Regiment (a Massachusetts unit) allowed his cobbler son to set up shop in Whitcomb's quarters. Whitcomb, in the Pennsylvanians' view, was guilty of "degrading his rank."[89] "Being warmed with wine," Lieutenant Colonel Thomas Craig led junior officers of the 2nd Pennsylvania Regiment in an attack on Whitcomb's headquarters in which they destroyed the cobbler's bench and beat up anyone within reach in a "riotous and mutinous Manner," including Colonel Whitcomb. Then they plundered the tents of the Massachusetts troops. Shots were fired when the aroused Massachusetts men fought back, and there were wounded on both sides. When common sense prevailed, the brawling stopped before anyone was killed.[90] This was a disciplinary breach of the first order, and Craig's action threatened the garrison's unity. There was no hiding the seriousness of the matter.

News of the event reverberated throughout the garrison. Craig claimed two of Whitcomb's men, Sergeant Samuel Benjamin and Major Daniel Whiting, had started the fracas by threatening him, but no one was buying it. Certainly Major Whiting wasn't. The outraged officer wrote directly to Schuyler demanding justice. Ebenezer Elmer, a junior officer in the 3rd New Jersey, was mystified that Craig's men would have "beat, stabbed, and most shamefully abused" Whitcomb (who had not been stabbed, although he suffered a cut ear) "for no reason at all, but to satisfy their drunken career." Thacher, one of Whitcomb's men, was mortified at Wayne's seeming reluctance to deal sternly with Craig, a fellow Pennsylvanian.[91] Even Craig, who professed to know nothing of what any other rioters had done, tacitly accepted responsibility when he agreed to pay all damages for looted and broken goods. It was quite a list, including various articles of clothing, shoes, buckles, blankets, two guns, and Colonel Whitcomb's sword—all coming to the then-hefty sum of £37 17s.[92]

Craig was arrested, but there was considerable reluctance to bring him to book. He wrote Schuyler a plaintive letter essentially begging for mercy. Schuyler apparently wanted the matter to go away—amid everything else going on, did he really need this?—and he likely took his cue from Wayne. And Wayne? He may not have wanted to exacerbate a situation already tense enough and that seemed to be healing. Craig, no doubt understanding he had gone too far, sent out a hunting party which shot a "fat bear"; he then hosted a banquet to which he invited Whitcomb and the Massachusetts officers. This papered over some of the wounded feelings, although not all of the New Englanders were placated. Whitcomb went home in January and called it a day—his army career was finished. Upon leaving, however, he withdrew his complaint against Craig, to which Thacher reacted philosophically. Whitcomb, Thacher considered, "is a serious, good man, but is more conversant with the economy of domestic life than the etiquette practiced in camp." While other Massachusetts officers wanted to crucify Craig and insisted on pressing charges, with Whitcomb's complaint gone, the attempt to discipline Craig eventually fizzled. He was briefly imprisoned in Albany, but in February a court-martial acquitted him. Indeed, his military career prospered. He won promotion to colonel in 1777 and served until 1783.[93]

In pondering the outcome of the Whitcomb-Craig incident, one is reminded of Paul Newman's line in the film *Harper*: "The bottom is loaded with nice people. . . . Only cream and bastards rise." But such were the personnel problems of the Ticonderoga commandant and the complications of garrison life on the northern frontier.

Anthony Wayne was anything but immune from Ticonderoga's morale problem. By spring 1777, he was exhausted and sick; and as the reader knows, he had long ago asked Gates to have him relieved. Schuyler was only too aware of Wayne's situation. In late January, he wrote Washington that the then-colonel wanted nothing more than to escape from a post he found miserable. Schuyler was willing to let the Pennsylvanian go, but he had no general officer available to replace him.[94] So Brigadier General Wayne waited, none too patiently, for news of a new assignment. Finally, to his immense relief, on April 25, Wayne received new orders. He was to join Washington's main army, then still in New Jersey, and assume command of a brigade of Pennsylvania Continentals. It was the field command he coveted, and in the coming campaign he would fight in his native Pennsylvania. Wayne departed on the twenty-ninth, stopped for the night at Fort George, and on the thirtieth headed south. He had been at Ticonderoga for some ten months, and he never looked back.

What can we say of those ten months? Wayne has come in for some criticism from historians, the argument being that he should have done more to improve Ticonderoga's defensive posture.[95] This is questionable. Wayne pushed his men hard to improve the French Lines, build new redoubts, erect works on Mount Independence, and complete the bridge and antishipping boom—although admittedly, the nature of his "pushing" certainly raised hackles. Once the logistics network began to function under Schuyler, Wayne apparently had the building materials and tools he needed, but the manpower problem—and that was not his fault—was a critical impediment.

The manpower issue was greater than the garrison's numbers. We need to bear in mind that Wayne never had the luxury of committing his entire troop strength to construction projects. Security concerns were quite real, and they required troop commitments, and not always far beyond his lines. On April 19, for example, a sentry fired on four Indians scouting in the vicinity of the sawmill on the La Chute.[96] Moreover, the frequent troop rotations were disruptive of construction projects, as were efforts to keep troops at the fort through the length of their enlistments or longer. Near the end of his tenure, garrison strength remained low; in late March, Wayne reported a total of only 1,200 regulars and militia, including the sick. And of those, four hundred militia were about to leave.[97] Had he stayed at Ticonderoga, Wayne might have accomplished more with an expanding workforce, but as it was he did about as well as circumstances allowed—although he never believed the unhappy garrison (morale was never really high) was large enough to hold the fort. In little more than two months, events proved him right.

Chapter 3

Commanders and Controversies

WHILE SCHUYLER AND WAYNE grappled with Ticonderoga's problems, and while Schuyler gave what attention he could to the rest of his Northern Department, a political battle was shaping up in Congress that roiled the northern command. In fact, that struggle, with Ticonderoga at its heart, reflected other disagreements over how and even whether to defend the fort. And these disputes surfaced at a time when patriot unity should have been at a premium, and as Ticonderoga struggled with preparations to meet an expected British assault. It was a narrative of petty politics, conflicting personalities, contradictory intelligence, and military frustration.

Never satisfied with his subordinate role to Schuyler in 1776, Horatio Gates stepped dramatically back onto the scene in March 1777. Gates's New England friends, notably John and Samuel Adams, had long felt highly of the major general; in fact, they had as much faith in Gates as they had little confidence in Schuyler. The Adamses and like-minded delegates—most, but not all of them, New Englanders—reasonably pointed to the leadership Gates had provided at Ticonderoga in 1776 and his popularity in New England. Unreasonably, they queried

Schuyler's ability, as a patrician New Yorker, to lead New England troops. True, Schuyler, as the reader knows, had expressed reservations about the discipline among New Englanders; yet his leadership of the Northern Army had been sound. This being the case, there seemed little Gates and his allied delegates could do to supersede or relieve Schuyler. That is, until Schuyler himself provided a political opportunity.

In early February, Schuyler's normal diplomatic demeanor snapped when Congress, without notifying him, dismissed the medical director of the Northern Department. Congress had acted based on a series of political machinations. Schuyler sent a carefully worded but candid letter of protest to Philadelphia. He should have known better. It was the opening Gates's allies had hoped for, and they pounced. Led by the New Englanders, Congress declared Schuyler's protest "highly derogatory to the honor of Congress."[1] Gates, who had tentatively agreed to rejoin Washington as adjutant general, now openly acknowledged his wish for command of the Northern Department. In resolutions of March 25 and 31, Congress gave it to him—almost.

"Almost" because the careless wording of the resolutions gave Gates an independent command at Ticonderoga but left the rest of the Northern Department to Schuyler. "Bizarre" is not too strong a word to characterize the situation; it is difficult to imagine a more dreadful violation of the military principle of unity of command. Nevertheless, Gates had orders to report immediately to Ticonderoga, taking with him a Frenchman in American service, Brigadier General Roche de Fermoy. At the same time, Congress directed Major General Arthur St. Clair to report to the fort to serve under Gates.[2] How Schuyler and Gates, two independent major generals, were supposed to interact within such a command structure was (and is) anyone's guess.

Actually, Schuyler was neither guessing nor even thinking of tolerating the situation. Shocked at learning of Gates's elevation, the nettled officer quickly repaired to the New York State Convention, then the state's governing body. The solons there, taking umbrage at the insult to a distinguished New Yorker, promptly elected Schuyler to Congress—to which Schuyler just as promptly reported to wage a personal political battle. It was a move Gates had not anticipated; one political ambush had begotten another. Schuyler tread carefully in Congress, but he put his case clearly and sought a formal investigation of his conduct in the North in order to justify his actions and to regain his command. Congress formed a committee with a member from each state to examine Schuyler's complaint, although, like most committees charged with a politically delicate task, this one made no haste.

In the meantime, the major general-congressman used his time wisely. In an astute move, he befriended Thomas Wharton, the president of Pennsylvania, who named Schuyler commander of all Pennsylvania forces. As a state officer—while still a member of Congress and commander of his share of the Northern Department—for two months Schuyler demonstrated considerable military prowess. He did yeoman work strengthening rebel defenses below Philadelphia on the Delaware River, and he capably marshaled and forwarded supplies and recruits to Washington's army in New Jersey. He regularly consulted with Congress on military affairs, and his performance no doubt bolstered his reputation.[3] At one point, however, angry that Congress was taking so long to investigate his conduct, he mused about resignation. But friends urged patience, and while he waited, he kept his hand actively in supply operations for forces in the North.[4] In fact he had by no means conceded the contest for the Northern Department to Horatio Gates, and given the value of Schuyler's ongoing military activities, it was hard for even Gates's staunchest allies to find fault with him.

While Schuyler maneuvered in Congress, labor on defensive works and security operations continued at Ticonderoga. In Schuyler's absence, Gates remained at Albany instead of following his orders to the letter and proceeding to the fort. It made sense. Albany offered a better location to direct logistics operations crucial to the Northern Department, of which Gates tacitly (but erroneously) assumed he now commanded. At Albany, he did not like what he saw; he complained to Washington that the Northern Army lacked key supplies, that its administrative affairs were a mess, and that the military chest was out of cash and unpaid troops were complaining.[5] The commander in chief matter-of-factly replied that no general was entirely happy with what he found upon assuming a new command and that Gates would have to deal with his own problems, although he did promise to send Gates some money.[6] In this letter one senses a hint of tension between the two senior generals—likely born of Gates's decision not to resume duty as Washington's adjutant general and of Washington's continuing regard for Schuyler—and it would not be the last hint.

Yet Gates was not idle. He pressed to get supplies moving to Ticonderoga from storage in Albany, and he fumed over dilatory shipments from New England. Gates was especially concerned about the garrison's living conditions. He wanted the decrepit barracks repaired, huts moved closer to defensive positions, and more tents available for temporary shelter. And Gates, like Schuyler and Wayne, wanted more men. Undoubtedly recalling the Ticonderoga garrison he commanded in 1776, he wanted 13,600 Continentals for the entire Northern Department; and of these fully 11,700 would garrison Ticonderoga, while to the south, Skenesborough and Fort Ann would share another 300 men.[7] In addition, Gates hoped for militia reinforcements. He was no happier than Schuyler and Wayne when the New England states appeared backward in filling their regiments, telling Congress that "a General Apathy seems to have pervaded our entire [recruiting] System."[8] Active as he was, however, Gates was no more able than Schuyler to strengthen the garrison.

While Gates understood the commander in chief could do little to solve Ticonderoga's manpower problems, he displayed more than a little petulance on another matter: tents (of all things). Given the bad blood that colored the Washington-Gates relationship later in the year, the incident was of more than passing interest. In early May, Gates had sent one of his aides, Major Robert Troup, to visit Washington and ask him to forward a supply of tents to Ticonderoga. The garrison needed additional shelter, and the request was reasonable. But the commander in chief demurred. He pointed out to Troup that in a recent (April 26) British raid on a patriot supply depot in Danbury, Connecticut, the largest supply of patriot tents had gone up in smoke. Consequently, Washington explained, the main army, a mobile force then in New Jersey, would be operating in the open field and needed most available tents to accommodate changing bivouacs.[9]

Gates reacted badly. He accused the commander in chief of favoring the army under Washington's immediate command—and he was snarky about it. To refuse the Northern Army "what you have not in your power to bestow, is one thing;" Gates retorted, "but saying This Army has not the same Necessities, or does not require the same Comforts, as the Southern Armies, is another; I can assure Your Excellency, that the Service to the Northward, requires Tents as much as any Service I ever saw: And whether it will be Our Fortune to Defeat the

Enemy, or theirs to Defeat us, remains to be decided; but in either Case, the ruining [of] the Enemy's Army, or saving Our Own, may in great Measure depend upon our being provided with Tents."[10] This was candor that crossed the line to insolence.

Washington did not receive Gates's letter until May 19. Four days earlier, however, obviously feeling he owed the major general an explanation of his interview with Troup, the Virginian dispatched a not-unfriendly message to Gates. The general noted his understanding that barracks and huts at Ticonderoga and Mount Independence could accommodate most of the garrison, which was a stationary force; and he reiterated the point he had made to Troup on the requirements of the main army. If Gates needed a small number of tents for the smaller posts between Albany and Ticonderoga, he could apply to the quartermaster at Peekskill, New York. But he entreated Gates to "draw as sparingly as possible."[11]

Then Washington received Gates's letter of the thirteenth. He clearly was taken aback at the belligerent tone, and his reply was a gloves-off stinger. He could not "help taking notice of some expressions" in Gates's message that appeared to be "an imputation of partiality in favr of this [Washington's] Army, to the disadvantage and inconvenience of the Northern. Can you suppose," he asked rhetorically, that "if there had been an ample supply of Tents for the whole Army, that I would have hesitated one moment in complying with your demand." Washington explained that he had told Troup about the impact of the Danbury raid, and that the main "Army would be a moving one, and that consequently nothing but Tents could serve our turn, and that therefore, as there was the greatest probability of your being stationary, you should endeavour to cover your Troops with Barracks and Huts. Certainly this was not a refusal of Tents," he insisted. Rather it was a "request" that, given the army's difficult circumstances, Gates should make every effort in his "Power to do without them, or at least with as few as possible." Washington pointedly informed the major general that "the Northern Army is, and ever has been, as much the object of my Care and Attention as the one immediately under my command, and I cannot recollect, that I ever omitted complying with the Requests, or supplying the Wants of the Commander in that department, when it lay in my power." The commander in chief adamantly denied "suffering partiality for either department." He promised to check on the availability of tents, and if there was a "sufficiency," Gates would get his share. "But if there is not, surely that Army, whose Movement is uncertain, must give up its claim for the present."[12] General George Washington was not happy with Major General Horatio Gates.

Gates had the last word. "Which Army will want Tents most," he retorted, "the Events of the Campaign will determine; but the Continent should be ransackd from Florida to Funda [Fundy], rather than any Army should be unsupply'd." As to the movements of Gates's army: if Washington meant it was to be "Stationary" and "fixed solely for the defence of a particular post" [Ticonderoga], Gates would be "Glad immediately to receive" the general's orders—and here Gates hinted at future truculence—as long as "your Excellency's Orders" didn't conflict with any congressional resolutions Gates had received on Ticonderoga's defense.[13] Washington dropped the matter, but he shipped no tents. What stands out here is that the seemingly mundane matter of tents for Ticonderoga was a prescient reflection of the deteriorating relationship between Washington and Gates. This was no small thing, and it represented a step toward the rancor that six months later shook patriot politics and the Continental officer corps in the so-called Conway Cabal.[14]

The squabble over tents, like the controversy between Gates and Schuyler, was something the patriot military effort did not need in spring 1777. With the thaw of Lake Champlain came signs of enemy activity. In March, there was at least one serious British raid out of Canada that penetrated as far as Lake George, and rebels were concerned royal commanders in Montreal would learn of "the Debilitated State" of the garrison from prisoners captured in the incursion. Later in the month, Anthony Wayne warned that with the lakes clear, the

Overleaf: "Plan of Ticonderoga and Mount Independence, including Mount Hope." Map drawn by British assistant engineer Lt. Charles Wintersmith, 1777. Wintersmith's map clearly shows the star fort at the top of the mountain (actually more a plateau), the bridge to Ticonderoga, East Creek (which proved navigable to British gunboats), defensive battery locations, and the track to the South leading to Skenesborough. (*John Carter Brown Library, Brown University*)

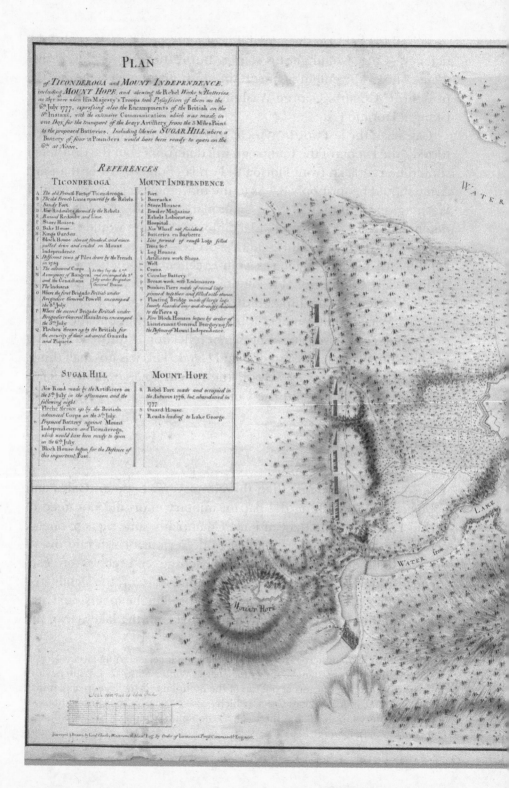

British would arrive "in full force" in three weeks at the outside.[15] In April he reported enemy probes around the outskirts of Ticonderoga's works, leading Richard Varick "to tremble" for the understrength garrison.[16] That the enemy did not come storming up the lake in the early spring did not abate fears that they might make a move at any time. In late April, John Adams's uncle by marriage, Isaac Smith Sr., feared the two thousand or so men at Ticonderoga would be no match for the British. "I Am A little affraid," he wrote Adams, "they will come Over [the open lake] too soon for us." Adams was every bit as anxious. He thought the garrison had "not a Thousand Men"; and despite assurances from the states that men were enlisting, he complained that "none of them, or next to none" actually reported to the army.[17]

Apprehensions were such that Congress considered abandoning the Ticonderoga peninsula. Rather than holding the fort in the face of an overwhelming attack, the delegates favored a concentration on Mount Independence and a defense of Lake George. Congress gave Gates permission to plan accordingly. If the major general thought best, he could move all patriot forces to the east shore of Champlain and prepare to contest the waters of Lake George if the British fought their way past Mount Independence. But if the rebels did leave the western peninsula, the congressional Committee for Foreign Affairs warned American diplomats that "the Enemy will probably give an Air of Triumph to the evacuation."[18] Unsaid was the obvious: Be prepared in European capitals to explain any abandonment of the fort as a logical defensive step, not an American defeat.

Despite these anxieties, however, by May the lack of any clear signals of a major British attack led to a surprising *sangfroid* among senior patriots. There always had been some faith among patriots that Ticonderoga would be too tough a nut for the British to crack.[19] Now, however, there was a perceptible shift in mood, one that evinced a confidence absent during the winter. Perhaps, as some rebels (including Washington) speculated, Ticonderoga would not be the enemy's primary target after all. Instead, if the British decided to send their Canadian troops by sea to reinforce Howe, Ticonderoga might face only a diversionary assault. This is what many in Congress, including President John Hancock, had come to believe based on what they deemed credible intelligence.[20] On May 10, Maryland delegate

Charles Carroll of Carrollton wrote his father that the British were "quiet" and that there were no indications Carleton was moving south. Virginia delegate Richard Henry Lee informed Governor Patrick Henry that Ticonderoga, reports to the contrary, was not threatened and "that we are no longer in pain for that Post."[21] John Adams, so frustrated only weeks before over the small garrison at Ticonderoga, waxed content by the first week in May. He wrote his wife, Abigail, "that all is well and quiet at Ticonderoga, that We have four Thousand Troops there, and that they were not afraid of Carleton." Adams said much the same thing to his friend Massachusetts politico and Continental army Paymaster General James Warren, noting "the Armies at Ti and in the Jersies begin to be very respectable."[22] These were cases of ignorance—Adams and Lee were misinformed about the size of the Ticonderoga garrison—being bliss; but they were not alone in this newfound optimism.

Gates, whose counsel carried great weight with Congress and who supposedly knew better than anyone the state of affairs in the North, offered an assessment every bit as chipper. When Congress suggested the evacuation of the fort in favor of Mount Independence, on May 11 he responded he was confident Ticonderoga was in no immediate peril. Quite the contrary. "I beg Sir you will in my Name assure Congress," he wrote John Hancock, "that at present I see no Reason for abandoning any part of the post of Ticonderoga; & further that there is good Grounds to hope, that we shall never be under the Necessity to evacuate or surrender any side or parcel thereof" if patriots could assemble their army and properly equip and provision it. If so, Gates believed "that Ticonderoga will be as safe this year, as it was the last."[23] Reading through this cheerful epistle one finds a number of "ifs" and contingencies: the fort was safe "at present"; the outlook was good *if* the fort received adequate supplies and *if* the rebels could assemble their troops on time. But there is little indication Congress chose to dwell on these imponderables. It is always easier—although not smarter—to focus on the good news. Gates's report was the sort of missive that lent credence to the public perception of Ticonderoga as the "bastion of the North."

Much of this wishful thinking was based on poor intelligence, and for a critical period even Washington shared the view that Ticonderoga could handle any perceived threat. As late as June 20, by which time early stages of the British invasion were well underway, the general fully reflected Gates's optimism. In a letter to Schuyler, Washington failed to credit the possibility that Burgoyne could bring more than five thousand men with him. With only that number, he predicted, any siege of Ticonderoga would entail all of Burgoyne's resources and preclude any British advance against other targets. The commander in chief was so confident he was right that he saw no point in sending additional regiments to the fort, thinking any new troops would only consume Ticonderoga's scarce provisions to no real purpose.[24] In short, virtually no one among senior patriots—in Congress or the military—really knew what the British were planning, and in their ignorance too many Americans assumed the Key to the Continent would stay locked.

This was the approximate state of affairs when, after Wayne's departure, the Ticonderoga command fell to the next senior officer present. This was Brigadier General John Paterson of Massachusetts. Paterson, often overlooked in the Ticonderoga story—he commanded the post only from April 29 to June 12—was a competent if typical general officer. That is, his career produced no fireworks, but no serious errors either. Paterson was a Connecticut native, a Yale graduate, and a successful lawyer before moving to Massachusetts in 1774. An early patriot, Paterson, as a militia colonel, had led troops to the siege of Boston; then as a Continental he participated in the ill-starred invasion of Canada. He was at Ticonderoga briefly in 1776 before moving south to fight at Trenton and Princeton. Congress promoted Paterson to brigadier general in February 1777.[25] In April he returned to Ticonderoga, reporting to Gates, who continued to maintain his headquarters in Albany.

What Gates thought of Paterson is unknown, although the reports he received were unflattering. In mid-May, Gates's aide, Lieutenant Colonel James Wilkinson, reported to the fort and quickly wrote a briefing letter. He informed Gates of his impressions of conditions at Ticonderoga—the defenses were not ready to face an attack and the garrison was too small—and he included a candid assessment of Paterson. The brigadier, in Wilkinson's view, was "a worthy good tem-

John Paterson (1744-1808). A Massachusetts Continental, Paterson was a stop-gap commander at Ticonderoga, "holding the fort" between the departure of Anthony Wayne in April 1777 and the arrival of Arthur St. Clair in mid-June. Paterson was a competent if unremarkable officer, and during his brief command he made little headway against the same manpower and supply shortages that plagued Ticonderoga commanders before and after him. Drawing based on a sculpture at Monmouth Battlefield. (*Monmouth Battlefield State Park*)

pered member of society, and a man I esteem, but so little of the general." The post commander had no opinions of his own, and "indeed he is one of the most humble characters I ever knew."[26] Certainly Paterson was no Anthony Wayne, although Gates probably didn't worry much about it inasmuch as he (Gates) planned on commanding personally at Ticonderoga once he had cleared up administrative matters in Albany.[27]

In fact, Paterson's command was generally unremarkable. He wrote back to Massachusetts with the normal list of complaints: not enough clothing, foul weather, depleted stores of rum and sugar, few blankets and shoes, shortages of small arms, and predictably, a very small garrison. He reported his roster as "very weak, not more than Nineteen Hundred Men sick and well, this Number composed of Soldiers, Carpenters, Seaman on board the Fleet, Blacksmiths, Armorers, etc."

Then a sentence Wayne could have written: "The Work necessary to put this place in a proper State of Defense is far from being complete, but I am pushing it on as fast as the Debilitated State of the Garrison will permit."[28] It was the same old story, and it gave no hint of any assembling force that Gates had assured Congress might hold Ticonderoga.

There was, however, at least one important addition to the garrison; on May 12, Jeduthan Baldwin noted the arrival of the French-trained Polish military engineer Thaddeus Kosciuszko.[29] A zealous adherent of the patriot cause, the young Kosciuszko had come to America after the failure of an abortive attempt to free his native Poland from Russian domination. He was a fine engineer, and the Americans, who desperately needed engineering professionals, commissioned him a colonel. Gates sent him to Ticonderoga to work with Baldwin; and the major general, who knew more than a little about political and personal sensibilities among officers, assured Paterson that Kosciuszko was reporting to assist, not to "supersede," the American engineer.[30]

Despite Gates's best hope, his well-meant introduction of the Pole did not avert yet another controversy (Ticonderoga seemed to breed them)—for Kosciuszko and Baldwin failed to hit it off. The Polish colonel eventually established a reputation as one of the finest military engineers in Continental service. However, that reputation lay in the future, and Baldwin soon found fault with some of the Pole's ideas; the American confided in his journal that he hoped Kosciuszko's planned works were never built. While Baldwin continued to push the construction of blockhouses and works on Mount Independence, Kosciuszko, who had an excellent eye for terrain, felt Baldwin was building in the wrong places.[31] Then the really serious dispute: the Polish engineer identified Ticonderoga's Achilles' heel—and reignited the debate over Mount Defiance.

Acting on a query from Gates, Kosciuszko took a new look at the mountain. After a careful study, he concluded that John Trumbull had been right in 1776: artillery on Mount Defiance would command the entire Ticonderoga complex, including Mount Independence. He recommended fortifying Defiance, and he so notified Gates in Albany. His opinion, however, put him at odds with Baldwin and most of Ticonderoga's officers. Kosciuszko's most recent (2009) biographer thinks professional jealously on the part of Baldwin and other American officers led to inaction on the Polish engineer's report.[32] It is likely, however, that a lack of manpower was equally responsible. Lieutenant Colonel Henry Beekman Livingston thought so. An aide to Schuyler, Livingston recalled that in 1776, rebels had "judged" the occupation of Mount Defiance "to be impracticable"; and in 1777, Livingston found American forces too weak to defend the "great extent" of Ticonderoga's lines.[33] Where would a garrison for Defiance come from when patriots lacked the troops to hold existing works?

Yet Kosciuszko had some support. Wilkinson, who had accompanied Kosciuszko to the fort, noted that Baldwin seemed focused on improving the French Lines, which made sense only if a new British commander chose to use Abercrombie's disastrous playbook.[34] But Wilkinson, along with Major John Armstrong, another Gates aide, thought the Pole was right. When Kosciuszko visited Gates in Albany to explain his concerns, Wilkinson wrote Gates urging support for the Polish soldier's plans to defend the high ground. "The works are now pushed on B[aldwin]'s unmeaning plan.—For God's sake," he pleaded, "let Kosciusko come back as soon as possible, with proper authority." Armstrong wrote that it was entirely possible to haul guns to the summit of Mount Defiance, and that a battery there "would completely cover the two forts, the bridge of communication and adjoining boat harbor." Gates agreed, and on May 28 he issued orders accordingly.[35]

But by then it was too late. Before anyone could act on his orders, Ticonderoga received shocking news: Major General Horatio Gates was no longer in command.

Philip Schuyler was back. On May 22, Congress, agreeing with the conclusions of its investigating committee, at last not only restored the major general to full command of the Northern Department but in so many words apologized for its shabby treatment of him in March. Congress specified that Schuyler's department would include Albany, Fort Stanwix in the Mohawk Valley, and Fort Ticonderoga. Schuyler was gratified, but he knew his victory was the result of a bruising political battle. Gates's supporters had gone down fighting. "Every possible opposition had been made by your friends," Jonathan Trumbull

assured Gates, "but in vain." Indeed, the recommendation to restore
Schuyler had carried by a single vote. But a win was a win, and the
major general reached Albany to resume active command on June 3.[36]

Gates, who during his roughly two months in command had got
no closer to Ticonderoga than Albany, took all of this with particularly
bad grace. He refused to serve again as Schuyler's subordinate, although he did provide Schuyler a status report on Ticonderoga. The
document lacked any of Gates's optimism of the previous month. In
a complete change of tone, it was a forecast of gloom, if not quite
doom: The garrison was still far too small, and timely reinforcements,
despite repeated appeals to the states, appeared unlikely. Defensive
works required six artillery companies, but there were only two. Poor
roads had impeded supply shipments. The British were probing, and
the fort was not provisioned to sustain a lengthy siege.[37] This briefing,
of course, was at stark variance with Gates's upbeat message to Congress of only weeks earlier. And one senses a defensive tone in all of
this; if the worst happened, Gates could always say "I told you so."

Gates was no happier with his sudden and unexplained replacement than Schuyler had been with his own treatment in March. In
mid-June, the disgruntled major general rode to Philadelphia and fu-
riously demanded entry to Congress. In a heated peroration to the
delegates, he objected to what he saw as a blow to his honor, and he
insisted that he always had intended to move his headquarters to "Tyconderoga." The fort was "the proper and only post for the Commander in Chief of the Northern Army," and only news of Schuyler's
return, he claimed, had prevented his going.[38] Friendly delegates privately professed sympathy for Gates, but his performance, at least according to Schuyler's congressional allies, did him no credit.
According to William Duer, one of Schuyler's closest New York associ-
ates, Gates's comments "became warm and contain'd many Reflections upon Congress," including personal attacks on individual
members. "His Manner was ungracious," Duer sourly reported, "and
Totally void of all Dignity." After a considerable "Clamour," the major
general withdrew, leaving a residue of ill feeling between Gates and
Schuyler partisans.[39] It was all a reminder that amid the instability in-
herent in revolutions, political power plays could have an impact on
military affairs every bit as profound as any action by the enemy. In
this case, Schuyler had won the skirmish, although Gates and his New

Arthur St. Clair (1737-1818). St. Clair's courageous decision to evacuate the indefensible Fort Ticonderoga and Mount Independence saved his small army, but caused a political uproar and stunned patriots across the rebellious colonies. Although a court martial later acquitted him "with honor," St. Clair's military reputation never fully recovered. Portrait by Charles Willson Peale, c. 1782. (*Independence National Historical Park*)

England allies were far from cowed. They would await a later moment to renew their campaign.

In the meantime, Schuyler went back to work. The newly restored department commander dealt quickly with the command situation at Ticonderoga. No one saw John Paterson as anything more than a stop-gap commandant, and his replacement arrived on June 12. This was Major General Arthur St. Clair. St. Clair was to have gone north with Gates in March, but Congress and Washington kept him in Philadelphia to help organize and forward new Continental units to Washington's army.[40] One assumes he worked fairly closely with Schuyler in this role. Certainly the men knew each other, and Schuyler promptly sent St. Clair north.

St. Clair's appointment, however, was itself a matter of controversy. In March, when Congress first mentioned St. Clair as Gates's subordinate at Ticonderoga, Major General John Sullivan protested. Sullivan was a New Hampshire Continental, and he had briefly commanded the troops retreating from Canada to Ticonderoga in 1776. As he (mistakenly) saw it, Ticonderoga would be an independent command, and in a frankly whining letter he told Washington he wanted the job. "I have been Informed that Genl St Clair is to take the Command at Ticondaroga [for] the Ensueing Campaign," he grumbled. "Though I Never Wish to Complain I cant help The Disagreeable feelings So Common to mankind when they find themselves Slighted & Neglected." "I know that Ticondaroga will become an Important object with the Enemy. They must Try for it & therefore he that has the Command there will have the Post of Honor—I do therefore Humbly claim it as my Right & as the first Seperate post Entrusted to my care [meaning his short tenure in 1776]—And cannot Think of the Command being given to a younger officer without Conceiving myself . . . Treated with neglect which I well know my conduct has not Deserved."[41] The commander in chief, with his hands full rebuilding his army in New Jersey, didn't want to hear it; it was the kind of bickering over precedence within the officer corps that drove him to distraction. Washington insisted Sullivan stop worrying about "imaginary slights" or involving "others in the perplexities you feel on that score." Ticonderoga was not going to be an independent command, and even if it was, there were officers "before you in point of rank, who have a right to claim a preference."[42] One did not have to read between the lines to find the general's real message: stop moaning and leave me in peace. Besides, Washington liked St. Clair.

Arthur St. Clair has fared poorly in the narrative of the Revolution. His fate at Ticonderoga (coming in chapter 5) left many rebels questioning his ability; but in 1791 his disastrous defeat in Ohio during the Northwest Indian War put the final blot on his military reputation. It was not always so. Early in the Revolution, patriots esteemed him as a competent and experienced soldier—which he was. St. Clair was another British veteran transplanted to America. He was born in Thurso, Scotland, in 1737. Details of his family background are sketchy, but his father, William St. Clair, was a successful merchant. William had means to support a medical education for his son and the connections to have him apprenticed to prominent London physician William Hunter. Instead of medicine, however, St. Clair chose the army, and in 1757, he purchased an ensign's commission in the 60th Foot, the Royal Americans. He saw action during the Seven Years' War, and in

1758, he served under British commander in chief Jeffery Amherst in the reduction of Louisbourg. The following year he was with James Wolfe at Quebec. He finished the war as a lieutenant, by all accounts an accomplished junior officer.[43]

But after the peace, the British army offered few prospects for junior officers, and St. Clair's postwar career followed a not-unusual path. Like Horatio Gates, Richard Montgomery, Charles Lee, and other British veterans with American service, he left the army and settled in the colonies. By 1770, St. Clair had become a major landowner and successful political figure in western Pennsylvania, and he identified with the colonial cause in the run-up to the Revolution. Given his military background, Pennsylvania commissioned him colonel of the 2nd Pennsylvania Battalion; he fought in Canada and then ably supported Washington during the Trenton-Princeton campaign. In February 1777, Congress promoted St. Clair to major general. Washington trusted him, and Gates spoke well of him. His reputation in the Continental army was solid when he took up the command at Ticonderoga.[44]

St. Clair did not inherit a happy command. Gates had been popular with the New England troops who made up the majority of the garrison, and there was no joy among them upon Schuyler's reappointment. Wilkinson, at the time a devoted Gates partisan, recalled "the mortification and dissatisfaction which marked their countenances on" learning of Gates's relief. Richard Varick, a Schuyler devotee also at the fort in June, recalled no one's "countenances," but he reported to Schuyler that the New England officers were prejudiced in favor of Gates.[45] No one held anything against St. Clair, but the garrison was in anything but high spirits.

St. Clair's senior command team was not altogether stellar. Beside Paterson, he had two other brigadiers, Enoch Poor and Matthias Alexis La Rochefermoy (Americans generally spelled it Roche de Fermoy). Poor was the best of them. A Massachusetts native, he fought in the French and Indian War as a private soldier, after which he moved to New Hampshire and prospered as a merchant and ship builder. An early patriot, he led troops at the siege of Boston and during the ill-fated patriot invasion of Canada. It was after the retreat from Canada that he first saw duty at Ticonderoga. He again reported to the fort on May 20, leading six hundred New Hampshire Continentals.

Intelligent and brave, he compiled a fine combat record before dying in New Jersey of typhus in 1780.[46] La Rochefermoy, however, was problematic. A French officer from the West Indies of dubious credentials—available evidence suggests he was never more than a captain of grenadiers—Congress commissioned him a brigadier general in November 1776. He inexplicably abandoned his command just before the Battle of Second Trenton, and over Washington's protests Congress sent him to Ticonderoga with Gates in March 1777. When St. Clair arrived, La Rochefermoy was in command at Mount Independence. Not speaking English, he could barely communicate with his distinctly unhappy officers.[47] The Frenchman would prove worse than useless.

In fact, whatever La Rochefermoy's shortcomings, Ticonderoga's defenses were anything but secure. To the untrained eye, however, they looked formidable, the end result of just over a year of patriot occupation and preparation. On the western shore of Lake Champlain, of course, was the old star fort, still very much recognizable as the original Fort Carillon. It served mostly as a depot, headquarters, barracks, and support facility; while it mounted artillery, the fort was not the heart of the defense. To the northwest, patriot breastworks and abatis had strengthened the old French Lines; a new blockhouse covered the lines as well. Two additional redoubts stood between the lines and the fort. To the southwest another blockhouse protected a medical post near the entrance to Lake George; and about a half-mile from the French Lines yet another blockhouse—Baldwin loved building blockhouses—covered the wooden bridge over the La Chute and the carrying place to Lake George, the nearby sawmills on the La Chute, and a small guard post. Mount Hope rose another half-mile northwest of the French Lines, and it boasted a strong redoubt. Finally, several batteries near the shore could bring artillery fire on vessels approaching the boom and bridge connecting Ticonderoga with Mount Independence.[48]

Schuyler and Congress placed considerable faith in the defensive value of the boom and bridge. The boom consisted of a double chain of one-and-a-half-inch-thick iron links suspended on floating timbers. Colonel Kosciuszko, frustrated at patriot reluctance to occupy Mount Defiance, had devoted much of his attention to finishing the bridge begun under Anthony Wayne's command.[49] By the end of June, it was nearing completion. A plank surface twelve feet wide rested on a series of equidistant floats some fifty feet long, all held together with chains and rivets. Ongoing work was fastening the plank surface to sunken piers. By June the unfinished structure was strong enough to support the transport of heavy equipment and artillery, and it allowed quick communication between the western and eastern defenses.

Mount Independence, as explained in the previous chapter, was really a large hill with a flat summit. At its base along the shore, a large breastwork with artillery embrasures protected against shipping coming up the lake. Troops had ringed these strong points with an abatis. Facing East Creek, itself a natural barrier, and curving south, a line of logs and an abatis ran the length of the summit's edge. The timber star fort lay roughly in the center of the summit, and at Schuyler's insistence, St. Clair had pushed the project to completion.[50] A rough military road, cut through the woods in 1776, led from the fort south to Skenesborough.

While extensive, the Ticonderoga-Mount Independence complex was actually quite vulnerable, and senior officers knew it. In mid-June, Varick found the works on Mount Independence far from adequate, and later in the month, St. Clair and his generals deemed them "very deficient." Despite all the work done to improve the French Lines, St. Clair feared the British could get around the American left. The commandant also reported the boom was only "very feebly secured for want of rope for the cables"; and while the bridge was at least useable, at the end of June, troops were still trying to finish it.[51] Ticonderoga was very much a work in progress.

Adding to St. Clair's burdens was an almost complete lack of concrete intelligence of British intentions. The garrison sent scouts out regularly, but they usually learned little of consequence. "The woods are so full of Indians," St. Clair told Schuyler in late June, "that it is difficult for parties to get through." And when they did get through, reconnoitering patrols usually had to fall back in the face of larger enemy detachments.[52] Credit the British with highly effective security operations. Sometimes the rebel scouts ran into real trouble. One patrol, returning from a mission and entering Ticonderoga's lines between the La Chute sawmill and the main fort, an area long considered completely safe, fell victim to an Indian ambush. One soldier reported that as many as thirty Indians were involved (that was likely an exaggeration) and that the patrol lost two killed and a soldier taken prisoner. That such an incident could occur virtually within patriot lines left everyone on edge.[53] All anyone could say with certainty was that British activity on both shores of Lake Champlain had become the norm, and enemy parties sometimes ventured as close to Ticonderoga as Crown Point.

St. Clair was conflicted. What were the British up to? On June 25, he surmised the increasing enemy activity indicated they were gathering intelligence or trying to harass the garrison rather than planning a major attack.[54] But the very next day he predicted the worst. "Inhabitants" told St. Clair of a thousand Indians and Tories stealing down the western shore of Champlain, skirting Ticonderoga, and intending to attack Fort George. Equally dire was additional intelligence indicating an imminent assault on Ticonderoga itself. St. Clair warned Schuyler that the British attack would come in only three days—on Sunday, June 29. That there was no march on Fort George did little to calm patriot trepidation, and as events soon proved, St. Clair's prediction of an attack on the twenty-ninth was wrong by only several days. "The scene thickens fast," St. Clair was sure, but neither he nor anyone else really knew what to expect or when to expect it.[55] At a time patriots needed to see clearly, they were virtually blind.

Moreover, there was a general agreement that in the event of a serious assault, the garrison was far too small to man the extensive works. As of June 20, there were only some 2,500 effective rank and file—not nearly enough, and not appreciably more than Anthony Wayne had commanded. "Had every man I had been disposed of in single file on the different works and along the lines of defense," wrote St. Clair, "they would have been scarcely within the reach of each other's voices." There was a growing consensus that in the face of a serious assault, the relatively few Americans wouldn't stand a chance. Prudence dictated abandoning the Ticonderoga peninsula in favor of a concentration on Mount Independence no matter what popular opinion might think.[56] Schuyler may have even toyed with the idea of pulling out of the entire Ticonderoga-Mount Independence complex and basing the Northern Army's defense on Fort George, although he fully understood such a move would spark public outrage.[57]

What was clear in all of this was that the mood at Ticonderoga was darker—much darker—than the relative optimism prevailing in Congress. Morale had cratered. On June 28, the arrival of a small party of reinforcements, St. Clair noted, "had a pleasing effect upon our people, who, never the most lively or gallant, began to show signs of dejection already. How they may hold out, God knows, but this has raised their spirits a little."[58] Hardly a sunny observation. In fact, a soldier who had lost his tentmates in the ambush near the mill apparently could take no more. Militiaman Jabez Colton reported what followed as a "sad accident." No. It was a suicide. What else are we to make of a soldier "standing by the side of the House having his hand hold of the end of his Gun and his mouth on the Muzzle . . . [when] the gun wen[t] of[f] through his head and blew out his brains against the side of the House." This was a flintlock musket, and it would not have been idly primed and cocked, and a soldier would not casually put the muzzle in his mouth. He "had a wife and three children," Colton lamented.[59]

St. Clair's outlook certainly was not suicidal, but it unquestionably was fatalistic. This he fully revealed in a letter of June 18 to his friend, Pennsylvania congressman James Wilson: "My dear friend, if you should not hear from me again, which may probably be the case, remember that I have given you this account of our situation, and do not suffer my reputation to be murdered after having been sacrificed myself. The prospect may clear up yet, for all this."[60] But the stoic major general doubted it.

None of this is to suggest that St. Clair was more or less paralyzed in the face of circumstances—a military equivalent of a deer caught in the headlights. While focusing on defensive measures, and decidedly glum about them, he was willing to consider offensive operations when circumstances appeared favorable. As late as June 28, when it was clear Burgoyne was coming, St. Clair decided to act on intelligence of a major Indian and Tory concentration near Otter Creek. The creek flowed from the direction of Rutland into the lake north of Mount Independence on the Vermont side. St. Clair supposed the enemy's mission was to cut communications with Skenesborough.[61] He ordered Colonel Seth Warner of the New Hampshire Grants (Vermont) to raise the regional militia, "attack and rout" the Indians, and report back to Ticonderoga. St. Clair was confident Warner would "give a good account of the enemy."[62] The Iroquois threat was not as great as reported, and in any event Warner was not able to engage, although he did reach Ticonderoga. It was yet another disappointment, but it did not change the fact that St. Clair had shown fight when he thought there was a chance to strike. He could not have known it was his last chance to take the initiative.

It was in this the somber atmosphere that Schuyler visited the fort on June 18.[63] After several days spent inspecting the works and discussing the state of affairs with the officers—and being informed that rebel intelligence had learned little of enemy intentions—Schuyler convened a council of war on the twentieth. In addition to Schuyler, St. Clair, Paterson, La Rochefermoy, and Poor attended. It was not an upbeat event. The council unanimously agreed that the garrison—numbering no more than 2,500 effectives—was too small to defend Ticonderoga and Mount Independence; prudence dictated that in the event of a major attack, the rebels should evacuate Ticonderoga and defend Mount Independence. That being the case, the garrison needed to redouble efforts to lay in necessary provisions, move all equipment and artillery not immediately necessary at the old fort to Mount Independence, and complete the water defenses and the works on Mount Independence. All of this, the council estimated, would take about six weeks. And just in case, the garrison needed a contingency plan for a retreat—that is, the officers understood that the American Gibraltar might fall.[64]

Such was the situation at Fort Ticonderoga on the eve of the British northern campaign of 1777. The political and military atmosphere was fraught. At the highest strategic levels, many in Congress entertained notions that the main British assault would not aim at the fort and that its defenses were adequate. The commander in chief was conflicted. Washington simply didn't know where the enemy would strike hardest and on that score questioned the dispatch of major Continen-

Opposite: "A Map of Ticonderoga with the Old and New Lines and Batteries," 1777. Many of the planned defenses shown on the map were never completed before the American evacuation in early July 1777. But the French Lines, to the fort's immediate northwest, are placed accurately. St. Clair never had enough men to hold them securely. (*Library of Congress*)

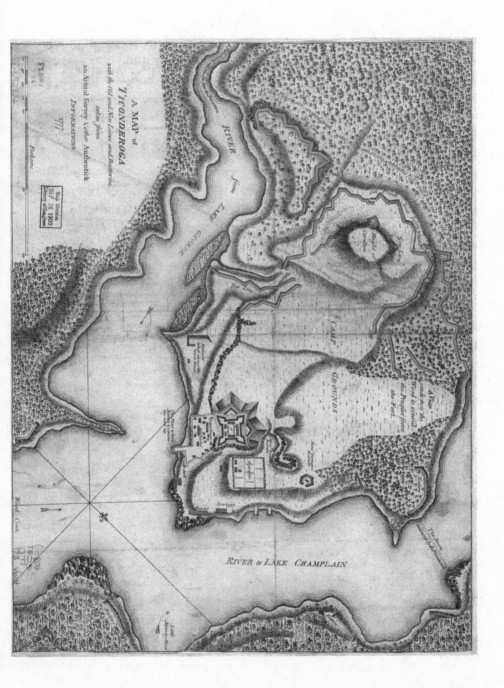

tal reinforcements to the Northern Department. The department itself was a political football. When command stability should have been at a premium, the respective partisans of Schuyler and Gates—and those of Gates were chiefly to blame—played high-stakes politics even as the garrison struggled with erratic supply deliveries, laggard recruiting efforts in the states, indifferent militia turnouts, and a perilous dearth of useful intelligence on enemy intentions and strength. The garrison remained dangerously small despite desperate pleas for more men by three post commandants over an eight-month period. In turn, the garrison's paltry numbers and the frequent rotation of militia and Continental units inhibited timely completion of Ticonderoga's extensive defensive works. And the fort's senior officers were at best philosophical about their chances against a serious assault—even to the point of planning for a possible retreat. Could the British have asked for a more inviting target?

Chapter 4

The Threat:
Lieutenant General John Burgoyne
and His Army

ERE WE MUST LEAVE the American army at Ticonderoga to its
worries and turn our attention to the source of those trepida-
tions. This, of course, was the British army in Canada. The imperial
campaign of 1776 had failed, but there was no thought among the
king's men of conceding the northern front to the Americans. Crown
forces would try again in the spring, and they looked forward to 1777
with increasing confidence. In fact, if the patriot outlook at Ticonderoga was bleak, spring 1777 found the mood among the British high
command positively buoyant. It is time to consider why and what they
intended for their opponents to the south. This, then, is the immediate background of Lieutenant General John Burgoyne's assault on
Fort Ticonderoga.

Upon its return to Canada, Carleton's army had gone into winter quarters, as one junior officer put it, "in different parts of the [Quebec]
Province." This generally meant in and around Montreal and in villages along the St. Lawrence all the way up to Quebec City. With few

adequate barracks in the cities, officers often quartered in private homes, if possible with families of the better sort (to use the contemporary term). Enlisted men often stayed in private homes as well, albeit more humble abodes, and sometimes in barns and other farm outbuildings. It was often a popular arrangement, as the troops gave up army rations in favor of meals from their "landlords." The supply services provided a majority of the troops with winter clothing, and officers were diligent in monitoring the soldiery's health and living conditions. As a result, the troops remained "remarkably healthy," and if sometimes cold, most of the army lived more or less comfortably through the winter.[1]

There were exceptions. Around Montreal, the spring saw an outbreak of dysentery among the Germans that caused some concern. But it resulted in few fatalities, and most soldiers recovered quickly enough; morale, according to a Brunswick ensign in the Prinz Friedrich Regiment, did not suffer. Lieutenant James Hadden of the Royal Artillery felt sorry for garrisons left behind to man the works at Isle au Noix and at St. John's. "The Barracks at these places not being completed 'till the beginning of January," he noted, "the Troops & Artificers suffer'd very much from the Cold." There were cases of frostbite, from which all of the afflicted recovered, although at Isle au Noix, a relatively isolated post, a scarcity of fresh food saw several fatalities to scurvy. But the spring thaw allowed the troops to catch fish, and with the timely arrival of supply shipments, including "*Spruce Beer*," the garrison's health was quickly on the mend.[2] Disease and low morale were not serious factors as the army looked toward a new campaign.

In fact, despite the disappointing outcome of the 1776 campaign, morale among the British and German soldiery remained remarkably high. Hadden was especially lucky. His artillery outfit had quarters in Montreal, where he found provisions plentiful and cheap. Officers enjoyed "Balls and Concerts composed of the best performers in the British and German Bands." The Canadian winter, while it had cold snaps, was bearable, and on good days the sun was "powerful and pleasant." Troops were able to clear roads through the snow over frozen rivers, opening communications between villages. The men skated on cleared ice, and almost everyone but "the very poor" went sleighing. In April, when much of the ice melted, Hadden was delighted to see how quickly greenery appeared in the countryside, and in June he was astonished to see "ripe strawberries" with snow still on the ground. "Upon the whole," the young artillerist concluded, "the Winter in Canada may be passed very pleasantly."[3] The difference between the situation in Canada and at Ticonderoga could hardly have been more apparent.

However "pleasant" the winter, there were reminders of the war. Naturally Carleton and his officers wanted to know what the rebels were doing at Ticonderoga, and British scouts, often loyalists or American Indians, occasionally secreted their ways down the lakes corridor toward the patriot bastion. The winter saw no major actions—in fact there were no armed clashes near Ticonderoga for many weeks after Valcour Island[4]—but the British did keep the Americans on edge. Wayne always suspected enemy scouts were out there, but it was impossible to know how often any reconnaissance missions actually put eyes on his works or what intelligence they gleaned. On the night of December 2, responding to scouting reports of British activity at Crown Point, Wayne put the fort and its outer works on full alert and had the men sleep with their arms. There were rumors of enemy raids over winter and early spring 1777, and the colonel warned his men to be on the lookout at all times.[5] It never paid for anyone, British or American, to let their guard down.

One of the British scouting missions was especially daring. Captain Samuel McKay (sometimes "MacKay") entered the army in 1755 as an ensign in the 62nd Foot (later renumbered the 60th, the Royal American Regiment); in 1775 he was a half-pay lieutenant on the rolls of the 60th, but he volunteered for active duty when the Americans invaded Canada. Appointed (not commissioned) a captain, as a scout McKay proved as resourceful as he was tough. He became known by friend and foe as a dangerous man in leading light operations, often involving loyalists and Indians. Eventually captured at St. John's in September 1775, McKay and a comrade escaped from a patriot lockup in Hartford, Connecticut, after months of captivity and made their way back to Canada. The rebels would regret his jailbreak.[6]

McKay was soon back in action. Over November 1776, he was busy recruiting a company of Canadian irregulars for service during the anticipated 1777 campaign. His most spectacular mission, however, came in March 1777. Departing Quebec, he led a sizable party, including Iroquois, south, passing Ticonderoga and traversing the carry to Lake George. Moving up the shore, on March 20 they encountered a group of some thirty mostly unarmed rebel recruits headed from Ticonderoga to Fort George. The ensuing skirmish wasn't pretty. The *Continental Journal* (Boston) told the tale, apparently quite accurately: McKay's men attacked the rebel encampment just before daybreak, achieving complete surprise. Four, possibly six, Americans quickly died by tomahawk, one officer was wounded, and most of the panicked survivors were taken prisoner. In the wider scope of the war, such raids were "trifling . . . in themselves," as Major General Schuyler reported to Washington, although he admitted that "their Consequences are very disagreeable."[7] They certainly were.

McKay got cleanly away. Despite rebel claims of inflicting casualties on the withdrawing party, a militia attempt to intercept McKay came to nothing. In Canada, the British made much of his exploit. They also confirmed from McKay's prisoners what the British already knew: "We learnt from them that the Enemy were preparing against an Attack from us at Tyconderoga."[8] This was no surprise, and no doubt McKay's prisoners also related what they knew of Wayne's numbers and defensive status. There were other intelligence missions as well, and other prisoners—and some deserters—to tell what they knew. And as winter turned to spring, the British certainly knew more about Wayne than Wayne knew about the British. Then again, because the British had occupied Ticonderoga for so long themselves, the royal commander already knew quite a bit about the post; but, professionals as they were, they were always interested in new details.

As both armies wintered in their respective regions and looked ahead to the new campaign they knew was coming, events were unfolding across the Atlantic. In London, the ministry of Frederick Lord North, after consulting with military and political figures as well as with George III, had decided on a sweeping plan of operations for 1777—a bold effort aimed at crushing the American rebellion once and for all. And Ticonderoga would figure prominently in it.

The plan called for an ambitious campaign on two broad fronts. One branch of the enterprise would marshal around Montreal, move to St. John's for final organizational and supply preparations, and then jump off following the traditional Lake Champlain-Lake George-Hudson River Valley corridor. The target was Albany, New York. In New York City, British forces would control the lower Hudson and move upriver to meet the Canadian army at Albany. Late in the planning, the British added a third force. A column including major contingents of Iroquois and Tories would advance from the west up the Mohawk Valley to Albany. The far-flung operation depended on the coordination of the different British forces, but Lord George Germain, secretary of state for the colonies and the minister most responsible for managing the British war effort, was confident of success.

The objective of the entire operation was to isolate the New England provinces, which the ministry considered the most truculent of the colonies. At the very least a successful junction of the armies at Albany would cut off (or make very difficult) the movement of troops and supplies between New England and colonies southward. With any luck, imperial forces could then defeat the Revolution piecemeal. As they moved toward Albany, the converging columns also would destroy any rebel forces encountered along the way. The plan had merit: it would force the rebels to split their forces and defend on three fronts; and as the British armies advanced, they would encourage loyalists to rise in the less-zealous colonies south of the Hudson. Any simultaneous British operations in the Middle Colonies could prevent Washington from reinforcing rebels in the North.[9] On paper at least, the new plan looked like a winner, and given Ticonderoga's critical location between Lakes Champlain and George, the fort would be the chief preliminary target—a prize in its own right—of the British drive south toward Albany.

The commander of the Canadian army would be Lieutenant General John Burgoyne. Burgoyne was a seasoned professional with a reputation of being one of Britain's best general officers. In 1775, he was one of three generals—the other two being William Howe and Henry Clinton—the Crown had dispatched to America to deal with the colonial rebellion, and as he was one of the leading personalities in the Ticonderoga story, we need to know about him.

The future general was born in 1722 in Bedfordshire, the son of a commoner army officer, although the family had wealthy friends.

Young John was especially close to children of the socially and politically influential Earl of Derby. John had an excellent education at the Westminster School and developed a lifelong love of literature and drama. As an adult he made many friends in literary and theatrical circles, and even while a soldier he established a modest reputation as a playwright. He was an intelligent and urbane individual.[10]

Burgoyne's military career, however, got off to an erratic start. Commissioned a cornet of dragoons in 1740, he soon purchased a lieutenancy. Three years later, after eloping with the Earl of Derby's daughter, Charlotte, he purchased a captaincy with his wife's money. But Burgoyne had to sell his commission after an angry Derby cut them off and Charlotte's money ran out. After a sojourn in Europe, and after making up with Derby and with his own family (the Burgoynes had not been happy with John's having offended Derby), in 1756, Burgoyne and his wife returned to England. He brought with him ideas on light cavalry gleaned from what he had seen on the continent. Quickly back in the army as a captain, he soon found a place in the elite Coldstream Foot Guards as a lieutenant colonel.[11] A posting to the prestigious Guards regiment was a career plum and had a great deal to do with being the son-in-law of the influential earl.

Yet Burgoyne was no military dilettante; he took his soldiering seriously. Acting on his interest in light horse, in 1759, he convinced the army to raise two new regiments of light dragoons, the first such units in British service. Burgoyne successfully organized and commanded one of them, which became the 16th Light Dragoons. Unlike previous dragoon units, the 16th was trained to fight mounted as light cavalry. Burgoyne subsequently served with distinction in Europe during the Seven Years' War. He led raids into France and, in 1762, as a brigadier general, he went to Portugal to help repel a Spanish invasion. The Portuguese assignment was the making of him as a senior officer. He led his men (including the 16th) in some daring actions. One was decisive: Burgoyne's victory over the Spanish at Villa Velha in October 1762 all but concluded the war in Portugal,[12] and he ended the conflict with a well-earned reputation as a gallant and genuinely talented commander.

In fact, even before the end of the war, Burgoyne's career trajectory had taken off. Elected to Parliament for Midhurst in 1761—again using the Derby connection—he took an active interest in military

John Burgoyne (1722-1792). Burgoyne's advance on Ticonderoga was thoroughly professional, and he was prepared to besiege Arthur St. Clair's army. The rebel retreat was unexpected, and Burgoyne's pursuit, while prompt, failed to catch all but a rear guard of the Americans, at Hubbardton, Vermont, on July 7. The difficulty of forwarding supplies from Ticonderoga delayed his march toward Albany for weeks, allowing the rebels to regroup and reinforce, contributing to the British defeat at Saratoga. Portrait by Joshua Reynolds, c. 1766. (*The Frick Collection*)

and foreign affairs. While still a sitting member (this time for Preston), he was promoted to major general in 1772; three years later his first play, *Maid of the Oaks*, was produced on the London stage. In fact, he enjoyed a certain celebrity.[13] There were plenty of British generals senior to Burgoyne, but few with his level of public name recognition. When the government sent him to the colonies, it did so with considerable confidence in its selection.

In America, Burgoyne got off to a slow start. Arriving in Boston in May 1775 with Howe and Clinton, he found himself without an independent command. He was a bystander during Bunker Hill and the early stages of the siege of Boston, and inaction left him irked and disenchanted. Seeing no prospect of a useful command under Howe, he returned to Britain in November 1775, well before the British evacuated the city in March 1776. In London, he lobbied the ministry for a senior command, but he was content to return to America, this time to Canada, as second-in-command to Quebec Governor and Lieutenant General Guy Carleton. This time he saw plenty of action. He arrived on June 1 at the head of a large contingent of reinforcements, and he promptly cooperated with Carleton in breaking the American siege of Quebec. By the end of June, the British counteroffensive had driven the rebels completely out of Canada, with Burgoyne, leading some four thousand troops, pursuing the beaten and demoralized patriots up the Richelieu. The American retreat did not stop until most of their battered units reached Ticonderoga (although a small garrison remained for a time at Crown Point). Burgoyne had every reason to be pleased with his performance.

Yet he was not pleased with Carleton's. In Burgoyne's opinion, the Americans were, in pugilistic terms, on the ropes and ripe for a knockout blow. This seemed especially true after Valcour Island. But, as the reader will recall, Carleton thought otherwise—much to Burgoyne's disgust. Carleton had by no means given up on an offensive. He was intent on moving up Lake Champlain, taking Ticonderoga, then moving on to Albany; he would still cut off New England from the colonies to the south, and he told London as much. Carleton planned an early start in 1777 to finish the job. But this was not good enough for Burgoyne, who thought Carleton had missed his chance in front of Ticonderoga and in any case lacked the requisite fighting spirit.

Peeved and frustrated with his superior, Burgoyne again returned to Britain, this time to fight a political battle. He had friends in high places—he was still a member of Parliament—and he knew how to use his connections. As senior officers of the day were wont to do, he wasted no time in castigating his former commanding officer, blasting what he considered Carleton's lack of initiative. (Of course Carleton, still in Canada, had no means to defend himself.) Burgoyne found ready listeners in the king, Lord North, and Lord Germain, all eager for some decisive action to bring the rebellion to a close. North asked for his ideas, and Burgoyne was forthcoming. He essentially endorsed Carleton's plan to move up the lakes to isolate New England, although he added detail; and he was instrumental in drafting the final plan for the 1777 campaign—that is, the advance from Canada meeting a simultaneous thrust up the Hudson, as well as a smaller force moving up the Mohawk Valley to Albany. And Burgoyne left no doubt he wanted the Canadian command.

There was just one wrinkle in this regard: Burgoyne was not the only senior officer home from America. Henry Clinton, who had served under Howe in the Middle Theater, was there too, and Clinton was as averse to remaining under Howe as Burgoyne was to remaining with Carleton. Clinton was senior to Burgoyne, thus Sir Henry had every right to ask for the new command. He didn't. He and Burgoyne were friends, and in London, Clinton spent time consoling Burgoyne on the loss of his wife. Charlotte had passed away in June as John was campaigning in Quebec, and he leaned heavily on Clinton, whose wife had died in 1772, as a kindred spirit. Clinton was interested in the Canadian assignment and even had some thoughts on how the campaign ought to unfold. The Canadian venture would be problematic, he thought, unless Howe's army moved up the Hudson in support. But understanding his bereaved comrade's wishes, he concluded he could not push his case. "I had a delicacy upon those matters"—the Canadian command—"that would not permit me to do anything of the kind."[14] With Clinton stepping back, Burgoyne received the command.

Burgoyne arrived in Quebec on May 6, 1777, and the event galvanized the army. Immediately, Lieutenant Hadden recorded, "preparations were . . . made for an Expedition under his Command, against Tyconderoga."[15] Carleton, however, would not be going. Germain's orders to Burgoyne were specific: Burgoyne was to command the invasion while Carleton remained behind to govern Quebec. Deeply offended, Carleton resigned the governorship on June 27, although he remained in office until his successor, Frederick Haldimand, arrived a full year later. In the meantime, good soldier that he was, he did his best to assist Burgoyne in organizing the invasion.

There was a great deal to do. Supplies of all kinds—rations, forage, pack animals, wagons and carts, gun carriages, beeves, bateaux for water transport, warships to deal with rebel gunboats, weapons, munitions—recruiting, and the other minutia of army administration all needed prompt attention. Burgoyne devoted considerable time to persuading Indian allies to accompany the expedition. Then there was the question of labor. There was simply too much to do using the soldiery alone, and at Burgoyne's request, Carleton resorted to corvée labor. This was a system left over from New France under which tenants owed unpaid service to their *seigneurs*—the semifeudal estate owners who still wielded enormous social influence in Canada. The corvée would do the backbreaking work of clearing roads through the forest, packing matériel, and any other heavy tasks the army required. As many as eight hundred French Canadians served in the corvée.[16]

While these preparations moved forward, Burgoyne organized his army. As of May 1, 1777, there were 11,608 regulars in Canada "fit for duty"—7,106 British and 4,502 Germans (Brunswickers). Of these, army returns indicate Burgoyne brought 8,118 troops with him (however, in what was probably a deliberate undercount, he would later claim he started with only 7,006).[17] Beyond troop strength, some 1,000 civilian camp followers—sutlers, families, the corvée—accompanied the Canadian army. Adding real punch was an impressive artillery train. Burgoyne was bringing 138 guns of various sizes capable of supporting action against enemy infantry or battering Ticonderoga's fixed fortifications.[18] This was a powerful force, but it was not overwhelming. Burgoyne's army was actually smaller than the Ticonderoga garrison Carleton had confronted in October 1776, although it was some three times larger than St. Clair's garrison of 2,500 or so effectives.

Burgoyne's order of battle was quite simple. The British troops were organized in three major units. There were two brigades, respectively under Brigadier Generals James Hamilton and Henry Watson Powell. In addition, Brigadier General Simon Fraser (Burgoyne spelled it "Frazer") commanded a highly mobile advanced corps intended as the army's vanguard. This corps had real striking power: Burgoyne assigned it a battalion each of elite British light infantry and grenadiers, as well as the 24th Regiment, "some Canadians and Savages, and ten pieces of Lt. Artillery" (three-pounders). In addition, there was a company of picked British marksmen and a battalion of German light infantry.[19] The rest of the expedition's Germans were organized in a division under Brunswick Major General Friedrich Adolf von Riedesel. Burgoyne had about five hundred American Indians, mostly Iroquois, attached to his various units, as well as some 250 Tories and Canadian militia.[20] Theoretically at least, the limited number of large units would make command and control relatively easy, although Burgoyne would find the Canadian militia of dubious

Friedrich Adolf von Riedesel (1738-1800). Riedesel commanded all of the German troops—overwhelmingly Brunswickers, not Hessians—with Burgoyne's army. While Burgoyne advanced down the west shore of Lake Champlain toward Ticonderoga, Riedesel led his Germans down the east shore toward Mount Independence. The Americans evacuated the Ticonderoga positions before Riedesel could engage, but he helped turn the tide in the Crown's favor at the Battle of Hubbardton on July 7. Engraving by M. Lammel. (*Library of Congress*)

reliability and the Indians, while the terror of the Americans, wont to pursue their own agendas.

Burgoyne was blessed with talented subordinates. His second-in-command was Major General William Phillips, an experienced field commander and artillerist. He had seen plenty of action in the Seven Years' War, and in 1776 at St. John's, he had supervised construction of the fleet that fought at Valcour Island. Until Burgoyne's return from Britain in May 1777, Phillips had exercised direct command of the army as Carleton's second. During the invasion, he would directly command the 1st and 2nd Brigades (Hamilton and Powell). He was competent and energetic, and he had no use for the rebels. He already had invoked patriot ire over the winter when he spurned receiving messengers from Ticonderoga sent to negotiate prisoner exchanges. Phillips refused any "communication with the American rebels—unless coming to implore the King's mercy."[21] Shortly he would give the Americans even greater reason to detest him.

The brigadiers were just as good. The British army had no permanent grade of brigadier general; the rank was temporary (brevet), conferred for special assignments such as the 1777 campaign or for service in a specific region. In Canada, Carleton had the authority to make brevet appointments, and the men he chose were all lieutenant colonels on the army list. Simon Fraser was a hardened veteran. He was a Scot whose military career began in the Dutch army in 1747; he joined the redcoats in 1755, and in the Seven Years' War served in America at Louisbourg and at Quebec. He remained in the army after the war and was promoted to lieutenant colonel in 1768. Carleton made him a brigadier in 1776, and on June 8, Fraser repaid him with a thumping victory over the Americans at Three Rivers (Trois-Rivières)—a battle that virtually ended the rebel invasion of Canada. No officer in the Canadian army enjoyed a better reputation than Fraser.

James Hamilton is lesser known, in part because the British army list had so many James Hamiltons that details of his early career were thoroughly obscured. The Hamilton with Burgoyne, however, likely began his army career in 1755, and he had means enough (most commissions being purchased through the rank of lieutenant colonel) and talent enough to advance to lieutenant colonel by 1772. In 1776, he took over a brigade in Canada upon the illness and death of its brigadier, and he did well enough for Carleton to promote him to brigadier general in November that year. Reading backward from his performance at Saratoga, where he did very well, we can safely assume Burgoyne found Hamilton a fully dependable brigade commander.[22]

We know more about Henry Watson Powell, and he has a special place in Ticonderoga's story. He had joined the army as a lieutenant in 1753, and during the Seven Years' War, he saw action in the West Indies. After duty on Gibraltar and in Ireland, in 1771 he was promoted to lieutenant colonel in command of the 53rd Foot and posted on the Mediterranean island of Minorca. Powell deployed to Canada in May 1776. The 53rd performed well at Trois-Rivières, and two days later Carleton appointed Powell a brigade commander with the rank of brigadier. In 1777, the brigadier led Burgoyne's 2nd Brigade.[23] Powell was a soldier's soldier, and he would prove as much at Ticonderoga.

For as we will see, he would be the only officer ever to defend "the old French fort" (as many contemporaries called it) from a direct assault.[24]

There is a final brigadier to consider. Lieutenant Colonel Barrimore (Barry) Matthew St. Leger would command the column advancing up the Mohawk Valley. For this assignment, Burgoyne brevetted him to brigadier. St. Leger was an Anglo-Irishman from County Kildare, Ireland. Well educated, he attended Eton and Cambridge (BA 1755, MA 1763) before joining the army in 1756. Like Fraser and Hamilton, he fought at Louisbourg and Quebec, and in 1776, his regiment (the 34th Foot) helped drive the Americans out of Canada. While Burgoyne moved on Ticonderoga, St. Leger's job was to lead a mixed force of British and German regulars, Iroquois and allied tribes (the Indians were the largest component of his force), and loyalists. Starting from Oswego, on Lake Ontario, they were to move up the Mohawk Valley to Albany, there to meet Burgoyne. We can note here that his mission failed. After a brutal but pyrrhic Iroquois victory over New York militia at Oriskany, St. Leger failed to take Fort Stanwix (near modern Rome, New York), which blocked the way east.[25] He gave up his quest for Albany and returned to Montreal. But much later he will return prominently to our narrative—at Ticonderoga.

The men under General Riedesel's command were mostly from the duchy of Braunschweig (Brunswick in English), thus contemporaries referred to them as Brunswickers and not Hessians (troops largely from Hesse-Kassel and Hesse-Hanau). Riedesel, born to a minor noble family, began his military service at age seventeen as an ensign in the army of the Landgrave of Hesse. He joined the staff of the Duke of Brunswick during the Seven Years' War and remained with the Brunswickers for the rest of his career. Newly promoted to major general, Riedesel arrived in America in 1776 as part of some four thousand Brunswick troops serving under a contract between the duke and George III. He quickly adapted to soldiering in America and led his men effectively as British forces pushed the invading Americans out of Canada. Burgoyne found the baron dependable and an able commander of German forces during the Ticonderoga-Saratoga campaign.[26]

Burgoyne also had a formidable naval commander. At St. John's, naval preparations went forward under Captain Skeffington Lutwidge—a Royal Navy sea dog if ever there was one. Indeed, a young Horatio Nelson was a midshipman under Lutwidge, and Nelson never lost his regard for the man. In 1773, Lutwidge commanded HMS *Carcass* on an Arctic exploratory expedition and then graduated to the twenty-eight-gun frigate *Triton*. He sailed it to America in 1775 and operated on the St. Lawrence in support of Carleton's counteroffensive in 1776. Carleton then brevetted Lutwidge to flag rank as commodore, placing him in charge of the Lake Champlain fleet. Lutwidge retained the command under Burgoyne and saw to the fitting out of hundreds of bateaux, gunboats of various types, and several larger men-of-war, including veterans of Valcour Island. Burgoyne's flagship was the twenty-gun (or twenty-six-gun, accounts differ) sloop *Royal George*. The fleet also included *Inflexible*, of eighteen or twenty-two guns, and *Thunderer*, a large and awkward flat-bottomed radeau designed to carry numerous cannon and tons of stores. Some 640 men served in the crews, and the fleet mounted a total of 133 guns.[27] The commodore's main job was to ferry Burgoyne's army up Lake Champlain and land it as close to Ticonderoga as safely possible. There was no real danger of a fleet action, as Lutwidge's ships vastly outnumbered and outgunned the five American survivors from 1776. And those five sheltered behind the antishipping boom and floating bridge; they wouldn't have stood a chance in battle. In effect, Lake Champlain had become Lake Lutwidge.

Thus, as Burgoyne readied his army, he worked with senior officers of genuine talent and experience. Those subordinates in turn commanded British and German staff and line officers who brought a level of professionalism to their tasks that St. Clair at Ticonderoga could only envy. Experience would reveal that Burgoyne's army and his preparations for the coming campaign were anything but perfect (he does end up at Saratoga!), but the British commander had every reason to feel his men were as prepared and well led as any troops could be for the mission that lay ahead.

By mid-June, Burgoyne was ready to move. Having assembled and prepared his army at St. John's, on June 20 and 21 the troops boarded the fleet and got underway.[28] Before pushing off himself, however, the lieutenant general took two opportunities to wax eloquent. On June 21,

Skeffington Lutwidge (1737-1814). Commodore (by brevet) Lutwidge commanded the Lake Champlain fleet in support of Burgoyne's invasion. After the Americans evacuated the fort and Mount Independence, Lutwidge's crews easily broke through the anti-shipping boom and bridge on the lake, enabling a quick pursuit of rebel vessels headed for Skenesborough. Portrait by Philip Jean, before 1802. (*Bonhams*)

he addressed an assembly of "Chiefs and Warriors" at Gilliland's Creek, also called the Boquet River, some forty-two miles above Ticonderoga. He reminded the Iroquois of the perfidy of the American "Apostates" and embraced the Indians as "Brothers in War." Burgoyne then established some rules for the coming campaign, which he summed up thusly: "I positively forbid bloodshed when you are not opposed in Arms. Aged Men, Women, Children and Prisoners must be held sacred from the Knife or Hatchet, even in the time of actual conflict."[29] It was a plea for restraint in war at variance with Indian cultural norms but aimed at assuring colonists the British army would keep the tribes under control. At Ticonderoga, St. Clair's scouts reported the large gathering at Gilliland's but couldn't get close enough to learn what was going on, let alone that Burgoyne himself was there.

Three days later, Burgoyne issued a "Manifesto" to Americans that, if anything, dwarfed in pomposity his address to the Iroquois. The royal commander opened with a virtual resume: he was "John Burgoyne Esquire, Lieutenant General of His Majesty's Armies in America, Colonel of the Queen's Regiment of Light Dragoons, Governor of Fort William in North Britain, and one of the Representatives of the Commons of Great Britain in Parliament, and commanding an Army & Fleet employ'd on an Expedition from Canada, &c, &c, &c." Then, in so many words—actually in very many words—he announced a mission of liberation. Burgoyne would end the "unnatural rebellion" and free Americans from the tyranny of Congress—"the compleatest system of Tyranny that ever God in his displeasure suffered for a time to be exercised over a forward & stubborn Generation." "Justice" and "wrath" awaited recalcitrant rebels, but as his army advanced he would protect the innocent; the unoffending should have no fear. This was Burgoyne the man of letters whose flare with words was probably unmatched in the British army—and perhaps in any army.[30]

Such eloquence (if it was that) became the stuff of ridicule in Britain and America. New Jersey Governor William Livingston, writing as "A New Jersey Man," heaped scorn on the manifesto in a satiric poem even longer than Burgoyne's epistle. A few lines from one of the final stanzas conveys the flavor of the whole:

PROCLAMATION. By John Burgoyne . . .
I will let loose the dogs of Hell,
Ten thousand Indians, who shall yell,
And foam and tear, and grin and roar,
And drench their maukesins in gore,
To these I'll give full scope and play
From *Ticondroge* to *Florida*;
They'll scalp your heads and kick your shins,
And rip your guts, and flay your skins,
And of your ears be nimble croppers,
And make your thumbs, tobacco-stoppers. . . .[31]

And so on (and *on*). Livingston's pen was as sharp as Burgoyne's. In Britain, Edmund Burke lampooned the address to the Indians on the floor of the Commons. Asking for Iroquois restraint, he scoffed, was akin to releasing wild animals from the zoo and then cautioning them, "My gentle lions, my humane bears, my sentimental wolves, my tenderhearted hyenas, go forth: but I exhort ye as ye are Christians and members of a civilized society, take care not to hurt man, woman, or child."[32]

But all of that was later. It is worth bearing in mind that the Iroquois prized oratory, especially on important occasions—such as going to war—and saw nothing funny in Burgoyne's speech. Philip Schuyler missed the humor in Burgoyne's literary productions as well. When he got hold of a copy of the "Manifesto" he feared the worst. As he explained to the commander in chief, Burgoyne had taken pains to circulate his proclamation "industriously . . . thro' the Country and I fear [it] will be attended with the most evil Consequences to us."[33] Henry Brockholst Livingston, William's son and variously an aide to Schuyler, St. Clair, and Arnold during the Ticonderoga-Saratoga campaign, initially missed his father's light take on the manifesto (if he ever saw it). "It is not by Arms alone, our Enemies mean to subdue us," he warned the senior Livingston. "Insidious Proclamations and the most cruel Threats are weapons they begin to brandish . . . but with what success we cannot yet determine. Burgoyne's Proclamation is fraught with the most scurrilous language."[34] These were exactly the reactions among patriots Burgoyne had intended.

As Burgoyne was making his speeches and issuing his proclamations, his army made its way up Lake Champlain. The voyage was unimpeded, and some of the soldiers thoroughly enjoyed themselves. Royal Artillery diarist Lieutenant James Hadden happily found himself aboard the same gunboat he had commanded the previous year at Valcour Island; and he remembered June 19 in particular as being "very fine and the passage pleasant, the *Lake* affording many beautiful prospects." On foggy days the drummers kept up a beat that served to keep the fleet together, and on good days the regimental musicians entertained the troops with "Music and Drums."[35] It seemed a leisurely sojourn to war.

But that was during the day; at night it was a different story. The army put ashore each night, and the Brunswick troops, used to the relatively open terrain of the settled areas of Quebec and Europe, found camping in New York a challenge. "The banks of the lake are covered with the thickest woods," recorded Lieutenant August Wilhelm Du Roi of the Prinz Friedrich Regiment, "and every time a camp had to be pitched, trees had to be cut down and the place cleared." The hard labor sapped morale. Moreover, men accustomed to cool Canadian and European evenings found the Champlain region's summer heat hard to bear. And they found the mosquitoes intolerable.

"We had already made the acquaintance of mosquitos in Canada," an exasperated Du Roi grumbled,

> but never before had we suffered from them as much as today, for these insects attacked us in such quantities that it was impossible to protect ourselves from them, neither smoking of tobacco, nor the smoke of a number of small fires all around the camp being of any avail. We nearly suffocated from the smoke and could not keep our eyes open. It was impossible to wrap ourselves up in blankets on account of the heat, and the blood-thirsty [sic] mosquito would sting even through three-fold linen (sheets). It is impossible to describe the torture, indeed, I think myself justified in stating that nobody could endure it continuously for more than a few days and nights without becoming insane. If anybody could have watched us from a distance with out being molested himself, or knowing what was going on, he would have thought the whole camp full of raving maniacs.[36]

But in late June, the time for "Music and Drums" was over, and for many the prospect of confronting the rebels was a welcome relief from the battle against the mosquitoes. The leading elements of the fleet reached Crown Point on June 24, and the entire army caught up by the thirtieth. Burgoyne then advanced to Four Mile Point—four miles north of Ticonderoga—on July 1, while Fraser led his advanced corps to Three Mile Point. For the men with Burgoyne and St. Clair, the moment of reckoning had come.

Chapter 5

Invasion:
The Key Unlocked

WITH HIS ARMY GATHERED at Crown Point, Burgoyne ordered the advance on Ticonderoga on July 1, 1777. Carleton had never brought his main forces to bear on the peninsula in 1776, so the new assault would be the first major action against Ticonderoga since Jeffery Amherst's approach had forced the French to abandon the post in 1759. It is an old military aphorism, however, that no plan survives contact with the enemy. And as events unfolded in July 1777, there were surprises aplenty for both the British and the rebels, with consequences few could have predicted.

John Burgoyne launched his attack with another literary flourish. At Crown Point on June 30, he spoke through general orders to his army, and it was a production Napoleon would have envied a generation later. "This Army," he proclaimed, "Embarks tomorrow to Approach the Enemy[.] We are to contend for the King and the constitution of Great Britain to vindicate Law and to relieve the Oppressed." There would be times, the theatrical general asserted, when even "life" was not "to be regarded. This Army must not retreat."[1] It is easy to read an implied exclamation point after that last sentence. In fact the royal army was moving already. As Burgoyne's general orders circulated at Crown Point, Simon Fraser's corps moved south to Four-Mile Point (so-called because of its distance from Ticonderoga); at the same time, Germans on the east shore moved south in parallel with Fraser. A day later, July 1, Fraser was at Three-Mile Point and ready to move farther south when, on the same day, Burgoyne put the rest of the army in motion. By the end of the day, his main body was at Four-Mile Creek, and Riedesel had his Germans as far south on the eastern shore of the lake. The attack on the entire Ticonderoga complex was on.

The redcoat commander had no intention of being another Abercrombie—there would be no frontal assault on Ticonderoga. While Burgoyne knew more about the Americans than the Americans knew about him, he was still unaware of exactly how strong the rebel defenses were, and he estimated rebel strength as appreciably higher than it was. The British and Germans thought they could be facing as many as five thousand opponents. Thus, instead of initiating any sudden direct attack, Burgoyne was prepared to move deliberately to cut off avenues of retreat, besiege the Americans, and batter them into submission with his powerful artillery train. With luck, he could bag the entire garrison before moving south to Lake George and on to Albany.

Burgoyne's plan was simple. Fraser would work around the American left and threaten rebel communications between Lake George and Lake Champlain. Simultaneously, Major General Phillips would move down the western shore of Champlain with Hamilton and Powell. They would support Fraser if necessary while threatening the works along the French Lines. Meanwhile, Riedesel would lead the Germans up the eastern shore. His mission was to get around Mount Independence and cut off any line of patriot retreat into Vermont. Vessels under Lutwidge would break through rebel water defenses and stymie any patriot escape up the lake. Cut off and surrounded, St. Clair would have no choice but to capitulate. It all seemed so straight-forward.[2]

At Ticonderoga, James Wilkinson already had privately reached the same conclusion. In a letter to Gates, he insisted St. Clair had too few men to mount an effective defense. And calling in more militia wouldn't help: available supplies were too meager to equip or to feed them—even trying would soon have everyone starving. Abandoning the fort to defend Mount Independence would only invite a siege in which Burgoyne was bound to prevail, and the Royal Navy would probably break through the lake obstructions, take Skenesborough, and thereby cut rebel communications to the South. He informed Gates that the only real chance the Americans had to impede Burgoyne was to pull out of Ticonderoga while they still could and fall back all the way to Fort George. "Should we attempt to support this place [Ticonderoga] in our present deficient situation, we lose *all*, and leave the country defenseless and exposed."[3] If pessimistic, Wilkinson's estimate of the situation was not unreasonable.

St. Clair, also a realist, was not yet so downbeat. Indeed, for a brief moment on July 1, the rebel commander not only misread available reports of British activity but actually thought it augured well for Ticonderoga. Scouts reported sighting what probably were Fraser's men at Three-Mile Point, and they informed the American general that the enemy was digging in. In addition, the same intelligence counted "two ships, eighteen gun-boats, and three sloops" anchored off the point and reported that they had floated a defensive boom. "This does not look like their being strong," St. Clair informed Schuyler. In fact, it looked as though Burgoyne was lying on the defensive—"Bravo!" the fort commandant concluded.[4] In all of patriot attempts to fathom what Burgoyne was up to, this estimate of the enemy situation stands as the classic example of the astoundingly wretched state of rebel intelligence efforts.

Later in the day, any rebel hopes of British hesitancy evaporated; in fact, they literally went up in smoke. Recovering quickly from his bout of euphoria, St. Clair realized the gravity of the situation as he learned of enemy movements on the west and east shores of the lake. He also knew—or at least suspected—that the British knew more about him than he knew about them, and he moved to tighten rebel security. Concerned that local civilians, who had access to the American camp, were passing information to Burgoyne, St. Clair ordered civilians living closest to the fort moved within American lines. He informed Schuyler that while he could not positively say "that they are our enemies, but they are certainly not our friends." He had them sent under guard to Skenesborough and then on to Albany.[5]

At this point the general's chief concern was for the safety of his exposed detachments and supplies at the sawmills and the Lake George landing. He ordered officers there to ship all stores to the fort, then to evacuate all remaining bateaux to Fort George. They were to burn any unneeded bateaux. The signal for departure would be smoke from the burning mills and nearby blockhouses, which St. Clair considered indefensible and ordered fired. The guards from the landings, mills, and blockhouses would then retreat to the French Lines.[6] The orders came not a moment too soon, as a small British scouting party tried its luck against a blockhouse near the mills. The Americans fought it off, but they knew they stood no chance against a larger assault. They prepared to get out while they could.[7]

The fires began early on July 2, and the smoke signaled the start of the first serious combat of the campaign. With the mills and blockhouses afire, the American bateaux pushed off for Fort George and the guard detachments prepared for the mile-and-a-half trek back to the patriot lines. But the British also saw the smoke, and redcoats probed forward. These were soldiers of an advanced party under Simon Fraser's nephew, Captain Alexander Fraser. The captain's were especially dangerous men, chosen from the army's infantry companies (two men from each) for their marksmanship.[8] As they neared Mount Hope, two things happened. First, rebels in the redoubt on Mount Hope saw them, and realizing St. Clair could not support their isolated post, they pulled out and made for the French Lines. This alone was a body blow to Ticonderoga's safety. Mount Hope was the key to communications with Lake George and the defense of the American left. The terrain west of the mount was trackless and rough, and moving a large body of troops around the mountain would have been difficult—prohibitively so if time was an important factor. Thus, with Mount Hope in patriot hands, a key approach to the fort was secure—but with its abandonment, the American left was wide open. Captain Fraser occupied the hill with a small force without firing a shot.

Opposite: "Part of the counties of Charlotte and Albany, in the Province of New York: being the seat of war between the King's forces under Lieut. Gen. Burgoyne and the rebel army."A 1778 map from the *London Magazine.* The detail of the blockhouses and other defensive works is remarkably accurate, although the roads look far more passable than they actually were. "Sugar Hill" (Sugar Loaf or Mount Defiance) is properly positioned but in reality extended farther south. (*Library of Congress*)

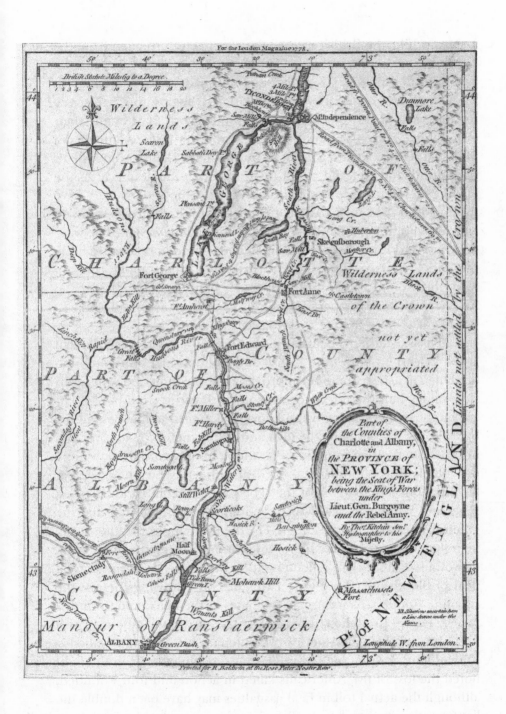

Meanwhile, the British spotted the Americans retreating from the burning blockhouses and mills. The terrain was relatively flat, and the rebels, some fifty to sixty strong, had not made it halfway to safety. Brigadier Fraser decided to cut them off. He was positioning his men for an attack when his accompanying Iroquois took matters into their own hands. Before the redcoats were ready, the Indians launched a wild charge. British and American sources later claimed the Indians were drunk and attacked under the influence. One doubts it. As the leading elements of Fraser's advanced party, the Indians may have reckoned on the rebels reaching safety before the redcoats came up and so acted independently. In any event the fight was on. The withdrawing Americans lost several killed and wounded before reaching the lines. Then the Indians and British light infantry took cover in heavy brush and traded fire with rebels behind their breastworks. American artillery peppered the British and Indians as well, some of whom got as close as sixty yards to the rebel lines.[9]

Call it a skirmish or small battle—either way it was a hot action that lasted at least an hour. The British and Iroquois had some five hundred men in action opposing approximately one thousand Americans (just under half the effective garrison) with eight cannon. St. Clair was on the scene, walking up and down the American line behind the breastworks, encouraging the men and telling them to take cover and not to waste their ammunition. Most took his advice, although there was still plenty of shooting. A great deal of the musketry, however, was anything but lethal. Many of the rebels were in combat for the first time, and Wilkinson, who was in action, later commented that the green troops tended to fire high. For the thousands of rounds fired, he noted, the patriots "could never learn that we killed a single man, or wounded more than a lieutenant!!!" But if there was not a great deal of bloodshed, there were casualties on both sides before the shooting stopped. As was usual, estimates of the killed and wounded varied. Henry Brockholst Livingston was "uncertain" about British losses but reported an American "Lieutenant & five privates killed— And a Lieut, & seven men wounded." A rebel lieutenant in the fight noted the loss of five Americans killed in action and four wounded, although the actual toll in fatal casualties may have been double the lieutenant's estimate.[10] If the British had contemplated a further attack, the stiff American resistance made them think better of it. The rebel performance gave Burgoyne no reason to deviate from his plan for a methodical envelopment and siege of the rebel positions.

In fact, the patriots had fought well. Whatever the human cost of the action, the rebels were encouraged. Livingston, then serving as aide to St. Clair, took an entirely practical view of the clash. Most of the rebel troops were green, he noted, and the skirmish on July 2 was something of an educational experience for the "raw, & undisciplined" men. Such small engagements "serve as Preparitives" for major combat, and Livingston (writing on July 3) was sure a real showdown with Burgoyne was imminent.[11] The brief action was hardly enough to make veterans of the Americans at Ticonderoga, but at least it was an important lesson in the realities of battle.

The fighting did produce an unusual intelligence coup for St. Clair. At some point during the action, Wilkinson noticed a redcoat firing repeatedly from behind a stump. He directed a rebel sergeant to pick him off, and the soldier dutifully took a shot—which set off a fusillade from other Continentals. When the smoke cleared the redcoat was down, and when the engagement ended, St. Clair ordered the body brought in—the brave enemy was to receive decent burial. A small party ventured out, only to find the supposedly dead soldier not only alive but untouched by rebel bullets (another example of the ineffectiveness of patriot musket fire). "The fellow was brought in; he belonged to the 47th light infantry," Wilkinson remembered, "and was intoxicated and insolent, refusing to give a word of information." But the insolent Briton did give it up. St. Clair had him locked up with an American officer posing as a captured Tory, and between more rum and the confidence of a supposed comrade, the light infantryman told "all he knew." That was quite a bit. In fact he largely confirmed information Schuyler had wrung out of a captured loyalist spy some weeks before. But for some detail on British units involved, however, it was little St. Clair didn't already know: Burgoyne had come in strength and meant to have Ticonderoga and everyone in it.[12]

This is not to say that St. Clair wasn't trying to find out as much as he could. He sent out his own spies, one of whom (according to local tradition) was New York militiaman Asa Douglas. (Douglas was the great grandfather of Stephen A. Douglas of Lincoln-Douglas fame.) July 3 saw a lull in the fighting, and it was on the third or fourth that Douglas slipped into British lines posing as a local (and likely Tory)

farmer. He walked around freely, but when he mounted his horse—
"Old Ti"—to leave, someone got suspicious. The cry went up: "'The old farmer is a spy!'" Fleeing gunfire, he supposedly told his mount, "'Old Ti, Ride for your life and if you get me home safely, you will never be saddled again.'" Douglas family lore has it that Asa kept his word, and that Old Ti "lived happily in the pasture for the rest of his life."[13] One really wants it to be true.

There is no record of what Douglas reported, if anything; he may not have been able to get back to American lines. But he must have seen plenty of activity. Proceeding with thoughts of a siege, the British tightened their grip on the western shore. They brought up additional supplies and artillery. On their right (the rebel left) Fraser moved up the rest of his advanced corps, and supported by one of Phillips' infantry brigades, consolidated the imperial hold on Mount Hope—not that the Americans were in any position to take it back. A second infantry brigade deployed to the right of the mount. A German unit from Riedesel's division came over from the eastern shore, allowing Burgoyne to have a solid line from the western shore of Champlain to beyond Mount Hope. Riedesel was moving on Mount Independence, but slowly in the face of difficult terrain. Rebel artillery maintained fire on all royal forces within range, but generally without fatal effect. Yet some shots on July 4 did tell. Accounts told of artillery fire actually holing tents in the British encampment; and on one occasion, reported Lieutenant Colonel Christian Prätorius, commander of the Prinz Friedrich Regiment, "3 English Artillerymen had their heads blown off."[14] Even so, by this time Burgoyne had sealed everything to the north and west of the fort, including the route to Lake George. If St. Clair tried to get away, the only remaining avenues of escape were the road south from Mount Independence and, using bateaux and what was left of the patriot fleet, the lake itself south of the protective boom and bridge. The ring was closing fast.

So things remained until July 5. The record is a bit hazy on who among the British had the bright idea: what about Sugar Loaf, the high ground just southwest of the fort the Americans called Mount Defiance? From their own intelligence sources, at least some of Burgoyne's officers knew that the rebels had discussed defending the mountain but had decided against it as impractical or too difficult. In any event, Burgoyne sent Major Griffith Williams and Lieutenant

Guns sited on Mount Defiance dominated Fort Ticonderoga, seen in the center distance, Mount Independence, a part of which is in the center right, as well as marine traffic. While the rebels dithered—they never made up their minds what to do about Defiance—in July 1777 the British quickly saw the mountain as key terrain and, to the Americans' surprise, hurriedly mounted 12-pounders near the summit. The British move convinced Arthur St. Clair the fort and Mount Independence were indefensible. (*Photo by Mwanner/Wikimedia Commons*)

William Twiss, Corps of Engineers, up Sugar Loaf to have a look. The lieutenant's report was electrifying. He concluded that getting artillery to the summit would be arduous but entirely possible. Moreover, it could be done in a day, and once done, a battery could command all rebel positions on the western and eastern sides of Lake Champlain as well as navigation on the lake itself. If Twiss was right, and Phillips— probably the best artilleryman in the entire British army—said he was, then a siege might be unnecessary. Enough guns on Mount Defiance could pound St. Clair into submission or oblivion.

After this, things moved quickly. Burgoyne put Phillips in charge of the operation, and with his now-famous quip—"Where a goat can go, a man can go. And where a man can go, he can drag a gun."—the determined major general soon had troops busy clearing a road to the summit of Defiance.[15] It was backbreaking work, and the resulting track was rough, but two twelve-pounders (or 18-pounders, accounts differ—but almost certainly twelves) were in place with plenty of daylight to spare. Those guns indeed could hit any rebel position below, although it would have taken more than two cannons to inflict decisive damage quickly, especially at long range. And the rough new road would have impeded ammunition deliveries sufficient for a heavy volume of fire.[16] Phillips was a bulldog, however, and eventually he would have hauled up whatever guns and munitions it took to blast the rebels to rubble. But he never got the chance.

Sometime during the mid-afternoon of July 5, patriots spotted the redcoats of the working parties on Mount Defiance. The Americans knew why they were up there—there could only be one reason—and the garrison's dismay was palpable. Morale evaporated. For St. Clair, the ominous development may have been the proverbial last straw. The major general was never a military genius, but neither was he a fool. With or without enemy artillery on Mount Defiance, St. Clair knew the noose was tightening around his command and that a painful decision—fight what would almost certainly be a losing battle, or flee while the rebels still could—was in the immediate offing. It was now time to decide, and fearing the game was up, he called a council of war. Brigadiers Paterson, La Rochefermoy, and Poor, and Continental Colonel Pierce Long (of New Hampshire) attended. The major general explained that British artillery would soon command all defensive works and that attacks on Ticonderoga and Mount Independence appeared imminent. In that case, neither part of the garrison could move to reinforce the other. Besides, it was only a matter of time before Riedesel worked his way around Mount Independence and cut the last overland escape route, effectively leaving the garrison surrounded. Surrender would be a matter of time, and patriots would lose not only Ticonderoga but the greater part of the Northern Army. Accordingly, the officers unanimously agreed that their position was hopeless and that only an evacuation could save the army.

We should note, however, that the final decision was St. Clair's—and that the major general displayed considerable courage in making it. He understood that abandoning the American Gibraltar would bring a public outcry; and in the honor-driven military ethos of the eighteenth century, commanders routinely confronted or even accepted death rather than sacrifice a personal reputation. In placing the salvation of the army first, St. Clair knew he risked a storm of criticism and personal dishonor. But he did the right thing. He was exhausted when he notified Schuyler of his decision: "Excuse this scrawl; I am so much in want of sleep that I am nodding as I write."[17]

St. Clair planned an orderly withdrawal using the water and overland routes. No one would leave until after dark on the fifth, and with any luck everyone would be gone before sunrise on the sixth. In the meantime, American artillery would redouble its fire, hopefully keeping British heads down and not guessing the Americans were pulling out. Indeed, security was tight enough to keep much of the garrison in the dark until the last minute. For many, if not most, of the rebel troops the decision to evacuate was as jarring as it was unexpected. Ebenezer Fletcher of New Hampshire recalled he and his comrades being awakened in the dark "early in the morning" of the sixth. Told to "strike our tents and swing our packs," Fletcher assumed he was "going to battle"; instead he found himself marching away from Mount Independence under Seth Warner. It all came as a complete surprise.[18]

Fletcher's experience was certainly typical. Livingston dolefully informed his father that "we retreated so or rather fled so precipitately that not an individual article, excepted the military chest [the army's funds], was saved. Not a single Officer saved any Part of his baggage but what he had on. Mine shared the fate of the rest." Luckier than most of his comrades, however, Livingston reported that he still had a personal "reserve" in Albany.[19] Lieutenant Thomas Blake of Colonel Joseph Cilley's 1st New Hampshire Regiment, shaken awake at 1:00 AM on July 6, found "everything in great confusion." Troops received orders to strike tents and assemble with packs and provisions and to get ready to march. But not all provisions were packed, and clothing chests were broken, with "clothing thrown about and carried off by all that were disposed to take it." As Blake hurriedly marched from Mount Independence, he learned that the British already were within the French Lines. Blake was with St. Clair's main body making for Castleton, Vermont, about thirty miles away, and he noted that the army's rear guard, encumbered with troops who could not keep up due to illness or wounds, had stopped about six miles short of Castleton at a place called Hubbardton.[20]

According to a nineteenth-century account, there was almost an altercation within American ranks during the early stages of the retreat. As the story goes, Kosciuszko could not find his horse as the evacuation began, so he grabbed the first mount that came to hand. On the march, however, he was accosted by the horse's owner, who happened to be Colonel Cilley's adjutant. When the adjutant demanded his horse, Kosciuszko refused. Angry words passed, and the New Hampshire officer allegedly challenged the Pole. Kosciuszko declined the challenge on the basis that a junior officer was "not of sufficient rank to meet" a senior. At this point, Cilley supposedly intervened and persuaded Kosciuszko to return the beast.[21] Could all (or any) of this have taken place in the midst of a precipitous withdrawal? Perhaps, but not likely. The story is a good one, but the affair has the same apocryphal ring as the heroics of Asa Douglas. The myth is simply another fragment of the folklore of the Revolution on the northern front.

The evacuation seemed a bit better organized on the Lake Champlain shore of Mount Independence. Surgeon's mate James Thacher remembered being shaken awake at midnight on July 5 at the general hospital and "informed that our army was in motion, and was instantly to abandon Ticonderoga and Mount Independence." His orders were to collect the sick and wounded and whatever supplies he could and get everyone down to the lakeshore. Hurriedly they boarded the already loaded and waiting bateaux and other vessels, and at 3:00 AM on the sixth, they embarked up the narrows of the lake for Skenesborough. The withdrawing flotilla was considerable. Thacher recalled sailing with five "armed gallies"—four of which were Valcour Island survivors—and two hundred "batteaux and boats deeply laden with cannons, tents, provisions, invalids and women." Six hundred infantry under Colonel Long escorted the convoy.[22] With the fleet's departure, the combat units began crossing the bridge from Ticonderoga to Mount Independence; linking up with troops there, and with St. Clair in the lead, they started on the road south toward Castleton, Vermont. After a stop at Castleton, St. Clair intended to meet Long at Skenesborough and reunite the army.

The American commander never got the chance. His evacuation plan, which was a good one, fell afoul of human error—or more ac-

Thaddeus Kosciuszko (1746-1817). Kosciuszko, a Polish patriot and French-trained military engineer, brought invaluable construction skills to Ticonderoga's defenses. He did not get on well with Jeduthan Baldwin, the American engineer, but he enjoyed the firm support of Major General Gates. Kosciuszko wanted to fortify Mount Defiance, but with resources barely adequate to defend the immediate works around the fort and on Mount Independence, his plans garnered little support. He escaped with St. Clair's army on July 6 and, like Baldwin, went on to work under Gates in the Saratoga campaign. Portrait by Karl Gottlieb Schweikart. (*National Museum, Warsaw*)

curately, of stupidity and dereliction of duty. On Mount Independence, a probably drunken La Rochefermoy had fallen asleep, and when awakened he torched his headquarters as he joined the evacuation. St. Clair had expressly forbidden fires as they risked signaling the American retreat to the British. Rochefermoy's blaze did just that. Riedesel saw it, surmised what was happening, and sent some of his men in boats to harass the rebels retreating across the bridge from Ticonderoga. The German also let Burgoyne know what was going on. Then came an even worse gaff. The withdrawing Americans failed to destroy the bridge as the last of the western garrison crossed. Blowing the bridge, or posting cannon on the eastern end to sweep it with grape, was an obvious precaution against a rapid British pursuit. Why didn't it happen? Did orders miscarry? Was there negligence on some officer's part in the haste and confusion of the retreat? We just don't know. We can only note that mistakes, even seemingly inexplicable mistakes, happen in the proverbial fog of war.

One fanciful explanation has remained stubbornly entrenched in the literature. According to Thomas Anburey, a junior officer in the 29th Foot and author of a highly dubious travelogue of his service in America, St. Clair indeed had posted artillery to hold the bridge if the British tried to follow. Grapeshot would have slaughtered the exposed redcoats. But the four American gunners, supposedly "allured by the sweets of plunder and liquor, instead of obeying their orders," were found "dead drunk by a cask of Madeira."[23] The British took them prisoner, repaired any minor damage to the bridge, and set off after St. Clair with Simon Fraser's men in the lead. It's an entertaining story, but it's nonsense—although a number of historians have believed it, and the absurd tale has refused to die. Another British officer, William Digby, surprised at finding the bridge intact and undefended, agreed that patriot guns protecting the bridge could have slaughtered anyone attempting a crossing. But Digby credibly recorded the fact that the withdrawing Americans had positioned no artillery.[24]

Whatever its cause, the American lapse—blunder is a better word—had serious and nearly immediate consequences. Fraser, probably surprised to find the bridge still intact, seized the moment. The enterprising brigadier quickly ordered his units across the unsecured span and, with only the supplies and ammunition his men were carrying, set out after St. Clair. Instead of having a comfortable head start on any British pursuit, the rebels, burdened with wounded and supplies, were only hours ahead of Fraser's fast-moving corps. As they trekked east, the retreating patriots initially had no idea they were being hotly pursued—still less did they suspect that at least some of them would have to fight to make good their escape.

Although St. Clair didn't know it, Colonel Long and his party were in a race as well. With the bridge and water boom now undefended, Lutwidge made short work of both. A few well-placed shots took care of the boom, and his crews quickly opened a gap in the bridge big enough to pass the fleet's largest ships. It took only half an hour. Thinking Burgoyne's army was safely behind, the Americans were enjoying the voyage. There seemed to be no rush, and Thacher recalled that the night was "moon-light and pleasant, the sun burst forth in the morning with uncommon lustre, the day was fine, and the water's surface serene and unruffled." There was a wonderful view of the scenic shoreline, and the surgeon's mate waxed almost rhapsodic, believing he had never beheld "a scene so enchantingly sublime." Drummers and fifers provided music, and the voyagers broke open bottles of wine they found among the hospital stores. It was all a lesson in the warning aphorism that if anything seems too good to be true, it probably is. "We were unsuspicious of danger," the unwary Thacher reminisced; "but, Behold! Burgoyne himself was at our heels."[25]

He certainly was. The general was aboard *Royal George,* his flagship and headquarters during the Ticonderoga operation. With the rest of the British flotilla, he was closing fast on the unsuspecting rebels. They were right behind as the Americans made it to Skenesborough, and as soon as they were in range, the British opened fire on their quarry. It was all the near-panicked rebels could do to try getting everyone ashore and started on the road south. Not everyone made it. In a brisk action, Burgoyne's navy destroyed or captured every vessel the Americans didn't scuttle. These included the five survivors of Benedict Arnold's little fleet. Tons of invaluable supplies were lost on the water, and still more at Skenesborough when the British came ashore.

The column with St. Clair fared better, but only after some real drama. The American commander had ordered his retreating units to Castleton, where he wanted to regroup before moving to Skenesborough and joining Long. Slowed by a large contingent of sick and wounded, however, the next day (July 7), St. Clair's rear guard, under Colonel Seth Warner, stopped to rest at Hubbardton, a few miles short of Castleton. It was there that Fraser, who had raced ahead of the following Riedesel, caught up with him. In a grueling action, Warner punished Fraser's unsupported attack, and the British prevailed, at a high cost, only when Riedesel's Germans arrived to turn the tide. Warner suffered 137 killed and wounded and lost almost 300 prisoners (mostly from among the sick and wounded in his column). But the engagement had cost the king's troops well over two hundred killed and wounded; and the Americans' stiff resistance prevented any further British pursuit of St. Clair.[26]

The Americans ultimately did regroup. Long made it to Fort Ann, where on July 8 he bloodied the nose of a too-eager British advance party. He then burned the post and retreated to Fort Edward, some twelve miles south and where Schuyler was gathering supplies and calling for militia reinforcements. With Skenesborough in British hands, St. Clair took a roundabout route through the Green Mountains and reached Fort Edward on the twelfth. It had been a close call, but the Northern Army, if battered, was still operational; and the troops that rendezvoused at Fort Edward made up the nucleus of the army that would confront Burgoyne at Saratoga.

On the morning of July 6, the Americans gone, the first of Burgoyne's troops marched into Fort Ticonderoga. These were the Brunswickers of the Prinz Friedrich Regiment, who moved in with "the band playing." They hauled down the American colors "at once" and hoisted the regimental colors. It was a proud moment for the Germans. After the ceremony, the regiment encamped outside the fort's walls, the barracks themselves being partially ruined and "very dirty." Slightly later the English 62nd Foot occupied Mount Independence.[27] His Majesty's troops had triumphed.

John Burgoyne was both pleased and surprised by his victory. It had come so fast and at so little cost. All of his planning for a siege was now academic. That he might have to pursue a retreating enemy, rather than bagging him in toto after a siege, seems never to have occurred to the royal commander. In fact, he was completely unprepared to follow up the American evacuation, and the pursuit was an ad hoc affair. As Fraser gave chase to St. Clair, he did so without medical supplies, extra rations, or additional ammunition; events had moved too quickly to plan for an extensive operation. Burgoyne's tons of supplies—and the carts, wagons, and animals necessary to move them—were being stockpiled near Ticonderoga, and he was in no position to speed them forward.[28] Indeed, it would take a full month to bring everything south. His supplies came by boat down Lake George and overland to Fort Edward (which Schuyler left on July 21), while the troops eventually marched overland from Skenesborough to Fort Edward. From there they renewed what became the Saratoga campaign. So while Burgoyne had captured Ticonderoga, the rebel army had escaped to fight another day, with weeks of grace in which to rest and reorganize. Burgoyne had conducted a competent operation, but as historian Michael Bellesiles has sagely observed (quoting

Napoleon), the lieutenant general had won only an "ordinary victory."[29]

Ordinary or not, Burgoyne made the most of it. Writing from Skenesborough on July 11, he dispatched a long communication to Germain (received August 23, 1777) giving a decidedly upbeat account of the Ticonderoga operation. His first paragraph, however, said it all: "I have the honour to acquaint your Lord Ship that the Enemy dislodged from Ticonderoga and Mount Independence on the 6th instant, and were driven on the same Day beyond Skenesborough on the right, and to Hubbardton on the Left, with the loss of a hundred and twenty eight pieces of Cannon; all their armed vessels and Batteaux, the greatest part of their baggage, and ammunition, Provision and Military Stores, to a very large amount."

It was a good summary of what had transpired, and Germain probably was little disturbed by a single sentence late in Burgoyne's epistle: "The remains of the Ticonderoga army are at Fort Edward where they have been joined by considerable corps of fresh troops."[30] In retrospect, of course, that sentence turned out to be gravely important; those "remains" would come back to haunt Burgoyne and Germain for the rest of their lives.

Yet in the immediate afterglow of Ticonderoga, the British gave little thought to a successful American rebound. The rebels were down, and it seemed they were all but out. Germain announced the seeming triumph in Parliament in the most glorious of terms, implying Burgoyne had landed a decisive blow. George III certainly thought so. "I have beat them!" he supposedly proclaimed to an astonished Queen Charlotte, caught *en chemise* in her apartment. "I have beat all the Americans!"[31] As far as we know, most Britons were equally delighted; certainly no one (at least publicly) entertained the thought that Ticonderoga, in fact, had been Lieutenant General Burgoyne's high tide. It certainly was, and they would find out that—and more—soon enough.

Americans, of course, learned of Burgoyne's triumph long before the king. Even so, in the days before "real-time" news, word of Ticonderoga's fall filtered to the rest of the rebellious colonies only gradually and only piecemeal. At Middle Brook, New Jersey, even the commander in chief was unsure of what was going on in the North. As the reader knows, over late June and early July, Washington was in fairly regular contact with Schuyler; and through Schuyler he thought he had a satisfactory understanding of St. Clair's status. But he didn't. In fact, Washington had not heard anything directly from St. Clair since June 26, and in the interim he assumed nothing in the North had really changed. Washington was still anything but sure of William Howe's intentions, but the Continental chief remained convinced the logical British move was a thrust up the Hudson in cooperation with Burgoyne. Washington just didn't know. That being the case, even as reports of Burgoyne operating around Ticonderoga made their ways south—and hearing nothing to the contrary from Ticonderoga—Washington clung to his hunch that any serious moves against the fort and its associated works likely would be diversions in favor of a more significant effort by Howe. He thought the same as late as July 7, when the fort already had fallen, and he so notified senior leadership in Congress and the states.[32]

A day later, however, he had second thoughts about Ticonderoga. Either late on July 7 or early on the eighth, he received word (we do not know from whom, although probably from Schuyler) that the British had occupied Mount Hope. This was six days after patriots had abandoned the post and Fraser's advanced troops had first reached it. As a precaution, Washington earlier had alerted several regiments to be ready to move north in case Ticonderoga faced real trouble. Now, as he awaited details from Schuyler, he ordered Major General John Sullivan, then in northern New Jersey, to get his division on the move. Sullivan was to link up with other rebel troops along the Hudson River and prepare to reinforce St. Clair. About the same time the Virginian received a letter from William Heath (dated July 7), who had heard from Schuyler. Heath's news was not good: he reported that Burgoyne was moving in strength against the fort.[33] These were the first solid indications Washington had that Ticonderoga just might be confronting more than a diversionary attack.

Then, in two letters to Washington of the seventh, Schuyler tried to dispel any ambiguity. The first note was a shocker: "I am extremely apprehensive," he warned, "that the greater part of the Garrisons of Tyconderoga and Mount Independance is in the Enemy's power and

George Washington (1732-1799). The commander-in-chief considered Ticonderoga vitally important to the northern flank of the revolution, and while he never visited the post during the years of active operations, he kept in touch with its various commanders. As the 1777 campaign loomed, Washington questioned whether Ticonderoga would be a primary British target and so decided he could not send major reinforcements to the fort. He was as shocked as anyone else when St. Clair evacuated the post. He finally visited the fort on a northern tour in July 1783 while awaiting word from Paris of the treaty of peace. Portrait by Charles Willson Peale, c. 1779–1781. (*Metropolitan Museum of Art*)

if they make a push they [the British] may do what they please." Then came some clarification: St. Clair had escaped, but the rebels had come off second best at Skenesborough, and St. Clair's whereabouts were unknown. In fact, Schuyler didn't hear from St. Clair until the tenth. The Continentals had "lost every Thing," Schuyler explained, and he urgently requested that Washington forward enough supplies for four thousand men, artillery and munitions, and "a good Engineer or two."[34] From a doubtful situation only days ago, events were unfolding as a full-blown disaster.

Incredibly, Washington still couldn't believe it. As of July 10, the general thought Schuyler was putting an unnecessarily grim interpretation on available reports. Washington suspected that news of a defeat probably referred to "some Misfortune that had befallen Colo.

Warner's party"—certainly a reference to Warner's aborted sally to Otter Creek, as Washington had not yet learned of the action at Hubbardton. A "total Defeat of our Army at Tyconderoga and Mount Independence" was unlikely, he told Schuyler. "If those posts were carried it must have been by Assault as the Time between the 3d & 5th [of July] was too short for it to be done by Blockade." It seems not to have occurred to Washington that St. Clair had evacuated Ticonderoga without a fight. In any event, he promised to send reinforcements north, although he was still convinced "that General Howe and Burgoyne certainly mean to cooperate." Nevertheless, Washington was concerned, and he assured the Northern Department commander that he was "exceedingly anxious to have more particulars from you. I hope a few Hours will put me out of Suspence."[35]

In Philadelphia, Congress was every bit in the dark. For long days the delegates had virtually no idea what had happened at Ticonderoga. Rumors and private letters, none with the full story, reached Philadelphia long before any official reports from Washington, much less from St. Clair or Schuyler. To be sure, the fort was much on the mind of the delegates. As late as July 8, unaware of St. Clair's evacuation and the bitter action at Hubbardton, members of Congress were sending urgent messages to their home states lamenting the thin rosters of their regiments at Ticonderoga and the lack of clothing, blankets, arms, and other supplies and matériel at the post. The Board of War wrote Washington of "inexplicable" gaffs in record keeping at the fort, questioning how 1,063 Continentals in the four New Hampshire regiments could receive 2,100 new French muskets and yet claim "they are in Want."[36] As late as the eleventh, Congress was still catching up with correspondence from Schuyler and St. Clair dated the first days of July, and the delegates failed to discern in these messages any threat from Burgoyne that Ticonderoga's garrison couldn't handle.[37] In fact, even as Burgoyne's men were chasing the retreating rebels into Vermont and up Lake Champlain, congressional concerns were of the minutiae of military administration and situation reports. There were no hints of impending disaster—much less that the disaster already had occurred.

It was not until July 12 that the first (that we know of) serious storm clouds reached Philadelphia. The New England delegates, whose frontiers had every reason to fear Burgoyne and who probably had the best informal of communication with the North, were the first to react. Writing to a colleague, New Hampshire Congressman George Frost sounded an ominous note. "I fear things don't go well with our Armey at Ticonderoga," he advised. But whatever news the New Hampshire politico had gleaned on northern affairs, it was not bad enough to prevent a rather chipper closing: "but we are in good spirits here."[38]

The next few days found other delegates similarly without a clue. On the thirteenth, John Adams wrote his wife, Abigail, that "we have a confused account, from the Northward, of Something Unlucky, at Ticonderoga, but cannot certainly tell what it is." However "confused" the account, Adams was sanguine. Even if the fort was lost, he assured Abigail, it would do Burgoyne little good; and besides, he now thought holding forts was a bad idea anyway. It would be better to draw the British into the interior and deal with them on patriot terms. Three days later, when the scope of what had happened was clarifying, his tone was more sober but still without any sense of calamity. This time he wrote Abigail that he had "wished that Post evacuated Three Months ago. We are Fools if We attempt . . . to maintain Posts, near navigable Water." James Lovell, a normally fiery Massachusetts delegate—he routinely deployed political invective as well as or better than anyone in patriot circles—was still quite calm. On the fifteenth, a full week after St. Clair's evacuation, Lovell, without any hint of alarm, inquired of his Connecticut friend Joseph Trumbull, son of Governor Jonathan Trumbull, hoping to learn "the matters of Ty in the *Northern Department*" ("Ty" was a frequent patriot shorthand for Ticonderoga).[39] In the near future, Lovell would wax positively phobic on "matters" of what he saw as inept Continental leadership, but not quite yet.

Below New York and New England the situation was equally vague outside the halls of Congress. In Reading, Pennsylvania, the questioning view of ironmaster and militia officer Mark Bird was probably typical of many in the Middle Colonies. On July 16, Bird wrote his friend Dr. Jonathan Potts—not knowing Potts already was long gone from Ticonderoga—of rumors circulating in his neighborhood that Ticonderoga was in British hands. He hoped it was untrue, but he did not dwell on the matter. Bird's chief interest lay in Sir William Howe's intentions. Howe's army, he noted, was still around New York City, and Bird was concerned the British would move up the Hudson to link up with Burgoyne.[40] At this juncture the Pennsylvanian saw affairs at

Ticonderoga as uncertain, but apparently not critical. Such sangfroid was not to last.

In fact, on July 12, Washington disabused Congress of any hopes that reports of a major defeat in the North were overblown. His letter probably reached Philadelphia on the thirteenth, and it confirmed the worst. "I hoped the Intelligence received respecting our Affairs in the Northern Department was not true," he told John Hancock, "or at least, that they were not so unfavourable, as they were then repre-sented; But the inclosed Copy of a Letter from Genl Schuyler, which came to hand Yesterday Evening, confirms it most unhappily for us in its fullest latitude." St. Clair's evacuation, "among the most unfortu-nate [events] that could have befallen us, is rendered more interesting by the manner in which it took place." This was certainly an allusion to the patriots withdrawing without a fight. But Washington confessed he had few details and that even Schuyler knew nothing with certainty, including whether the Northern Army was now captive. He feared that such a calamity was entirely possible.[41]

With this message, and the increasing arrival of other intelligence from the North, the dam broke. Nothing had prepared the public for such an eventuality, and a wave of consternation swept the New Eng-land and Middle Colonies. What had happened? How did it happen? Who was responsible? With St. Clair temporarily out of touch, no one knew. Washington shared the alarm, admitting he had no idea why the garrison had retreated and that nothing, in his view, was less ex-pected. He had thought highly of Arthur St. Clair, but he freely shared his conviction that a full investigation and public accounting was in order.[42] Schuyler, who had clearly understood Ticonderoga's vulner-ability and had endorsed pulling out of the western defenses in favor of holding Mount Independence, professed amazement at events. Per-haps seeking to distance himself from the outcry, he was quick to point out he had never issued orders for a full evacuation. Schuyler later stoutly defended St. Clair's conduct, but his immediate reaction was one of self-defense.[43]

A full-scale blame game developed quickly. Long after the fact, Connecticut Governor Trumbull perfectly captured the sentiments of July 1777: "The dread, with which this unexpected blow filled the whole country," he recalled, "was as extravagant, as their rage against the commanding officer, who, in the language of the day, had sold, or given away, the most important fortress on the continent."[44] John Adams, then chairing the congressional Board of War, was furious. "Don't you pitty me to be wasting my Life," he moaned to Abigail, "in laborious Exertions, to procure Cannon, Ammunition, Stores, Baggage, Cloathing &c. &c. &c. &c., for Armies, who give them all away to the Enemy, without firing a Gun."[45] He was even less restrained in a letter to Horatio Gates: "We shall never hold a post until we shoot a general." The loss of Ticonderoga "Calls for Inquiry," he demanded. Innocent officers should be acquitted, but those guilty should "meet their Deserts. I see no Medium, I confess, between honourable Acquittal and capital Punishment."[46] Samuel Adams, John's distant cousin and a fire-eating Massachusetts radical, was of the same mind. He never mentioned shooting anyone, but he was enraged that less-strident sentiments might "baulk" an inquiry into the conduct of Ticonderoga's senior officers.[47] Worse, the Reverend William Gordon, a future historian of the Revolution and a relatively recent acquaintance of Washington's, reported rumors circulating in New England to the effect that St. Clair and Schuyler had sold out to the enemy—that the loss of Ticonderoga was the spawn of "silver bullets" and of "Bribery & treachery."[48] Life was going to be difficult for Arthur St. Clair and, for that matter, Philip Schuyler.

Upon reflection, Washington had his own view of where the blame fell, views at stark variance from the Adams cousins. In fact, he pointed fingers squarely at the New England states that had failed to fill their Continental regiments or to marshal sufficient militia forces. If Ticonderoga's garrison had been unequal to the task, "even moderate exertions of the states more immediately interested" should have been enough to stop Burgoyne. Now, however, the general counseled patience and a renewed effort to raise the forces necessary "to convert the advantages he [Burgoyne] has gained into his ruin." In New York, which understandably shared some of New England's angst, prominent state leaders, including John Jay and Gouverneur Morris, followed Washington's lead and did their best to calm public alarm.[49] In doing so, however, they were swimming against a deep-running and virulent popular tide.

That tide swept away Arthur St. Clair and Philip Schuyler. In and outside of Congress the popular rage, especially in New England, was such that the delegates in Philadelphia had to act. In two resolutions in late July and early August they recalled both major generals and ordered all general officers formerly at Ticonderoga to report to Washington's headquarters.[50] There they would await official inquiries or courts-martial into their conduct. Fortunately, no hearings occurred in the heat of political passions; rather, courts-martial in autumn 1778 acquitted St. Clair and Schuyler with "honor." The trials demonstrated conclusively that both men had done their best with the Northern Army and that the loss of Ticonderoga stemmed from a lack of patriot manpower and resources, not from anyone's dereliction of duty (much less from treachery). Both men returned to duty.[51] Schuyler eventually served again in the North, while St. Clair, Paterson, and Poor (the latter two were never tried) remained with Washington. The useless La Rochefermoy had the temerity to ask for promotion to major general and resigned when Congress wisely refused.[52]

In the meantime, the northern war continued. When Washington demurred on appointing a new commander of the Northern Department, Congress promptly looked to the darling of the New Englanders: Horatio Gates. Samuel Adams led the charge. The Massachusetts zealot disparaged Schuyler at every opportunity and lauded Gates to the skies. "Gates is the Man of my choice; He is *honest* and *true*, & has the Art of *gaining the love of his Soldiers* principally because he is *always present* and shares with them in *Fatigue & Danger.*"[53] So it was done, and Gates relieved Schuyler at Albany on August 19.[54] The army that the new department commander inherited was growing as Continental and militia reinforcements reported, built around the regiments St. Clair had saved from Ticonderoga. Gates even made excellent use of Ticonderoga's two engineers, Baldwin and Kosciuszko. Politics had foiled Gates's wish to confront Burgoyne at Ticonderoga, and politics now determined that he would do so at Saratoga.

So who was to blame for the loss of Ticonderoga? Not Schuyler or St. Clair. On the American side the issue really came down to one thing: numbers—or the lack of numbers. The garrison never had enough men to hold the extensive works. Given their lean rosters, the situation on the western Ticonderoga peninsula was virtually impossible. Even if patriots had pegged their defense on holding Mount Hope in force, thus negating a British occupation of Mount Defiance, rebel lines would have been stretched too thin to hold elsewhere, or even to relieve Mount Hope if it fell under siege. And what of an American concentration on Mount Independence? This might have delayed but not stopped Burgoyne's victory. The British controlled the lake, and eventually they would have cut off the overland escape route from the mountain. Riedesel's Germans were moving slowly, but they were moving, and their mission was to cut the road to Skenesborough. Under the circumstances, an attempt to hold Mount Independence would have risked the loss of St. Clair's entire force, and patriots were in no position to relieve the post with reinforcements from elsewhere. It was all a numbers game, and the Americans lost it.

Was there some way St. Clair might have put up a fight with his limited forces? If patriots had concentrated on Mount Hope and Mount Defiance—and mounted strong batteries on Defiance—they might have seriously impeded Burgoyne's movement to Lake George. Rebel guns on Defiance would have enjoyed the advantages Burgoyne's artillery gained on July 5, and American fire would have imperiled any British occupation of the Ticonderoga peninsula and Mount Independence as well as royal navigation of the narrows of Lake Champlain. And if, as would have been probable, protracted operations finally compelled a patriot withdrawal, St. Clair could have safely retreated up Lake George or overland down the western shore of the lake. But all of this is rank speculation. Such a patriot defense would have taken weeks (or more) of preparation, time St. Clair simply did not have. Recall that he arrived at the fort only weeks before Burgoyne arrived in front of his lines. St. Clair also would have faced persuading his officers and Schuyler to give up on defensive preparations in progress since fall 1776, which would have been a tough sell. Moreover, had St. Clair based a defense on Mounts Hope and Defiance, he would have done so with the certain knowledge that his decision to abandon the Gibraltar of the North would ignite a popular and political uproar. On July 5, Major General Arthur St. Clair made the only reasonable choice available to him; it is impossible to conclude otherwise.

But the real blame for the loss of Ticonderoga—or credit, depending on one's perspective—lay with Lieutenant General John Burgoyne. He executed a nearly flawless operation at Ticonderoga, although the chance occupation of Mount Defiance saved him the trouble of conducting an actual siege. His advance was skillful, and he deployed his forces appropriately. His key subordinates were high quality, and he managed his logistics effectively; his troops had what they needed to sustain their mission. Burgoyne's intelligence was generally good—he certainly knew the layout of Ticonderoga's defensive works—and his counterintelligence operations were first rate. With few exceptions, patriot scouts were unable to penetrate Burgoyne's screening forces. And these were generally Iroquois, whose deployment had an unnerving effect on many rebels. The later march to Saratoga would reveal a less sure and hardly as competent John Burgoyne—but the general who took Ticonderoga knew his business.

Chapter 6

Counterattack:
Ticonderoga Assaulted

WHILE AMERICANS BEMOANED the loss of Ticonderoga, the war entered a brief hiatus as Burgoyne caught his breath at Skenesborough. The royal commander took almost a month gathering supplies and arranging transport, and he saw little reason to hurry inasmuch as he considered St. Clair's army scattered and ineffectual. But the long delay had forestalled any possibility of rapidly exploiting his victory at Ticonderoga, and the situation was in great measure the lieutenant general's own fault. He had badly underestimated his transport needs, and it took time to assemble the necessary carts, wagons, and teams to support his march south. While he waited, Burgoyne pondered his next moves. He briefly looked east at virtually undefended New England; it seemed an inviting target. But Burgoyne considered his original orders binding, so when his troops were ready he would proceed to Albany.

But how would he get there? He considered two routes. The first was to return from Skenesborough to Ticonderoga. From the fort, his army would take the short road to the Lake George landing, pass the lake by boat, then march the relatively undemanding overland passage to Fort Edward on the Hudson River. This was the easiest alternative.

But he disliked the idea of the seeming retrograde to Ticonderoga, fearing a move north might sap morale. After all, he had grandiosely proclaimed, "This Army must not retreat."[1] Accordingly, Burgoyne chose a second option. He directed Phillips to forward the heavy artillery and supplies via Lake George—establishing a depot on Diamond Island, over two-thirds of the way up the lake—while the army would march overland to Fort Edward. The only road from Skenesborough to Fort Ann was rudimentary and the terrain was rough, but the previous year the Americans had improved the route from Fort Ann to Fort Edward. There was always the chance the rebels would harass his progress, and he counted on Schuyler felling trees and demolishing bridges to obstruct the road. But Burgoyne considered he could deal with that sort of thing—which in fact he did—and on July 25, his army marched out of Skenesborough.[2] They would trek twenty-three miles south to Fort Edward, reaching the post on the twenty-ninth.

While Burgoyne prepared to march, Phillips tackled the daunting task of marshaling and transporting the army's tons of matériel and provisions. Most of the supplies were stored at Ticonderoga. Nothing, however, moved quickly from the fort. It took weeks to improve the road over the portage from Lake Champlain to Lake George, and the major general made free use of American prisoners of war to complete the job. With supplies finally moving over the rough road, personnel (including the prisoners of war) then transferred everything onto hundreds of bateaux and other small craft. The shipping then moved slowly up Lake George, some crews stopping at Diamond Island to establish the reserve depot, while the rest proceeded to Fort George at the top of the lake. At Fort George, cargoes were loaded onto carts and wagons—of which the army had too few—that lum-

Detail from "A map of the country in which the army under Lt. General Burgoyne acted in the campaign of 1777, shewing the marches of the army & the places of the principal actions," William Faden, 1780. The map shows the key positions and various engagements (crossed swords) of the campaign, as well as the routes of main troop movements. Fraser's pursuit of St. Clair's army is clearly marked, as is the clash at Hubbardton and St. Clair's rendezvous at Castleton. Mount Defiance is labeled Sugar Hill and is clearly shown to the immediate south of Fort Ticonderoga. (*Norman B. Leventhal Map & Education Center, Boston Public Library*)

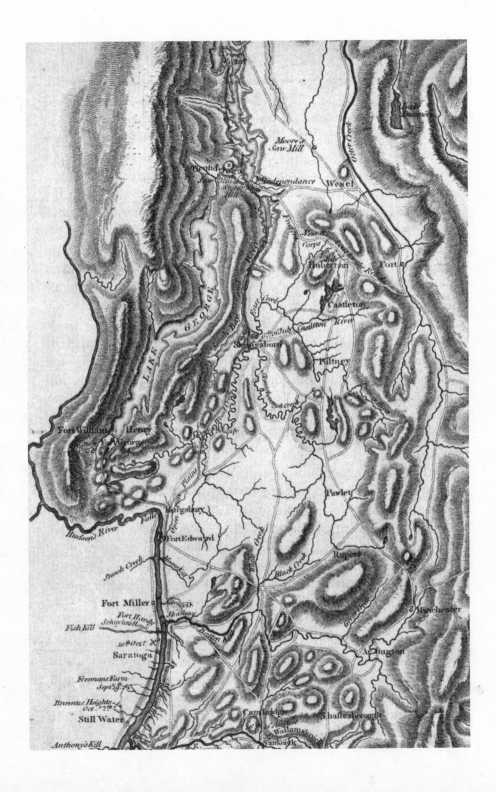

bered overland to Fort Edward on the Hudson. Phillips was a superb administrator and hard taskmaster, but it took well into September before Burgoyne finally received the thirty days of supplies he considered necessary to support the advance to Albany. The British crossed the Hudson from Fort Edward only on September 13.

Observing from New York City, Burgoyne's good friend Sir Henry Clinton thought crossing the Hudson was a mistake. Rebel strength was mobilizing, and he felt Burgoyne should have stayed at Fort Edward until assured of support from the south. As it was, Clinton believed all he could do on Burgoyne's behalf was to threaten a move up the Hudson that might distract the Americans, thus "easing his [Burgoyne's] retreat back to Ticonderoga." And Clinton feared a withdrawal to the fort was a real possibility.[3] It was good advice. But even if he had communicated as much to his friend there is little evidence it would have done any good—Burgoyne was committed.

Burgoyne's sojourns at Skenesborough and Fort Edward were costly if not, as events would prove, fatal delays. Given a respite, competent leadership, and at least minimal reinforcement and resupply, even a wounded army can heal. Burgoyne's delay provided the respite, and the healing process started for the Northern Army in mid-July as Schuyler and St. Clair finally rendezvoused at Fort Edward. They subsequently dropped back to Stillwater as militia began to rally in numbers and as Schuyler frantically called on regional patriots for reinforcements and supplies. The situation stabilized further in mid-August as Gates arrived to take command and Washington sent sizable Continental detachments north. Instead of a demoralized rabble, Burgoyne marched toward a reorganized, reinforced, competently led, and determined patriot army. If the British appeared unstoppable in early July, some six weeks later the fortunes of war were changing.

The story of Burgoyne's march to defeat and humiliation at Saratoga is an oft-told tale. Burgoyne's army moved only slowly, plagued by growing militia harassment and the desertion of Indian allies. An effort to seize rebel supplies in the New Hampshire Grants (modern Vermont) cost the British some nine hundred men at the disastrous Battle of Bennington. Then, to Burgoyne's distress, in mid-August he learned definitively that Sir William Howe would not be coming north to meet him. Nor was help coming from the west. In the Mohawk Valley, faced with a stubborn rebel defense of Fort Stanwix and the desertion of his allied Indians (who feared false reports of massive Continental reinforcements headed up the valley), on August 22, St. Leger gave up his advance and headed back to Canada. If Burgoyne was to reach Albany, he would have to do so alone.

That was not all. While Gates prepared a defensive stand blocking his path to Albany, word came south from Ticonderoga that patriot forces had actually gone over to the offensive. Burgoyne's lines of communication to Canada—vital if he was to receive reinforcements or new supplies, or if necessary, serve as an avenue of retreat—were threatened. In fact, for the first time in its history, Fort Ticonderoga had come under direct assault.

By August 19, Gates had established his headquarters at Van Schaick's Island in the Mohawk River (close to the Mohawk's junction with the Hudson River) not far from Albany. He would shortly move to Stillwater some twenty-three miles north of Albany and squarely in Burgoyne's path. He exuded an air of confidence as he organized a reception for the royal army. He did so, not incidentally, with the assistance of both of Ticonderoga's military engineers: Kosciusko and Baldwin were on the job. The Polish soldier took primary responsibility for planning Gates's defensive works, while Baldwin built a floating bridge across the Hudson. No one was underestimating the magnitude of Burgoyne's threat, but the wave of panic that had swept patriots after the loss of Ticonderoga was long gone.

As Gates prepared, Washington did his best to monitor developments in the North. From his vantage in Bucks County, Pennsylvania, where he was trying to divine Howe's intentions, he remained in touch with Gates. While rushing reinforcements north, the commander in chief also broached the possibility of limited offensive operations; in particular, he felt the interdiction of the lengthening British supply lines would play havoc with Burgoyne's advance. Washington had already sent Major General Benjamin Lincoln of Massachusetts to assist Schuyler (and subsequently Gates), and he knew Lincoln had gathered a considerable force of New England militia in Vermont to the north of Gates's army. Put Lincoln in action, he wrote Gates, and "I am in hopes you will find yourself at least equal to Stop the Progress of Mr Burgoyne." Hitting Burgoyne's supply lines, the patriot commander believed, would "render his Situation very ineligible." Gates responded quickly and promised to send Lincoln along with New Hampshire's John Stark—the victor at Bennington three weeks before—"to act upon the Flank, and Rear of the Enemy, while the main Army opposes them in Front."[4] Gates, whose relationship with Washington at this point is best described as ambivalent—within months they would fall out bitterly—was as good as his word and ordered Lincoln to his headquarters to discuss possible operations. The meeting took place August 24.[5]

In fact, Lincoln was a step ahead. Only days earlier, he had conferred with Stark on the possibility of using militia against Burgoyne's lines of communication. Lincoln explained as much to Gates, noting that even if they could not actually interdict enemy supply operations, they could at least compel Burgoyne to divert precious manpower to protect his communications. That alone would be a blow to the British. Gates was enthusiastic and told Lincoln to go to it, and the Massachusetts Continental promptly rode to Bennington to lay his plans, gather supplies, and rally militia.[6] For the better part of the next month, Lincoln would operate as an independent commander.

Lincoln was the right man for the job. The scion of a prosperous and politically active family in Hingham, Massachusetts, before the war he served in local office and held a militia commission. Casting his lot with the patriot cause, after Lexington and Concord, Lincoln played an important role in supplying the rebel forces besieging Boston. Named a major general of the Massachusetts militia, in February 1777 he received a Continental commission at the same rank. Never a brilliant officer, he proved steady in combat, and he held important commands in Washington's army over 1776 and early 1777.[7] He was always popular with New England militia and proved adept at making the most of available resources. This was a good thing, as after meeting with Gates he found Stark uncooperative. Stark, a militia officer, was a great fighter but he felt slighted at not receiving a Continental commission; he wanted nothing to do with serving under Lincoln and went his own way.[8] If the temperamental Stark upset him, Lincoln never let on; instead, he went ahead with his own planning and mapped out a truly bold operation. Lincoln aimed at nothing less than stopping British supply operations at their source: Fort Ticonderoga.

Benjamin Lincoln (1733-1810). Tasked with disrupting British communications and supply lines between Ticonderoga and Burgoyne's army moving toward Albany, Lincoln planned and launched the Pawlet Expedition in September 1777. John Brown's raid on Ticonderoga was the expedition's most important and successful component. Lincoln then moved south to join Gates in the fighting around Saratoga. Portrait by Charles Willson Peale, 1784. (*Independence National Historical Park*)

In early September, Lincoln moved his headquarters from Bennington to Pawlet, also in modern Vermont. With him were some two thousand troops, mostly Massachusetts militia but with smaller contingents from Connecticut, New Hampshire, and Vermont. There also were small numbers of Continentals, including ranger units. The major general had chosen Pawlet for its location. It was some fifty miles south of Ticonderoga, and about the same distance from Gates's army at Stillwater. At need, Lincoln could move in either direction. The rugged terrain around the village also made it a defensible location in the event the enemy came after him. It was at Pawlet that he finalized plans for what became known as the Pawlet Expedition.

The plan was complicated, the bane of too many operations. But Lincoln based his thinking on intelligence indicating there were fewer than a thousand British at Ticonderoga, and that these men were dispersed between the old fort and its immediate outworks, Mount Independence, Mount Defiance, and the Lake George landing. Lincoln planned on remaining at Pawlet with four hundred or so men while the rest of his command would split into three columns of five hundred men each. Colonel John Brown of Massachusetts would lead the main effort. He would assault the Lake George landing and send a party against the small British outpost on Mount Defiance; his orders were to free the American prisoners held at the landing, then move toward the fort, engaging enemy troops and destroying or capturing supplies. If he could do so without undue risk, Brown was authorized to assault and capture the fort itself. Another party under Colonel Samuel Johnson would attack Mount Independence, taking it if possible but at least serving as a diversion in support of Brown's movement. The third column, under Massachusetts Colonel Benjamin Ruggles Woodbridge, a veteran of Bunker Hill, would occupy Skenesborough.[9] The British already had pulled out of the town, but Woodbridge would be in position to support Brown's later withdrawal. He was also to move cautiously south to Fort Ann and on to Fort Edward (which the British were about to abandon), in effect following Burgoyne's track and feeling for any British presence. If Brown and Johnson could hit by surprise, they would have the advantage of numbers at each point of attack. All of this was nothing if not daring.

Inasmuch as John Brown was the chief actor in what was to follow, we need to know him better. Brown was an early and committed revolutionary. He attended Yale—where he became best of friends with David Humphreys, a future Continental army officer and one of Washington's military secretaries—graduating in 1771. After briefly practicing law in modern Johnstown, New York, he moved to Pittsfield in western Massachusetts where he won election to the colonial General Court (the legislature). As the revolution loomed, Massachusetts patriots sent Brown to Canada to assess prospects for enticing Canadians to the revolutionary cause (for which he reported little hope), and he was one of the first to insist patriots seize Fort Ticonderoga. In May 1775, Brown joined the expedition under Ethan Allen and Benedict Arnold that took the fort. He subsequently served actively in a variety of operations against the British in Quebec province, including the captures of Fort Chambly (in an operation Brown led) and Montreal.[10] It was during this campaign that he came to distrust Arnold, accusing him of plundering captured goods among a laundry list of

Benjamin Ruggles Woodbridge (1739-1819). A Massachusetts militia colonel, Woodbridge was variously a farmer, rum distiller, physician, and lawyer. He was a Bunker Hill veteran, and during the Pawlet Expedition Woodbridge commanded the covering force that occupied Skenesborough while John Brown attacked Ticonderoga. From Sophie E. Eastman, *In Old South Hadley* (Chicago: Blakely Print Co., 1912), 140.

other alleged misdeeds, some of which were outlandish. Most senior officers and congressional delegates found little merit in these complaints, but Brown remained Arnold's implacable enemy. Still, Brown's service record was first rate, and he rose to lieutenant colonel. Angry that he could not rally political support against Arnold, he resigned his Continental commission in March 1777 but remained active as a colonel in the Massachusetts militia.[11] It was likely Brown's leadership experience that convinced Lincoln to entrust him with the expedition's main attack.

Brown's and Johnson's men were a mixed lot. Most of the troops came from an assortment of militia regiments. But since Brown and Johnson were most likely to engage the British, Lincoln made sure both colonels had some veteran Continentals to stiffen the less experienced militia. Most of the regulars, divided more-or-less evenly between Brown and Johnson, came from Colonel Seth Warner's regiment (although Warner was not with the attacking columns);

these were mostly New Hampshire and Vermont men, with some New Yorkers. Brown also had a small detachment of Continental rangers under Captain Ebenezer Allen who specialized in scouting missions.[12]

By mid-September, Lincoln was ready to strike. With his plans finalized, his subordinates briefed, available intelligence shared, and the three detachments equipped, the major general issued final instructions on September 12. He wanted to avoid major combat. Success, as historian Edward A. Hoyt has pointed out, would depend on the patriot units moving quickly and overwhelming any opposition before it could mount a determined defense. Accordingly, Brown, Johnson, and Woodbridge moved carrying only "bare essentials" of equipment and ammunition and without artillery or carts.[13] Once again Lincoln told Brown to hit the Lake George landing, free the American prisoners of war (POWs), and then do what damage to British stores and equipment "as may fall within your power." If the original plan proved unfeasible, Brown still was to do all he could to "annoy, divide, and distract the enemy." The three colonels moved from Pawlet on September 13—the same day Burgoyne began crossing to the west bank of the Hudson—although Brown was still hustling to deal with last-minute organizational, intelligence, and supply details on the fourteenth.[14] With the expedition underway, Lincoln informed Gates, adding hopefully that Ticonderoga's defenses appeared "weak."[15]

No doubt Gates was glad to learn as much, but he was too busy to quickly reply—he was only days away from combat himself. On the nineteenth he would fight Burgoyne to a standstill at Freeman's Farm, the first Battle of Saratoga. Thus, with Lincoln's columns on the move, the British were facing trouble in front and rear.

At Ticonderoga, the British suspected nothing. When he marched south, Burgoyne left Brigadier General James Hamilton in command at the fort, along with the 62nd Foot and the Germans of the Prinz Friedrich Regiment. The regiments spent most of their time moving supplies from the fort to shipping on Lake George and guarding and supervising American prisoners who did much of the work. Hamilton saw to it that his men treated the POWs humanely. The brigadier deployed the bulk of the 62nd to the Lake George landing and the Germans to Mount Independence, although over July, both regiments had details shifting position as senior officers assigned particular tasks. Small detachments (numbers varied), for example, occupied a lookout on Mount Defiance; in late July it consisted of only a corporal and four men of the 62nd, although Hamilton increased it to fifteen in early August. About the same time, Hamilton sent a mixed detachment of the 62nd and the Prinz Friedrich to Hubbardton to recover British wounded from a field hospital near the battlefield (the wounded were sent to the hospital on Mount Independence). The old fort—"the citadel"—itself initially held POWs, but at the end of July, the Brunswickers moved the prisoners to a large barn near the landing, cleaned the damaged fort's barracks, and made some much-needed repairs. Most of the Germans, with a Royal Artillery company, then took post on Mount Independence. Thereafter, the fort usually held only a "captain's guard" of a Brunswick officer and some thirty rank and file. At one point, however, the guard, such as it was, was "only one sentinel."[16] The brigadier also had Commodore Lutwidge station gunboats to defend the water and land approaches to Mount Independence (the road to Skenesborough ran close to the lake)—a decision that proved prescient.[17]

Thus British-occupied Ticonderoga was a hive of activity, although Hamilton suffered from the same disability as Arthur St. Clair: the garrison was far too small to mount an effective defense if confronted with a serious attack. The British could mount few security patrols beyond the fort's immediate outworks, and they made no effort to defend the old French Lines or most of the works and block houses Jeduthan Baldwin had constructed. They simply lacked the manpower. In due time, the Americans took notice.

In August, Burgoyne had second thoughts about the Ticonderoga garrison. He ordered Hamilton and the 62nd to join him at Fort Edward. As replacements, the lieutenant general sent the 53rd Foot back to Ticonderoga. The reason? It seems the 53rd had a large number of sick, including the better part of four companies seized with "an epidemic of fever."[18] Burgoyne could ill afford any spread of contagion and needed to get most of the 53rd away from his main army as quickly as possible. The 62nd started up Lake George on July 24, with most of the regiment following on August 1; the brigadier himself left with the small balance of the regiment on the twelfth.[19] Replacing the "dignified" Hamilton, as Ensign von Hille put it, was the "not very refined" Brigadier General Henry Watson Powell. Whatever the basis for von Hille's reservations, Powell, as we know (chapter 5), was an experienced officer and would prove a tough man when tested. At Fort Edward, the 53rd learned of its transfer with mixed feelings. Lieutenant William Digby, a veteran of the Canadian campaigns, lamented the orders—"very disagreeable news"—as it meant separation from his fellow officers, many of whom shared his feelings. Digby remained with Burgoyne (to share his fate at Saratoga) as his comrades sullenly headed north, not knowing how lucky they were. At this point the Prinz Friedrich Regiment had taken up positions on Mount Independence, and until the 53rd started arriving on August 18, the Ticonderoga peninsula was virtually undefended.[20]

Powell inherited Hamilton's manpower problem: too much ground to cover and too few troops to cover it. Of the able-bodied men of the 53rd, he posted a hundred—four small companies—at or near the Lake George landing under Captain James Davis. A contemporary map shows their camp not far from the western slope of Mount Defiance.[21] There they guarded over one hundred American prisoners. Approximately a hundred Canadians were on the Ticonderoga side of Lake Champlain as well. The bulk of Powell's troops were on Mount Independence, where the brigadier made his headquarters. The Prinz Friedrich Regiment was there, along with part of the 53rd. Powell also retained the Royal Artillery company along with a small number of Royal Navy personnel manning vessels on Lake Champlain and Lake George, including a sloop at the landing mounting three six-pounders. The brigadier also kept a guard of fifteen on Mount Defiance, where Canadian corvée labored to build a blockhouse. An officer and thirty-three enlisted Brunswickers garrisoned the fort. Altogether Powell had some seven hundred to nine hundred men (accounts differ, although it really didn't matter).[22]

Powell was an experienced soldier, but with the real action of the day seemingly focused to the south with Burgoyne, he foresaw no problems at Ticonderoga. He could only hope there were none; given the paltry size of his command he had few defensive options in the event of trouble. The brigadier really had little choice but to disperse his few troops—St. Clair, with about three times Powell's force, had faced a similar problem—and they would have little opportunity to concentrate in the face of any threat.

But Powell's security measures were lax on the Ticonderoga side of Lake Champlain, and that was his fault. Lieutenant John Starke of the Royal Navy reported that army officers allowed civilians to come and go from the fort as they pleased and that the garrison troops were "so secure . . . in their own prowess" that officers never sent out scouts to gather intelligence.[23] This seems a bit hard to credit, but if security patrols went out and sentries stood watch, one wonders how seriously patrols scoured the fort's environs or if sentries peered beyond their immediate posts. The poor security seems all the more remarkable since as early as September 10, a Prinz Friedrich ensign recorded that Powell had suspicions of a patriot operation.[24] This may have been a misperception on the young Brunswicker's part—how would an ensign know what a brigadier general was privy to?—but even Burgoyne later would lament "so fatal a lack of Vigilance" at Ticonderoga.[25] When all was said and done, one wonders how Powell escaped court-martial for dereliction of duty.

Colonel Brown arrived on the high ground overlooking the Lake George landing (the western slope of Mount Defiance) on September 17. His trek from Pawlet had not been easy. He crossed Lake Champlain undetected at the narrows about ten miles above Skenesborough, then followed a rough track along the shore toward Ticonderoga.[26] The eighteen-mile trek was not easy. Difficult terrain made for tricky footing and occasionally scattered the column. Too often men started at the unnerving sound of rattlesnakes. The region was rife with them (the French had called Defiance "Rattle Snake Hill"). In an effort to maintain silence, officers sent men with coughs to the rear, then gave up on the measure when coughing became general.[27] Still, the column got into position on the lower western slope of Mount Defiance unnoticed—testimony to rebel skill as well as poor British security. Brown gave his men a chance to rest while he spent the seventeenth reconnoitering.[28] Powell's men never caught on; indeed, they later thought the Americans had been watching them from the woods for the better part of two days. The Americans, well concealed on the heavily wooded hillside, were close enough to see virtually all significant activities in the British encampment, even to the point of witnessing the flogging of a redcoat near the fort for some disciplinary infraction. Lieutenant Starke, who left a full account of the raid from the British perspective, admitted that British security had been deplorable and that Brown "had seen every transaction at the Portage"—the road to the landing—and in Captain Davis's camp.[29] When he attacked, Brown knew exactly where he was going.

The rebels struck just before first light on the eighteenth, achieving complete surprise. The action opened with Brown sending a small company of the Green Mountain Continental Rangers up Mount Defiance. Their commander, Captain Ebenezer Allen, was an interesting man, and from time to time he will reappear in these pages. He was one of the Green Mountain Boys—much later, along with some of Seth Warner's Continentals, reconstituted as Continental rangers—who followed his cousin Ethan Allen in the capture of Fort Ticonderoga. In 1776, he was a member of an extralegal convention that declared Vermont independent of New York State. In August 1777, Allen took a prominent part in the fighting at Bennington, and as a ranger he saw arduous frontier duty before and after Brown's Ticonderoga operation.[30] Allen knew his business as a small unit leader—in fact he was one of the best such officers the northern theater produced.

After a silent climb up Mount Defiance, Allen's rangers made short work of minimal opposition. They quickly overwhelmed the thoroughly stunned sergeant's guard. Some of the British were barely awake. But there was fighting. Allen's men suffered no casualties but killed or wounded several redcoats, captured about twenty, while others of the enemy—mainly the workers building the blockhouse—managed to escape, legging it for the safety of the boats on Lake Champlain. Allen also captured the guns that had prompted St. Clair's evacuation in July.[31] It was a grim but successful piece of work.

Meanwhile, Colonel Brown led his main body toward the Lake George landing. Along the way he scooped up the men of the 53rd who had been sleeping in the camp and in a nearby barn. Struck without warning, they had no choice but surrender. At the landing itself, the swarming rebels confronted a shocked group of sailors. Here there was some shooting as well; American fire killed one sailor and wounded another before two officers and ten other seamen gave up. Again, the choices were surrender or death.

Brown's men then turned north up the road toward the La Chute crossing—the very road on which Major General Phillips had put the American POWs to work. This advance met no opposition. Indeed, one modern history has likened the Americans, supposedly giddy with success, to "a wild exultant mob."[32] This is unlikely. No doubt morale was high, and Lemuel Roberts, a former Continental captain now serving as a volunteer, recorded some confusion during the advance. As they turned to head north after their assaults on the landing and on the camp of the 53rd, in a few instances junior officers seemingly lost control of their men. But the situation was not widespread and only temporary. Roberts noted that he and other officers quickly dealt with any disorder.[33] There is no real evidence that in the excitement Brown had lost command and control. To the contrary, the colonel clearly had his men in hand. As the situation developed, he quickly secured over a hundred British prisoners, dealt with the released American POWs, and then led an organized advance to the La Chute crossing. This was crucial; a disorganized "mob" would have reached the crossing piecemeal, greatly negating any chance of surprising opponents across the river. As it was, the rebels closed on the bridge in strength with the La Chute rapids loud enough to partially mask the sound of their approach; they hit the British detachment in the blockhouse near the crossing without warning. The small redcoat detail under Lieutenant Simeon Lord of the 53rd, overwhelmed, capitulated after a brief but obstinate defense.[34] Brown's men then freed more rebel prisoners held in another barn as they surged toward the old fort itself. The jubilant Americans made it all the way to the French Lines meeting only minimal opposition. This was the work of a well-led and determined command.

The panicked arrival of the few redcoats who had escaped Brown was the first inkling those inside the fort had of the startling events unfolding outside its walls. They soon had more evidence: the rebels dragged two captured six-pounders to the French Lines and opened fire on the fort. The fire of two guns was hardly a barrage, but a captured twelve-pounder on Mount Defiance later joined in, forcing everyone in the fort to keep their heads down.[35] When the captured guns ran out of ammunition, the rebels found others and continued a leisurely fire. Brown's raid was over for the moment, but it had been an exciting hour or so.

Brown had orchestrated a tactical masterpiece. His men had swept all before them, and on the western side of Lake Champlain, the British retained only the fort itself and the artillery battery (the Grenadier Battery) covering the floating bridge connecting the New York shore to Mount Independence. The raid had freed over 100 American prisoners while capturing almost 300 of the enemy, including 143 British troops ("gentlemen and privates" as well as NCOs)— mostly men of the four understrength companies of the 53rd—119 Canadians, and 18 "artificers." In addition to the sloop at the landing, Brown also took 200 bateaux on Lake George, 17 gunboats, a large amount of baggage and "plunder," and about 200 stands of small arms, some of which armed the released American prisoners. To the delight of Major General Lincoln, Brown also recovered some American colors lost the previous July. All of this came at the cost of four or five Americans killed in action, and about the same for the British.[36] It was quite a haul, and Brown wasn't finished.

Flushed with success, the patriot colonel turned his thoughts to the fort itself. He never seriously considered storming it—but could he force Powell to surrender? As soon as he could, Brown wrote to Johnson informing his fellow colonel of events and hoping Johnson was doing as well (he wasn't, as we will see). Obviously, Brown could not expect a quick answer, but if Mount Independence had fallen or was in real danger, Powell's predicament would have been desperate. Thus, with nothing to lose, and hoping Powell saw his chances as impossible, at about 11:00 AM, Brown sent in a flag and rather grandly "demanded the immediate surrender of Ticonderoga & Mount Independence."[37]

Brigadier Powell, across the water on Mount Independence, had been caught flat-footed. His untoward circumstances owed much to his own lax security, but the furious brigadier was not about to compound his mistakes. Informed of the raid, he had made his way across Baldwin's bridge to the fort, where he quickly spurned Brown's demand. "The garrison entrusted to my care," he replied, "I shall defend to the last."[38] The indignant response likely failed to surprise the tough American, who would have said much the same in Powell's place. The next day (September 19) Brown tried again, this time asking for a prisoner exchange. "Refused," was Powell's retort.

Powell was made of stern stuff, and on the nineteenth he dealt with yet another surrender demand—by not dealing with it. This time the Americans sent a flag to Mount Independence with a note from Massachusetts militia Brigadier Jonathan Warner, who had joined Johnson. "I am here with a large Body of Troops & have large Numbers more marching to my Assistance," the brigadier warned. "I now demand an immediate surrender of Mount Independance, & Ticonderoga. On your compliance with the Above request you may depend upon good Quarters. Otherwise you must abide the Consequence." Powell ignored the bluff, and there is no evidence he even formally responded. A German account indicates that if there was a response, it was a blunt refusal.[39]

Brown's surrender demand requires further comment. The colonel's letters to Johnson and Lincoln of the eighteenth are clear: He sent his initial demand to Powell on that date, and Powell refused on the same date. There is no doubt on this score. Yet some historical accounts date the matter on September 21 and paint the story with considerably more drama. Supposedly Powell personally ordered his men to fire on Brown's flag, killing three of five Americans in the party. The story relies on an alleged British eyewitness.[40] All of this is highly improbable. A British general officer was also a "gentleman," and gentlemen were supposedly bound by the restraints of the eighteenth-century rules of "civilized warfare." This meant that a gentleman simply would not fire on a flag of truce without incurring the obloquy not only of his enemies but of much of his own side as well.[41] It just wasn't done, at least not by general officers. If Powell had done it, the matter would have been a propaganda coup for the Americans on the scale of the infamous Jane McCrea incident that so embarrassed John Burgoyne. (When Indian allies of Burgoyne murdered McCrea, the fiancée of a loyalist officer, Burgoyne was mortified. Patriots, ignoring McCrea's Tory affiliation, loudly blamed the general and inflamed public opinion against the British in the run-up to the Saratoga battles.) Brown or some other American at the scene certainly would have trumpeted the news and made the most of it, and no patriot ever did. Because it didn't happen. But such is the stubborn mythology of war.

The two sides settled into a largely ineffectual mutual cannonade interspersed with occasional musketry, some of it intense. Brown lacked heavy siege artillery, and his captured guns were too light to do more than bury shot in Ticonderoga's wooden and earthen walls, although rebel fire did kill two unfortunates inside the fort. In one melancholy case, a rebel cannonball took off the legs of "Musk[eteer] Wilke" of the Prinz Friedrich Regiment, killing him instantly. Dropping into the fort's interior as it did, one assumes the shot came from a twelve-pounder on Mount Defiance. Almost simultaneously, an exploding powder keg mortally burned three other Prinz Friedrich soldiers, including a "Lieut. Volckmar" who had brought some of the fort's artillery into action against Brown.[42] Other incidents were not as grim. Outside the fort a patriot doctor, "feeling considerably valiant," rushed from his medical post to the front (probably along the French Lines). He wanted to get in on the fighting. As he arrived, a British cannonball struck next to him and threw up enough dirt to almost bury him. Rebel soldiers dug out the sputtering doctor, who returned to his medical duties—his thirst for martial glory well and truly quenched. Lemuel Roberts and his comrades thought the episode was hilarious.[43] This continued for four days while Brown took stock of the situation and planned his next moves.

So did Powell, although his options were limited. He had reacted quickly to the American attack, rushing the unfortunate Lieutenant Volckmar and forty enlisted Germans to the fort from Mount Independence. The brigadier also sent three officers and some "50 convalescing Englishmen" of the 53rd. These reinforcements, along with the existing guard at Ticonderoga, gave Powell about 130 men. He issued orders to resort to the bayonet if the Americans managed to close with British positions; and if the rebels broke through on Mount Independence, the garrison was to fall back to the American-built barracks and fight on. Powell's defense was not entirely static. Forces on Mount Independence launched at least one raid across Lake Champlain, seeking to spike some rebel artillery on the Ticonderoga side—only to have Americans swarm out of "ditches and holes" to beat back the Brunswickers. Nevertheless, Powell was determined to hold. He did his best to keep up morale, issuing extra rum rations "as a large bonus" (although Major von Hille thought "fresh meat, vegetables, and rice would have been better"), and he reinforced the battery guarding the bridge between the fort and Mount Independence. For five nights his troops, English and German, slept at their "alarm places."[44] They were long nights.

While exchanging cannon fire with Powell, Brown learned what had transpired on the Vermont side of the lake. Colonel Johnson's attack on Mount Independence never came off. Johnson got started late—around 6:00 AM, about an hour after Brown's men were on the move. It was all the difference. The firing on Mount Defiance had alerted the garrison on Mount Independence that something was up, and when Johnson's men appeared at the base of the mountain, the element of surprise was gone. The Germans were ready. Besides, the rebel approach was hardly silent. The patriots, according to Lieutenant Starke, had come up the Skenesborough road announcing their arrival with musket fire and "Indian war Crys."[45] The rebel approach was loud enough to attract the attention of British gunboats moored in the lake, including the two largest in the fleet, the fourteen-gun *Maria* (with Starke commanding) and the twelve-gun *Carleton*. Two smaller gunboats that had worked their way up East Creek also brought their guns to bear on the patriot right.[46] Thus from two directions, British sailors blazed away at the patriots with grapeshot, inflicting no fatalities but forcing the rebels to keep their heads down. In fact, aside from some long-range musket fire, Johnson's command wisely never tested the formidable German defenses.

With their position secure, British artillery crews on the Vermont side joined the cannonade at Ticonderoga. Various works near the shore and on top of Mount Independence mounted twenty-four-, eighteen-, and twelve-pounders, and the guns blindly hurled solid shot across Lake Champlain. Much of the artillery fire and musketry was just as blind at shorter range. To prove the point, on the twenty-first, a cow wandered near the German lines after dark; nervous gunners, thinking the Americans were coming, loosed an angry fusillade into the night. Eventually they realized their mistake. Cautiously venturing from their guns, they also discovered that for all of the expended powder and shot, they had never hit the cow. They did catch the meandering bovine, however, and the unfortunate beast likely ended up supplementing garrison rations.[47] Johnson's men, under cover well below the enemy guns, must have wondered at all the racket.

With the rebel attack stymied, Johnson realized there was no point in remaining below the mountain. Brigadier General Warner had arrived to assume command, and Johnson's men subsequently withdrew toward Skenesborough after the Brunswickers had refused Warner's surrender demand. Thus, as far as any additional combat was concerned, John Brown was on his own.

Brown had few choices. One was simply to pack up his plunder, burn what he couldn't carry away, evacuate his prisoners, and head to Pawlet to rejoin Lincoln—a rather anticlimactic end to a nearly flawless mission. Then there was the fort. Brown believed he could have stormed Ticonderoga, but only at prohibitively high cost, and Lincoln's orders had warned specifically against such a risky and expensive action. Besides, Powell was getting no weaker. In his letter of the eighteenth to Lincoln, Brown had alerted the major general that enemy reinforcements might be on the way. In fact, as early as the nineteenth, a lieutenant and eight men arrived at Ticonderoga from Canada. Then, on the twenty-first, an additional 150 Brunswick troops arrived. They had been training in Canada, and according to the Prinz Friedrich adjutant, Lieutenant August Wilhelm Du Roi, they just "happened to arrive and were willing to join us." Imagine their surprise to find themselves walking straight into battle.[48] There were also rumors of more serious British reinforcements. After his disappointment in the Mohawk, Lieutenant Colonel St. Leger (no longer a brevet brigadier) had returned to Montreal; from there he planned to march six hundred troops south to reinforce Burgoyne, passing through Ticonderoga. As events played out, he would never reach Burgoyne (who was only weeks away from surrender), but as we will find, Ticonderoga eventually would see a great deal more of Barry St. Leger. In the meantime, even the minimal new arrivals made a patriot attack on the fort an even less promising idea, so Brown shifted his attention to another target he had mentioned to Lincoln: the British supply depot on Diamond Island in Lake George.

Diamond Island lay some twenty-five miles from Ticonderoga up Lake George, about three miles from Fort George at the head of the lake. Burgoyne had ordered the depot established on the island rather than at Fort George out of security concerns. Fort George, with only a small garrison, was too vulnerable to attack, while the island location was easily defended. But how many men were on the island? Burgoyne had left a guard of two companies of the 47th Foot—about seventy or eighty redcoats—under Captain Thomas Aubrey. However, according to at least one detailed contemporary source, Aubrey also had six cannons and a detachment of ninety Germans under an Ensign Godecke.[49] Yet it is difficult to imagine so many men stuffed onto a relatively small island, or for that matter a command of ninety men under a lowly ensign. And no other source has placed Godecke there. Barring the discovery of new sources, we simply cannot verify the full size of the Diamond Island garrison. But whatever the captain's numbers, it would be enough.

We have a more certain view of Aubrey. He was a veteran of Bunker Hill and the northern campaigns in Canada, and events would prove he had lost none of the nerve he displayed in those battles. Had he heard of the events at Ticonderoga? Given the sound of cannon fire over several days and the fact that some British must have escaped Brown's dragnet on the eighteenth, we have to assume Aubrey was not totally in the dark. The captain probably was on the alert, but just as probably he had not learned he was a potential target. He would learn soon enough.

Brown planned to leave Ticonderoga on the afternoon of the twenty-second, hoping to repeat his success of the eighteenth—another early morning surprise. In preparation, he had his prisoners marched away under heavy guard (per Gates's orders, they ultimately ended up in Boston) and then ordered any carts, wagons, baggage, and other captured matériel unneeded or too difficult to take with him burned. All but fifty of the captured bateaux went up in smoke as well. Then Brown and 420 men piled into the remaining bateaux and three armed craft, including the three-gun sloop, and set sail up the lake. With any luck they would overwhelm Aubrey in a quick strike.[50]

But there was no luck—at least no good luck. The weather turned sour, forcing the patriot fleet to shelter ashore about midnight. There would be no attack on the twenty-third. Worse luck followed. As Brown sailed south on the twenty-second, he had intercepted a sutler—"one Ferry" (or "Terry")—coming north from Fort George. The colonel, obviously suspecting the loyalty of anyone coming from a British post, paroled Ferry but compelled him to come with the Americans for the night. Ferry, however, slipped away in the dark and sailed to warn Aubrey. And Ferry was not alone. Several other individuals—perhaps

American deserters—had learned of Brown's plans and had alerted Aubrey, for which they later received cash rewards.[51] Forewarned is indeed forearmed: Captain Aubrey's men had plenty of time to throw up breastworks and mount their guns. Without the element of surprise, Brown was in for a warm welcome.

In fact, Aubrey had time to spare. Continued foul weather forced Brown to lie up for yet another night, this time at 12 Mile Island, about seven miles shy of Diamond. Finally, Brown closed on Diamond at about 9:00 AM on September 24. While the sloop and two gunboats engaged Aubrey's guns, troops in the bateaux sought opportunities to land. There were none. British defenses were too strong, and artillery fire began to tell on Brown's vessels. The duel lasted about an hour and a half. Brown, aboard the sloop, returned fire in "good earnest . . . giving the Enemy as hot a fire as in my Power." But Aubrey, his gun crews fighting from behind excellent protection, got the best of the contest. Lemuel Roberts, in one of the rebel bateaux, recalled the enemy guns firing to "so good advantage, that we were constrained to retire" with many craft badly damaged and many men wounded. Brown reported two men killed and two others mortally wounded, with still others so badly hurt he had to leave them in the care of local inhabitants. Soundly beaten, the rebels broke off and headed for the eastern shore of the lake. There Brown burned his boats and "all the Baggage that was not portable" and struck out for Skenesborough and eventually to Pawlet.[52] He was convinced he had faced some three hundred British during the fighting on the lake.

Despite the setback on Diamond Island, John Brown had every reason to be pleased with his performance. His tactical leadership was first rate, and, with a minimum of casualties, he had more than ful-

Opposite: Lieutenant John Starke's manuscript map of John Brown's attack on Fort Ticonderoga in the Fall of 1777. Starke's was one of the most accurate contemporary maps of Ticonderoga and its dependencies. The lieutenant was a veteran of Valcour Island in 1776, and in 1777, he commanded the 14-gun *Maria* on Lake Champlain, which saw action against the rebels attacking Mount Independence during John Brown's raid. Starke's map carefully located and identified virtually all significant positions around the fort. The fact that Brown was able to get his entire command in position on Mount Defiance unnoticed (and then sweep down by surprise on the encamped companies of the 53rd Foot, shown clearly to the left of the mountain) was testimony not only to Brown's tactical acumen but also to the lax British security Starke found so deplorable. (*Fort Ticonderoga Museum Collection*)

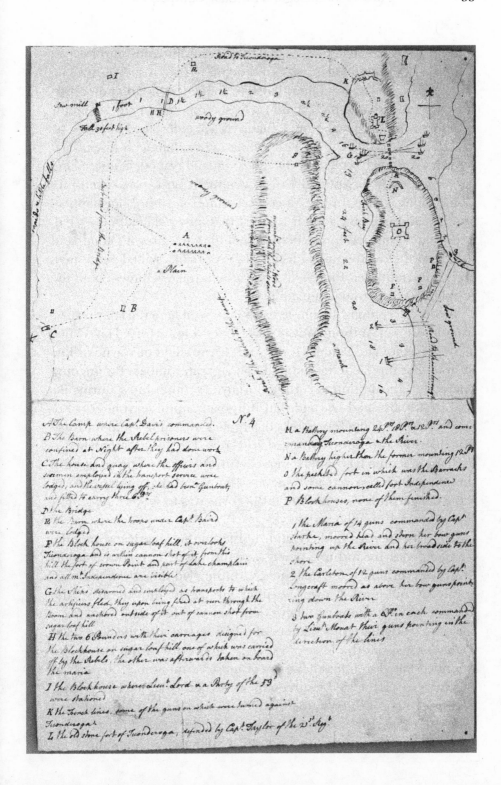

N.º 4

A The Camp where Capt. Davis commanded.

B The Barn where the Rebel prisoners were confined at Night after they had done work

C The house and quay where the officers and seamen employed in the transport service were lodged, and the vessel lying off, she had been a Gunboat, and fitted to carry three 6 Pº.

D the Bridge

E the Barn where the troops under Capt. Baird were lodged

F the Block house on sugar loaf hill, it overlooks Ticonderoga and is within cannon shot of it, from this hill the fort of crown Point and part of Lake champlain and all mt. Independence are visible

G the Ships disarmed and employed as transports to which the artificers fled, they upon being fired at ran through the Boom and anchored outside of it out of cannon shot from sugar loaf hill

H the two 6 Pounders with their carriages designed for the Blockhouse on sugar loaf hill, one of which was carried off by the Rebels, the other was afterwards taken on board the maria

I the Block house where Lieut. Lord & a Party of the 53 were stationed

K the French lines, some of the guns on which were turned against Ticonderoga

L the old stone fort of Ticonderoga, defended by Capt. Taylor of the 21 Reg.t

M a Battery mounting 24 Pº 18 Pº & 12 Pº and commanding Ticonderoga & the River.

N a Battery higher than the former mounting 12 Pª

O the picketed fort in which was the Barracks and some cannon, called fort Independence

P Block houses, none of them finished.

1 the Maria of 14 guns commanded by Capt. Starke, moored head and stern her bow guns pointing up the River and her broadside to the shore

2 the Carleton of 12 guns commanded by Capt. Longcraft moored as above her bow guns pointing down the River

3 two Gunboats with a 24 Pº in each commanded by Lieut. Monat their guns pointing in the direction of the lines

filled the mission assigned by Major General Lincoln (and bear in mind that Diamond Island was an "add-on"—Brown's idea, not Lincoln's). Besides freeing fellow patriots, he had stunned and embarrassed the British and had cut off (at least temporarily) any possibility of resupplying Burgoyne from Canada via Ticonderoga. Moreover, he had done all of this largely with militia rather than with disciplined regulars. And such regulars as he did command had been, not so long ago, the loosely disciplined Green Mountain Boys, now taken into Continental service. In war, of course, almost anything can happen, and it would be going too far to insist that only a skilled, motivated, and competently led force could have done what Brown's command did. Nevertheless, the raid indeed was the work of a skilled, motivated, and competently led force—and that alone spoke volumes about the problems facing royal commanders.

Brown's accomplishment was easily comparable to the later respective successes of Anthony Wayne and Henry "Light Horse Harry" Lee at Stoney Point and Paulus Hook. And it is no slight of Wayne or Lee to note that the Ticonderoga raid had a greater impact on ongoing operations. In addition to cutting Burgoyne's supply lines, during his raid Brown also had learned that Burgoyne, upon leaving Fort Edward, had only some four weeks of supplies with him—vital information patriots promptly conveyed to Gates. For John Burgoyne, as Richard Ketchum has wisely observed, Brown's raid was proof positive that the British rear was anything but secure and that a retreat north was a dangerously risky option. If Burgoyne was to survive, he almost had to break through to Albany.[53]

The Ticonderoga raid certainly bolstered the Americans' morale, and it did so as the fortunes of war were turning in their favor. Patriots in nearby Vermont were delighted with the glad tidings, as fairly accurate accounts of Brown's exploit circulated quickly after the colonel's return. Along with news of Brown's exploit came word of casualties among Vermont soldiers who had served with the colonel at Ticonderoga; but the losses were light, and word of the killed and wounded failed to temper the joy of most Vermonters.[54] Reports of Brown's success traveled south on the heels of the Battle of Freeman's Farm, the first of the Saratoga battles, in which the Americans had fought Burgoyne to a bloody standstill. The first definitive word apparently reached the American camp at Stillwater on September 21.

As slippery a character as Lieutenant Colonel James Wilkinson was—
he was then an aide to Major General Gates, as well as a genuine
knave—in this instance his reaction in a letter to Arthur St. Clair seems
to have captured the moment:

> We are just this moment informed of the success of a descent on Lake
> George by a detachment from a body of militia under General Lincoln,
> which was in the rear of Mr. Burgoyne. It was commanded by the fa-
> mous Colonel Brown. He very dashingly carried the post at the landing
> and at the saw-mills, took two captains, nine subordinates, and two
> hundred and ninety-three privates, of the 53d British regiment, and
> released a hundred and nine prisoners. He had in possession the
> French lines, and had sent a flag to demand the surrender of the fort,
> but had no artillery to enforce his demand. He has taken two hundred
> bateaux, twenty odd gunboats, some armed vessels, etc.[55]

If Wilkinson's statistics were off, his assessment of Brown's operation was accurate enough. Gates, now increasingly confident, made
the most of events at Ticonderoga. On the night of the twenty-first,
he had his army celebrate "by prolonged cheering and a salute of thirteen guns." In Burgoyne's camp, Lieutenant Digby of the 53rd "heard
them huzzaing. . . . [W]e found it was a Feu de joy but for what we
could not tell."[56] Showing an astute understanding of the psychologi-
cal element in warfare, the American commander released a British
POW to carry an explanation. Gates was rubbing it in, almost certainly
enjoying himself.

Just as certainly, Burgoyne was not. Until September 21, he had no
inkling that the rebels had attacked Ticonderoga and that his supply
and communications lines northward were in trouble. In fact, in two
letters of September 20 and 21, Burgoyne had written to Powell boasting
of a solid victory at Freeman's Farm (Gates would have scoffed at this)
and asking that Powell relay the glad tidings to Carleton in Canada. He
also called Powell's attention to a reported militia concentration at
Pawlet, never imagining that the Americans had mounted a raid from
the village. It appears, however, that these messages never reached the
fort. American troops intercepted the letter of the twentieth, and in all
likelihood the same fate met the note of the twenty-first.[57]

Later on the twenty-first, however, and obviously after Burgoyne
had sent his second letter north, alarming news reached his headquar-

ters, then at Stillwater near Saratoga. A German officer from Ticonderoga had slipped past the Americans, probably at considerable peril,
to confirm—if confirmation was needed—the story related by the prisoner Gates had released. This was disturbing, but the messenger may
have soft-pedaled the impact of Brown's raid. (Powell may well have
emphasized the fact that he had held the fort and Mount Independence. What brigadier wants to tell a lieutenant general the enemy had
caught him flat-footed?) Based on the officer's report, Riedesel
thought the raid "had been unsuccessful," but he had to admit that
the troops with Gates seemed delighted.[58] The Brunswicker had *that*
right, but it seems not to have fully dawned on him that key communications between Ticonderoga and Burgoyne's army were anything
but secure.

In Pennsylvania, northwest of Philadelphia where Washington's
men were nursing their wounds after the Battle of Brandywine, the
commander in chief seized on the good news. In general orders on
September 28, he proclaimed the "success of the American Arms" at
Freeman's Farm, and then he congratulated the army "on the success
of a detachment from the northern army under Col. Browne."
Brown's men had "attacked and carried several of the enemy's posts,
& have got possession of the old french lines at Ticonderoga." They
took "293 of the enemy prisoners with their arms," freed "more than
100 of our men," and captured over 200 bateaux and other vessels
with "cannon—ammunition &c.—&c." In celebration, Washington ordered "that at four o'clock this afternoon all the troops be paraded
and served with a gill of rum a man—and that at the same time there
be a discharge of *Thirteen* pieces of artillery at the park."[59] No doubt
the general's men were glad of the happy news, but we can as easily
assume they were just as glad of the "gill of rum."

Washington himself, now planning his counterattack on the British
at Germantown, was enthusiastic about rebel prospects in the North.
On September 20, he wrote Major General William Heath in Boston
of his hopes that Ticonderoga itself would fall to the Americans. At
the very least he recognized that Burgoyne would have a very hard
time if he headed back north, and it appeared to the rebel chief that
if Burgoyne did try to retreat, he would have to do so under "circumstances that threaten his ruin."[60] This, of course, was not exactly how
events played out, and from the remove of over two centuries it is easy

to conclude Washington had overestimated the impact of the Ticonderoga raid. But it is just as clear that at the time, he credited John
Brown with throwing a major wrench into British operations at a critical moment.

The Ticonderoga operation reflected well on all levels of the patriot
war effort. Washington had stressed the merits of going after Burgoyne's rear and disrupting British communications and supply efforts; and Gates, the theater commander, had agreed and tasked a
capable subordinate (Lincoln) with devising and executing an appropriate mission. Lincoln rose to the occasion. The entire plan had been
his: he had identified the targets, labored to gather intelligence, assembled the necessary troops, chosen the tactical commanders, and
made sure they were properly equipped and supplied. If Johnson was
unable to take Mount Independence, Brown had more than made up
for Johnson's disappointment. Worthy of note was Lincoln's ability to
meld militia and Continentals in a unified effort. From start to finish,
the operation evinced a mature command performance (at a time, as
we have noted, when Washington and Gates were becoming increasingly leery of one another), something Burgoyne, much less Powell,
never expected to confront.

Lincoln's work was not done. He had received orders from Gates
on September 19—the day of Freeman's Farm—directing him to collect his men and come south as quickly as possible. Lincoln wrote
Brown informing him as much,[61] but Brown, of course, was out of
touch and didn't learn of Lincoln's departure until after escaping Diamond Island. By then the rest of Lincoln's command, including the
troops of Johnson and Woodbridge, were on the march toward Gates's
army confronting Burgoyne at Stillwater. They arrived in time to form
a key part of Gates's right wing and were in position to block any effort
an increasingly desperate Lieutenant General Burgoyne might make
to get back across the Hudson and head north.[62] Brown, however, was
not idle. On the thirtieth, Lincoln got back in touch. He ordered the
colonel to raise as much militia as he could and to cut off any British
communications and supply efforts between Forts George and Edward.[63] Thus, as further combat loomed near Stillwater, Brown con-

tinued to play a key role in tightening the noose around the nearly surrounded royal army.

Among Burgoyne's increasingly anxious junior officers, Fort Ticonderoga was out of sight but not out of mind. They knew that Burgoyne was receiving dispatches from Powell, one of which was an account of Brown's raid. The contents of other communications were a mystery to the lieutenants and captains, and rumors ran through the regiments that the army would attempt a breakout to the North and make a dash for Ticonderoga. In fact, on October 7, Digby reported that "our design of retreating to Ticonderoga" had become "public."[64] The old fort, once a British target, now appeared a place of refuge for the army that had captured it almost four months earlier.

It was not to be. Burgoyne surrendered at Saratoga on October 17, bringing to a close one of the most remarkable campaigns in American (and perhaps world) military history. Ticonderoga's war, however, was far from over. Gates, seeking to follow up his victory, looked north with a view to a winter campaign against the fort. He had veteran troops, and lots of them, most of them sent by Washington from the Middle Theater. And he wanted to keep them. The problem now was that Washington wanted them back; he had his own battles to fight against General Howe. After some personal cajoling by Alexander Hamilton, one of Washington's favorite aides, Gates rather grudgingly began sending the requested brigades south in mid-November, his hopes for a strike at Ticonderoga disappointed.[65] He need not have worried. The British, having seen the Americans take Burgoyne's entire force and, thanks to John Brown, fully aware of the rebel ability to launch operations around Ticonderoga, decided not to risk another disaster.

In Quebec, Governor Carleton probably learned of Brown's raid on September 20 (but no later than the twenty-first). It was a shock, and he reacted immediately. In a flurry of orders and communications to subordinates, he informed senior officials of events at Ticonderoga and set in motion plans to relieve the besieged Brigadier Powell. Carleton ordered Brigadier Allan Maclean—a former Jacobite and Culloden veteran but serving in the British army since the 1750s—to hasten St. Leger's troops to Ticonderoga and to go south himself. For Maclean, this was bitter irony: in 1758, as a junior officer of the 60th Foot, he had survived Abercrombie's debacle in front of the French Lines.[66] The governor now wanted Maclean to join forces with Powell and secure British control of Lake George, of which at this point Carleton mistakenly believed the Americans were "masters." He wrote separately to Powell, informing him Maclean was on the way and when St. Leger arrived, he (St. Leger) was to follow any orders from Burgoyne. Carleton also told Powell that if he had to surrender before being relieved, he was first to destroy all shipping on the lakes to prevent it falling into rebel hands.[67] Of course by the time Powell received these instructions, Colonel Brown had long since withdrawn, but the governor could not have known it. As it was, Carleton had done all he could in the face of a crisis he had hardly expected—and at a time when the British still considered the security of Ticonderoga as bearing on the success of Burgoyne's operations.

Maclean's mission served only to confirm the success of John Brown's raid. By the time the brigadier arrived at Ticonderoga, St. Leger was already there with his reinforcements. But Maclean (on September 30) wrote Carleton that the situation was bleak. The Scot had heard from Burgoyne with a report of the initial fighting near Saratoga at Freeman's Farm (September 19). The lieutenant general had suffered casualties and wanted help. However, while certainly sympathetic to Burgoyne, Maclean told Carleton that for the present, forwarding St. Leger's command to the South was simply impractical. Brown had left quartermaster operations at Ticonderoga in tatters; carts, shipping, and batteaux were damaged or destroyed, and moving men and matériel would take time.[68] It was time, of course, that Burgoyne did not have.

News of Burgoyne's surrender changed any thoughts of anyone moving south from Ticonderoga. Quite the contrary. Now there seemed little point to holding on to what had become an isolated post vulnerable to rebel assault (and as the reader knows, Gates was indeed thinking about just such a possibility). The ability to hold against a determined American attack was problematic, and with Burgoyne's invasion thwarted, the British had no further use for Ticonderoga as a supply or staging post anyway. It was time to leave. Maclean, learning of Powell's intentions, returned to Crown Point, where he rejoined the troops who had accompanied him, and he then retraced his route to Canada. Powell and St. Leger evacuated Fort Ticonderoga and Mount Independence on November 8. The departing troops burned facilities, structures, and all baggage and equipment they couldn't carry away. Then, as a dramatic grand finale, they lit a fuse to fifty barrels of powder and blew much of the old fort sky high.[69] The few outpost troops at Crown Point left at the same time.[70]

But the British did not get cleanly away. Brown had burned the British bateaux on Lake Champlain, and apparently there were too few watercraft remaining to transport the joint commands of Powell and St. Leger down Champlain. That meant some British, as well as some regional loyalists who left Ticonderoga with them, had to walk. And as they headed north, they had to fight off rebel harassment, some of it very effective. The worst came from the Green Mountain rangers of Captain Ebenezer Allen (these were Continentals)—the same Ebenezer Allen who had led the daring assault on Mount Defiance. According to Thomas Chittenden—one of the leading patriots in the New Hampshire Grants and soon-to-be president of the self-declared Vermont Republic—Allen took forty-nine prisoners, over a hundred horses, and some livestock. In another instance, patriots took to the water to intercept the boats of a large group of fleeing Tories.[71] Henry Watson Powell could be excused for never wanting to see Ticonderoga again.

There is a final word in order on Captain Allen. Numbered among the prisoners his rangers took during the British retreat were two black slaves—Dinah Mattis and her infant daughter, Nancy—the "property" of a fleeing Tory. Under congressionally approved prize law, Allen and his men could legally seize and claim ownership of certain enemy property. With the agreement of his rangers, Allen claimed Dinah and Nancy; then, also with the approval of his men, the captain stated and did the following: "I being conscious that it is not right in the sight of God to keep slaves—I therefore obtaining leave of the detachment under my command to give her and her child their freedom—I do therefore give the said Dinah Mattis and Nancy her child their freedom to pass any where through the United States of America . . . and to trade for herself and child as though she was born free without being molested by any person or persons." He filed the statement of manumission with the town clerk of Bennington, Vermont. Dinah and Nancy were free.[72] Ebenezer Allen was a superb soldier, and one gathers from this episode that he was also a very decent human being.

The departure of Powell's soldiers, Ticonderoga's last garrison of any real duration, marked the end of the old fort's days as a military stronghold. Indeed, after the British withdrawal, the Americans never bothered to reoccupy or repair the fort, its various outworks, or Mount Independence. At least twice during the war's remaining years, patriots talked of renewed efforts against Canada. Had talks proceeded to operations, Ticonderoga might have played a role, but they never did. From time to time, as we will see, the British would be back. But they never came back with any intention of staying permanently, and for the time being the war left the fort to the solitude of the lakes and surrounding mountains.

Chapter 7

A War Continued:
Frederick Haldimand and
Aggressive Defense

THE BRITISH DEPARTURE from Ticonderoga did not signal the
end of the war in the North. Far from it. If the Crown had given
up the fort, the Provincial Navy still controlled the lakes, and after the
dust had settled on the Burgoyne fiasco, British vessels began fairly
regular patrols. Sailing mostly out of St. John's and Isle aux Noix, they
had Lake Champlain to themselves, and eventually they pushed into
Lake George as well. The patriots—no longer with a fleet of their own,
with few Continental units in the region (and these only small ranger
outfits), and with most militia having dispersed after Saratoga—had
little means of stopping this activity. But for that matter, at first there
seemed little reason for Americans to worry about it. The British patrols, knowing full well that patriots at various times had expressed
considerable interest in invading Canada, were defensive and kept a
keen eye out for any signs of a rebel offensive. The ships of the Provincial Navy hardly seemed precursors of another invasion from the
North—until British vessels began bringing royal troops up Lake
Champlain. Again.

Prior to spring 1778, the northern frontier in the Ticonderoga region was relatively quiet, but there were some broad hints of change. Alarmed at the fate of Burgoyne and worried about Canadian security, in December 1777, Governor Carleton inaugurated a new and proactive intelligence effort. Above all he sought to avoid any rebel surprises. What were they planning after defeating Burgoyne? Would they target Canada again? Seeking any and all information on what the rebels were up to, he ordered a series of scouting patrols into northern New York and Vermont to create what historian Gavin K. Watt has aptly termed an "an early warning system." The first reconnaissance party set out in early February 1778. Carleton's goal was information, not combat; and in fact, there was little fighting. On March 12, a brief Indian-loyalist raid on Shelburne, Vermont, resulted in a couple of casualties on both sides, but for the rest of the spring, the Champlain Valley saw little bloodshed.[1] The war had not yet returned to Ticonderoga.

Still, both sides remained on guard, and in April it appeared things were heating up. Philip Schuyler wrote Washington that he expected no major British operations in the region; yet without a significant patriot military presence, roving "scalping parties" had many residents living in fear. Some families even abandoned their homes for safer areas. Worse, he reported disturbing British activity on Lake Champlain. "Five or seven of the Enemy's largest Vessels on Champlain are arrived at Tyconderoga," he related, "and, it is said, have debarked a Body of Troops at that place." Five hundred more had "landed opposite Crown Point and in their March towards Mount Independence fell in with Captain Allen"—the stalwart Ebenezer again—"who commanded a Scouting party of one hundred Militia." Allen supposedly forced the British "to Retreat with some Loss."[2] Even so, this was ominous news.

Yet it seems Schuyler had reacted to faulty or incomplete intelligence. Royal vessels were active around Ticonderoga and Crown Point in April, but if they landed troops at either place the landing parties were not in strength and did not stay long. More accurate intelligence informed Governor George Clinton that the British presence at Ticonderoga in April involved as few as two boats, sent to assist fleeing loy-alists trying to reach St. John's.[3] If the British put ashore at all it was probably for a quick check on the state of the fortifications—had the rebels undertaken any repairs?—which were pretty much in ruins. There was no record of any shooting. Ebenezer Allen was indeed ac-tive in Vermont. He was busy keeping a roving lookout for British ac-tivity and helping families in exposed areas move to safety, but as far as we know he wasn't fighting anyone at the time.[4] Whatever else it may have been, the mission Schuyler reported doubtless was part of Carleton's early warning system. In any event, the *Quebec Gazette* re-ported speculation—completely off the mark—that the Americans were rattled to the extent that they had installed a new garrison at Ticonderoga.[5]

Carleton's program of active patrolling did not end with his governor-ship. Indeed, his successor wholeheartedly embraced the policy. The new man was Lieutenant General Frederick Haldimand. He was no stranger to North America or to Canada in particular. Born in Switzer-land to a German family of modest means, from his youth Haldimand apparently considered no direction in life but a career in arms. He started as a junior officer in the Prussian army and then saw consider-able action in the Dutch army during the War of Austrian Succession. In 1756, he entered British service as a lieutenant colonel in the 62nd Foot (renamed, as noted earlier, the 60th Foot, the Royal American Regiment). Deployed to America, two years later Haldimand was wounded commanding grenadiers in James Abercrombie's disastrous attack on Fort Carillon; upon recovery he compiled a distinguished record during the rest of the Seven Years' War. A full colonel by 1762, he displayed administrative talents in temporary military governor-ships in Montreal, Trois-Riviéres, and Pensacola, West Florida, before coming north as a major general and joining Lieutenant General Thomas Gage as his second-in-command in North America. Haldimand even served as acting commander in chief when Gage re-turned briefly to Great Britain. He left Boston the day before Bunker Hill, but he returned to America in 1778, replacing Guy Carleton as governor and commander in chief in Quebec. Never a British subject,

Frederick Haldimand (1718-1791). Haldimand was lieutenant general and, from 1778 to 1786, governor of Quebec province. He actively promoted offensive military operations in northern New York, which he saw as essential to the defense of Canada. Haldimand also pursued political discussions (ultimately unsuccessful) with the Allen brothers and other Vermont leaders, sounding them out on a Vermont return to royal allegiance. He permitted prisoner exchanges after the war. Portrait by Joshua Reynolds, c. 1778. (*National Portrait Gallery*)

technically he was a soldier for hire, or mercenary, if you will (and this was no pejorative in eighteen-century Europe). Haldimand was honest, competent, tough, loyal, and one of the most respected members of the British officer corps.[6]

The new governor's chief concern was the security of Quebec, which he knew had been an American target. He arrived in the province in June 1778, when it was common knowledge that the Continental Congress had seriously contemplated an "irruption into Canada." The intended operation never took place—patriots lacked the troops and resources, and Washington vigorously opposed it—but Haldimand had to plan for the worst. His available manpower was a concern in 1778, but the numbers built gradually as redcoat and German reinforcements arrived and loyalist troop strength increased. By 1780–81, his muster rolls listed some 3,500 redcoats, 5,000 Germans, and about 2,800 provincials for a total of 11,300 (although numbers varied monthly as units rotated). However, the vast geographical reach of Quebec province left these troops scattered widely in posts from the St. Lawrence Valley to Michilimackinac in the far west. Any troop concentration in one area would leave threadbare defensive coverage in others. Moreover, sick rolls were usually considerable, and the training status of new units often limited the number of effective rank and file. The governor-general seldom felt he had sufficient provisions and matériel, much less the transport capabilities, to sustain major operations. All of these factors would have made it difficult for Haldimand to collect forces enough at any given time or place to either launch a major offensive or fend off a serious attack. As late as 1781, he informed Germain that he could, in a pinch, field only some 2,500 effectives for major defensive operations, much less to mount an offensive. And he added that he had the resources to maintain active operations with those 2,500 for only two months. One careful study of the governor's manpower has concluded that he could have marshaled the strength for an invasion of northern New York or Vermont only well after Yorktown—and by then, of course, there was no point.[7]

Thus, his military posture, of necessity, could "only be defensive." He poured his time and his initially scant resources into shoring up the defensive works at St. John's and on Isle aux Noix in the Richelieu River; these posts, as the reader knows, covered the traditional communications route from Lake Champlain to Canada. In this he worked closely with William Twiss, the engineer officer who had found it practicable to build the fateful road up Mount Defiance the previous year.[8] The new governor, like Carleton, maintained naval patrols on the lake. But Haldimand—as if bearing in mind the old military aphorism that "the best defense is a good offense"—went further. He expanded the policy of patrolling into rebel territory to include active raiding. That is, the governor would pursue the tactical offensive to secure a strategic defense.

We can accurately call Haldimand's course of action aggressive defense, and the policy made sense. With minimal forces the governor could inflict serious damage on rebel agriculture, support loyalists (and help them escape), take prisoners, and intimidate regional patriots. If he could mount effective raids into the Mohawk River Valley, he could seriously disrupt agricultural production in what was one of the breadbaskets of the Continental army. Such operations also would keep patriots off balance and feeling defensive, and thus less likely to initiate offensives of their own. In the face of surprise raids, the patriots could rally militia, but not necessarily quickly and not necessarily in force.

Haldimand lost no time: In July, only weeks after his arrival, he sent a party of Indians and loyalists under New Hampshire Grants Tory John Peters (although Peters was Connecticut-born) into Vermont with orders to strike at harvests in settlements closest to the Canadian border. The governor informed Germain that the mission destroyed some barns and mills in the Onion (now Winooski) River region. Haldimand claimed the raid would have accomplished more had not the white and Indian participants quarreled (over exactly what we don't fully know) and headed back to Canada.[9] But the governor was only starting. He explained to Germain that he intended to strike around Ticonderoga and Crown Point with "respectable" parties "covered by some of the ships and Gun Boats." He would do so late in the year, making it difficult for rebels to repair damage and replace crops.[10] In short, Haldimand would try to make the most of scant military resources while inflicting maximum material damage on the rebels, throwing them off balance, and keeping them guessing as to British intentions.

Reconnaissance missions kept Haldimand informed of the enemy situation to the south of Quebec as he looked for an opportunity to stage the more "respectable" operation. In early to mid-October, a preliminary scout of the Champlain area reported "All quiet at Ticonderoga and Skenesborough," so obviously the Americans had not put a new garrison into the fort.[11] And it appeared that the rebels were in strength nowhere in the region. Thus, it was time, the governor concluded, to mount his major raid.

The operation took place in late October and into November. The "principal object" of the mission, as Haldimand told Brigadier Henry Watson Powell (who commanded at Montreal after his evacuation of Ticonderoga), was the devastation of "everything that can afford the Rebels resources upon the Lake [Champlain]."[12] The governor wanted crops, livestock, matériel, food and fodder stores, munitions and powder—anything that might support patriot operations against Canada—captured or destroyed. Major Christopher Carleton would command. Carleton was a highly respected veteran of light operations with extensive experience in Indian affairs (he had an Indian wife); he also was Guy Carleton's nephew.[13] The raiders, 454 strong, including regulars, loyalists, and about 80 Indians, set out up the lake from Isle aux Noix early on October 24. For a week they based out of Crown Point and West Bay doing little more than gathering intelligence. Then, over the first days of November, Carleton launched destructive raids into Vermont and New York. Although two British scouting parties reached Ticonderoga, all of the action occurred well to the north of the ungarrisoned old stronghold.

The British got away virtually unscathed, returning to Isle aux Noix on November 14. The American response was too little and too late. A small party of patriot rangers headed down the lake to chase Carleton and sailed past the empty fort, but they failed to catch the withdrawing major. In fact, Carleton was long gone before any rebel militia could take the field, and he demonstrated just how effective Haldimand's aggressive defensive policy could be. At minimal cost, Carleton had struck hard. He estimated he had inflicted enough damage in destroyed structures, food stocks, forage, and livestock to forestall a potential four-month campaign by twelve thousand Americans.[14] Mission accomplished—and the governor was delighted.

A year of relative quiet followed Carleton's foray as Americans, British, and Indians focused on events in western New York. It was there that violence erupted with renewed fury. Answering the pleas of frantic settlers, the Continental army finally moved against the Iroquois. Over summer and early fall 1779, Major General John Sullivan's destructive expedition into Iroquois country inflicted payment in kind for earlier Indian and Tory raids on the New York and Pennsylvania frontiers. If out of the immediate fray, however, Ticonderoga was not out of mind. On Christmas, Washington queried Schuyler on the possibility of a raid on St. John's and other small British posts. Would it be possible to collect six hundred men at Ticonderoga, plus necessary sleds and supplies, and stage a winter coup against these relatively isolated garrisons?[15] Such a surprise attack had certainly worked at Trenton three years earlier, and it seems the Virginian was thinking along similar lines. Nothing came of Washington's idea—the resources weren't available. But even in such musing, the general recognized the importance of the fort's critical location if the rebels were ever to stage a significant movement north.

This relative calm ended grimly in 1780. From January through August, raiders struck patriot settlements and militia posts across western New York. Some of the strikes wreaked genuine havoc. In late May, as loyalist commander Sir John Johnson campaigned in the Mohawk Valley, George Clinton—the New York governor and Continental general—planned to give chase and ordered troops to rendezvous at Ticonderoga. But by the time some 240 men (including Ebenezer Allen) had assembled at the fort, Johnson was well away.[16] In fact, despite occasional stubborn patriot opposition, during the first half of 1780, the raiders had things pretty much their own way.

Thus encouraged, in the autumn, Haldimand approved a more ambitious operation. This time the implications for the Lake Champlain-Lake George region would be serious. Again it was a raid—the governor had no intention of invading and holding territory—but it was to be a big raid. The mission was a three-pronged assault. From the west, Sir John Johnson, Joseph Brant, and other Tory and American Indian leaders would lead a mixed force of loyalists, regulars, and Indians into the Mohawk and Schoharie Valleys. To the east, in order to divert rebel attention from Johnson and Brant, a small column would hit central Vermont. A third and much larger effort, operating in several groups, would push up Champlain and strike targets to the east and west of the lake, then move up Lake George and probe south of Fort Edward.[17] Haldimand aimed to hit hard and fast over a broad geographical expanse—the better to confuse and divide patriot defensive efforts.

Johnson and Brant were in motion by late September. The Iroquois in particular were burning to avenge the devastation wrought by Sullivan the previous year. By the end of October, their raids had dispossessed thousands of inhabitants, destroyed several villages and hundreds of farms, and burned out a region vital for the food supply of patriot armed forces. They finally withdrew in the face of mounting rebel opposition, but not before Johnson's men had killed John Brown—"a notorious and active rebel," according to Haldimand—on October 19 in a vicious fight at Stone Arabia. For good reason, future generations referred to the campaign as "The Burning of the Valleys."[18]

The other raiders were active as well. In mid-October, Lieutenant Richard Houghton of the 53rd, with six redcoats (or one grenadier or twenty loyalists—accounts differ) and some 270 to 300 Mohawk and Abenaki Indians, struck into central Vermont. In the Royalton Raid, they trekked up the White River, burning the villages of Royalton, Sharon, and Tunbridge along the way. In addition to torching homes and barns, they destroyed crops and livestock and captured dozens of civilian prisoners. Houghton escaped to Canada after a brief clash with militiamen who, fearing harm to the prisoners, gave up a close pursuit.[19] The militia reaction was actually quite efficient, and the raid, while devastating to the three settlements, proved of little long-term consequence.

Major Christopher Carleton commanded the thrust up the traditional Lake Champlain-Lake George military corridor, his second such venture in two years. This time he led just under a thousand men, again a mixed force of redcoats, loyalists, and Indians.[20] The party left St. John's on September 28. Brigadier General Powell accompanied the party as far as Isle aux Noix, where he formally reviewed the troops. Carleton reached Bulwagga (West) Bay in back of Crown Point on October 7, where the expedition divided. Loyalist Captain John Munro took some 260 Tories and Indians and headed southwest, intending to raid Schenectady and then cooperate with Johnson's command. (More on Munro later.) Carleton then took to the lake with his main body, sailing toward Fort Ticonderoga and on past to Skenesborough.

Most of the expedition's forces enjoyed an uneventful voyage—but not all of them. Carleton's fleet made its way up the lake in single file, sailing into the late evening. Near the end of the long line of vessels, a craft commanded by Ensign John Enys, a young Cornishman in the 29th Foot, approached the gap between Ticonderoga and Mount Independence. He got no farther. His boat snagged on an underwater obstruction—Enys had hit one of the sunken piers that had supported Jeduthan Baldwin's uncompleted bridge connecting the east and west shores of the lake. Brigadier Powell's troops had destroyed the bridge when he evacuated the fort in November 1777. Here was irony: after three years, a remnant of the bridge had finally impeded a British ship. Eventually pulling free, Enys could not catch up with the rest of the fleet. Along with other boats equally lost, the ensign sought shelter for the night below the fort in the broad mouth of the La Chute, where the waters of Lake George emptied into Champlain. It was an unlucky attempt; Enys found that supposed haven blocked by two rows of "pickets." He and the other stragglers spent the night on the lake before a search vessel found them in the morning.[21] They caught up with Carleton at Skenesborough, where the major was staging his men for a march south.

Carleton reached the southern end of the lake without trouble. He decided, however, to secure his route north when he finally withdrew, especially if he had to do so under pressure. The major sent the fleet back to Ticonderoga; aboard were Captain Malcolm Fraser, two officers, and a hundred rank and file. They were to secure the fort, which would serve as a stopping point upon Carleton's return. Fraser also had orders to send a party of thirty soldiers (Lieutenant Robert McFarlane commanding) to the Lake George landing; once there McFarlane's men would ferry two small mortars up the lake. They were to meet Carleton for an attack on Fort George.[22] Counting Munro's men, Carleton had detached almost half of his total numbers.

It didn't matter. Carleton's remaining troops and Indian allies moved down Champlain's eastern shore meeting no effective opposition. On October 10, they forced the surrender of Fort Ann and then burned out the Kingsbury and Queensbury districts of New York, pressing all the way to the Hudson River. The major then sent a party of Tories "to destroy the country about Fort Edward."[23] The Tories returned by the eleventh, when Carleton converged on Fort George. Part of the patriot garrison sortied to meet him, which was a mistake. They suffered a shattering defeat as Carleton's Indians overwhelmed them at the Battle of Bloody Pond. Almost thirty Americans died. The garrison's small remnant then surrendered after Carleton agreed to generous terms. Shortly afterward, McFarlane's party arrived, too late to see combat. The royal forces had accomplished a great deal at minimal cost: the fighting at Forts Ann and George had cost them only three killed (including one Indian), four wounded, and two men deserted.[24]

The following day, Carleton's unified command began its march back to Ticonderoga. They traveled "Rogers Road," a rudimentary track that paralleled the western shore of Lake George. (This was likely the route John Brown's raiders had followed in 1777.) Robert Rogers's famous rangers supposedly had cut the road during the Seven Years' War. Ensign Enys recalled it as barely passable in places, and the going was slow and treacherous. But the expedition met no opposition, and on October 15, after three grueling days, the column arrived tired but safe at Fort Ticonderoga. The British caught their breath and reorganized before pushing on to Crown Point on the sixteenth. There they awaited the return of Captain Munro's party.[25]

While Carleton waited, Munro was busy. His was the only column without regulars. The loyalists and Indians had trekked west of the Ticonderoga peninsula heading southwest; they intended to raid Schenectady and then coordinate operations with Johnson. Those plans fell through. Schenectady's defenses were too strong, and it proved impracticable to link up with Johnson, so Munro settled for the village of Ballston, some ninety miles southwest of Ticonderoga and thirty miles north of Albany. On October 16, guided by loyalists with roots in the Ballston area (who may have had private scores to settle with local patriots), the raiders burned and plundered much of the town and carried off thirty prisoners, including civilians and several militia officers. Heading north, they rendezvoused with Carleton at Crown Point on the twenty-fourth.[26]

With his mission seemingly accomplished, Carleton's united command took ship, intending a return to Canada and winter quarters. Haldimand had other ideas. Evidently unsure of American intentions after the raids—would there be retaliatory strikes?—he sent an "express" to Carleton ordering him to "keep on the Lake [Champlain] as long as possible." And orders were orders, a resigned Enys noted, "however disagreeable." The fleet put about, stopping for a meal at Mount Independence on October 30. Before pushing on late in the day, the troops set ablaze some piles of brush as well as the post's decaying abatis. That night they enjoyed the fire's glow on the horizon, complemented by a striking display of the aurora borealis—the northern lights.

The next day, a small rebel party appeared at Ticonderoga under a flag. They proposed allowing some Tory families to travel to Canada with Carleton. Satisfied the rebels intended nothing underhanded, the major took in the refugees.[27] But word of Carleton at the fort, however temporarily, again raised patriot alarm bells. Schuyler, apparently misinterpreting news of Carleton's presence, warned Washington, who in turn mistakenly warned Congress, that the British had returned in force to Ticonderoga. Did the British intend some larger operation? Unsure of enemy intentions, Washington was concerned enough at Schuyler's intelligence to send a brigade of Continentals from West Point to Albany—just in case.[28]

But there was no need. With cold weather setting in, Carleton again led his fleet north, arriving at Isle aux Noix on November 14.[29] From there the expedition passed up the Richelieu and on to winter quarters in Quebec province. It had been an exciting couple of months, and Governor Haldimand again was delighted. Carleton in particular, he proudly informed Germain, had "shown great zeal and activity in this affair, having fully answered the purposes for which he . . . [was] sent."[30] Aggressive defense was doing everything the governor had hoped.

For the rebels, those months had been costly and confusing. The scale and scope of the various raids left some Americans questioning whether Haldimand's initiatives were not part of some larger plan. In mid-October, Governor Clinton thought the British operations were somehow connected with Benedict Arnold's recent treason and that the raiders would retreat upon learning that Arnold's effort to betray West Point had failed. There was nothing to this, and even Clinton expressed his doubts as he worried about it. But his anxiety was indicative of how off balance the rebels had become.[31] Property losses alone were staggering. A "moderate Computation," Clinton thought, listed some two hundred dwellings destroyed; one hundred fifty thousand bushels of wheat, other grains, and forage lost; and many families deserting "from the northern parts of the state" as fast as they could. American casualties had been high when measured against the numbers engaged: a conservative count found 79 American military and civilian dead (and the civilian deaths are certainly undercounted), an undetermined number of wounded, and at least 225 captured over the month of October. Surveying the work of the three enemy parties—Johnson-Brant, Houghton, and Carleton—a distressed George Clinton put it mildly when he informed Washington, "The—Injuries we have sustained by these different Incursions of the Enemy will be most severely felt."[32] It was no exaggeration.

Chapter 8

A War Not Ended:
From Military to Political Battle

CHRISTOPHER CARLETON's withdrawal did not end Ticonderoga's war. The British came again in 1781, twice, although these missions were quite different. Neither episode was a combat operation; in fact, Haldimand wanted nothing more than to avoid fighting. His raids—his aggressive defense—had served their purpose, but the war went on as the rebels absorbed their losses and clung doggedly to their pursuit of independence. It was time to try something new, and the Crown issued instructions accordingly: the governor was to try luring Vermont back to the empire. While still fighting on other fronts, the British would wage the war in and around Ticonderoga in the political arena. Aggressive defense would yield to a peace offensive.

Even as the British turned their thoughts to Vermont, however, reconnaissance missions still sortied from Canada. If the Crown was to change policy in a crucial theater, it had to know as much as possible of American intentions and capabilities. It was no time to scant intelligence operations. There were also loose ends left over from previous

British operations to clean up. Haldimand's first operation of 1781 on Lake Champlain was just such a clean-up effort. The mission took place in secrecy, and details are sketchy, but it brought royal forces back to Ticonderoga in the late winter. According to the official history of the 31st Foot, on March 12, Captain Andrew Ross of the 31st landed quietly at Ticonderoga. With him were the light troops of the 31st, a party of Indians, and a loyalist contingent. Ross was not a raider. His job was to investigate reports of supplies left at the fort when Powell evacuated in 1777, destroy whatever he found, and get back to Canada. The winter was cold, and the mission was arduous enough to induce desertions among the provincials and Indians, leaving Ross with only his lights.[1] There is no existing record (at least that we know of) of what, if anything, the captain discovered at Ticonderoga, but apparently he was able to slip in and out of the fort without patriots learning of his presence. Indeed, the speed of Ross's arrival and departure would indicate he found nothing worth the time to burn or demolish. But the fact that there were no rebels around the area to oppose a British probe was valuable news in and of itself. For his part, Ross, brevetted to major, would be back at Fort Ticonderoga with his light infantry soon enough.

A second mission also had a secret component. This was Haldimand's major effort, and it involved Ticonderoga in events considerably more political than military. The story centered on Vermont—the New Hampshire Grants. The Grants had fought alongside the thirteen colonies against the British; indeed, Ethan Allen's 1775 raid on Ticonderoga was staged from the Grants and had been a largely Vermont operation. But Vermont's status as an independent state was disputed. While New Hampshire and Massachusetts also had claims on the region, New York was most vociferous in its objections to Vermont statehood. From Albany, New Yorkers insisted on their rightful ownership of most of the disputed territory and loudly protested that Vermont land claims were illegal. New York's refusal to recognize Vermont as a separate political entity had prevented Congress from receiving delegates from the would-be state. Instead, the Grants operated as the self-proclaimed and independent Republic of Vermont without congressional representation but with plenty of frustration and anger at New York and Congress. As time went on, some leading Vermonters became frustrated and angry enough to flirt with the British, either to reach a separate political accommodation with the Crown—would Vermont become a province of Britain?—or to use that possibility to pressure Congress into recognizing Vermont.[2]

This is not the place to reprise the complicated story of the British-Vermont negotiations, which actually extended with varying degrees of intensity from 1780 through 1783. The resulting documentary record has left historians with plenty to debate. Some have argued that a circle of Vermont leaders, including Vermont President Thomas Chittenden and Ethan Allen and his brother Ira, were serious about returning to British allegiance in return for the Crown granting Vermont separate provincial status and guaranteeing the land titles of Vermont residents and real estate speculators. Others have concluded Vermonters (at least the majority of them) were never serious about reconciling with the empire. Rather, they used the negotiations to stave off a British invasion or to bluff Congress into recognizing Vermont as a state.[3] For our purposes, it is enough to know that Haldimand took seriously the possibility that given generous terms, Vermont might be enticed back to the royal standard. Even failed negotiations, however, were valuable. While talks continued, they would keep the peace along the Canadian-Vermont border, thus contributing to Canadian security and allowing Haldimand to deploy his scarce manpower to other fronts. And holding Canada for the empire was, of course, Haldimand's chief concern. Viewed in this respect, the negotiations were very much a part of the governor's defensive outlook.[4]

Haldimand approached the Vermont issue cautiously. He was fully aware of the tensions between the Grants and Congress, not to mention the Grants' outright hostility toward New York. With the full approval of Germain and the rest of the ministry, he decided to take advantage if he could find the right avenue. As early as March 1779, Haldimand notified Germain that he was going to encourage Vermont independence, and later in the year, Ethan Allen did have some sort of discussion with royal authorities. Yet the governor made no really significant move until September 1780. That month he received a letter from Chittenden asking about the possibility of a POW exchange. Haldimand agreed to negotiations and further considered that this was an opportunity to raise the subject of Vermont's political status.[5] But how to proceed?

Enter Major Carleton. The governor tasked the major with contacting Ethan Allen during his 1780 raid. Following orders, Carleton wrote to Allen from Crown Point, informing him that Haldimand had authorized loyalist Captain Justus Sherwood, an old friend of Allen's, to open talks regarding a return of Vermont to the British fold. After preliminary meetings and correspondence, the Vermont rebel noted that any such political development would take considerable time—a lot of Vermont minds would have to change—but he agreed to suspend militia operations against the British in return for a POW exchange and a truce. (To his credit, Allen wanted the truce extended to the New York frontiers as well; when agreed upon, the truce with Vermont generally held.) These talks were secret, but rumors of contacts between Haldimand and Vermont circulated, and in late October, when Carleton subsequently put in at Fort Ticonderoga, some patriots feared continued negotiations would lead to a decisive Vermont turn toward the British.[6] And if Vermont turned, would it be an example to other war-weary states? Given Benedict Arnold's recent treason, Washington and Schuyler seriously discussed the possibility that Allen indeed had cast his lot with the Crown.[7] Such fears were overblown, but patriot angst was genuine.

Haldimand was generally pleased with the 1780 talks. They had, in effect, pacified the Canadian-Vermont frontier. However, he launched his maximum effort with Vermont in 1781: a diplomatic overture backed by a considerable military presence. Early in the year, British authorities put high-profile New York loyalist Beverley Robinson in touch with Allen. Robinson, who had been in league with Arnold, actively courted Allen with the clear intention of returning Vermont to royal allegiance.[8] Robinson's initiative produced no real progress, but Haldimand was encouraged enough to send other emissaries. By July, however, when successive talks produced no results, a frustrated governor decided to put some muscle behind the British negotiators.[9]

In autumn, he again dispatched Justus Sherwood, this time accompanied by George Smyth, a Tory doctor from Albany. In mid-September, they arrived from Canada at Ticonderoga to open new talks. Once more the contacts were secret, restricted to a narrow circle of Vermont leaders around Chittenden and the Allen brothers. Again, the ostensible subject was a prisoner exchange, but the real political agenda remained the same. With headquarters at the old fort, the two envoys laboriously pursued talks and communications variously with the Allens and Joseph Fay, one of the early Green Mountain Boys and the Vermont secretary of state.[10] Sherwood even traveled to Skenesborough for one meeting. There was little progress, which they blamed on patriot meddling from Albany, although exactly what the New York rebels were supposedly doing to obstruct the talks is unclear.[11] It is also a bit foggy as to when Smyth and Sherwood learned Haldimand was about to back them up with a military expedition.

In fact, the governor had decided to dramatically increase the British military presence on Lake Champlain. He wrote Henry Clinton he intended to send "a strong detachment" to Crown Point, one large enough to leave no doubt of the Crown's interest in Vermont.[12] Hopefully this would lend credibility to Sherwood's efforts and would signal Haldimand's determination to assist Vermont leaders in the event they openly decided to reunite with the empire. A significant military force in the region, he further believed, also would encourage all Vermont loyalists. There had been no serious fighting in the Lake Champlain-Lake George region since the 1780 raids, which largely had spared the New Hampshire Grants anyway (there had been, of course, the Royalton Raid). But it was time to demonstrate what a large-scale British effort could do. So, while negotiations continued with Vermont—coupled with a military presence—the governor intended to launch a simultaneous operation in the Mohawk Valley. The fighting in 1780 had devastated the valleys west of Albany, but the royal governor wanted to keep the pressure on the New York frontier.

Unfortunately, while we know Haldimand planned a significant operation, the record of exactly what he wanted to do remains somewhat vague. The most complete contemporary account of the British plan, at least as some commanders in the field understood it, is from a German officer who accompanied part of the expedition to Lake Champlain. This was Lieutenant Colonel Carl Adolf Christopher von Creutzburg (sometimes Kreuzbourg), commander of the Hanau Jaeger Corps. (These men were from Hesse Hanau; thus, unlike the now familiar Brunswickers, they were Hessians.) According to Creutzburg, who had his information from his commanding officer, Colonel Barry St. Leger, Haldimand envisioned a two-pronged operation. He wanted to send a party into the Mohawk Valley via the traditional route from Oswego. The commander of this force was veteran brevet Major John Ross of the 34th Foot (no relation to Andrew Ross) and of the King's Royal Regiment of New York. Ross was to push all the way to the Saratoga area. At the same time, a second force, this one under St. Leger, would move up Lake Champlain. This was the group Haldimand had mentioned to Henry Clinton in relation to Crown Point. In addition to supporting continuing negotiations with Vermont, if all went well, St. Leger's force was somehow to link up with Ross near Saratoga and help evacuate loyalists from the Albany area. Then in spring 1782, everyone would move east against Boston in conjunction with a force from New York City under Clinton.[13] Subsequent after-action reports by Ross and St. Leger, as well as correspondence between Haldimand and Germain, confirmed the broad strokes of von Creutzburg's understanding, minus any mention of how St. Leger and Ross were to coordinate any joint operations or any operation against Boston in 1782.[14]

All of this reflects optimism well beyond British capabilities or intentions this late in the war. Certainly, Henry Clinton's memoirs make no mention of an attack on Boston in cooperation with Haldimand. In late September, however, through Baron Riedesel (who had been exchanged after his capture at Saratoga and was in Canada with Haldimand), Clinton did share his thoughts with the Quebec governor. Sir Henry endorsed (but did not order) operations in the Mohawk Valley via Oswego—without mentioning a push to Saratoga—as well as an advance up Lakes Champlain and George. These undertakings might divert American resources and attention while Clinton launched operations in the Chesapeake or against Pennsylvania.[15]

Haldimand acted, although not fully along the lines St. Leger and von Creutzburg understood. In October, he sent Ross with a large contingent of regulars and Indians into the Mohawk region with orders to do what damage they could. They did plenty in Warrensborough (modern Warrensburg), burning out a path seven miles long. But unlike the feeble patriot response to the raids of 1780, rebels under Colonel Marinus Willett rallied to stop Ross at the Battle of Johnstown on October 25. Five days later, Willett's command battered a component of Ross's dispersing raiders; in this action they killed the notorious Tory partisan Walter Butler.[16] Nevertheless, and well before learning of Ross's fate, per his understanding with Clinton the governor also dispatched the Lake Champlain expedition. St. Leger (who was promoted to full colonel in 1780), as the reader knows, was no stranger to Ticonderoga. But as events unfolded, St. Leger would have little better luck than Ross.

Hoping for maximum political impact, Haldimand timed St. Leger's operation to coincide with the convening of Vermont's legislature in early October.[17] This was the session in which, if Sherwood had been reading the signals from the Allens and others correctly, Vermont would vote to come over to the Crown. Haldimand had meant the expedition to be a secret—why give rebels a chance to react?—but word leaked quickly that the British were coming south again. Troops moved by detachments from Canada over late September and early October, and by October 16, some 900 men—comprising the light companies of three (or four, again accounts differ) British regiments, 100 additional redcoats, 121 Hanau jaegers, and some 300 loyalists—had assembled at Pointe au Fer on the New York shore of Lake Champlain. This was just over the border from Quebec province and a bit under ninety miles north of Ticonderoga. Pointe au Fer was a small outpost, but in late 1781 it was the southernmost British fortification on the lake.

On October 17, St. Leger arrived to take command. After an uneventful voyage south, the small army made a stop at Crown Point before pushing on to Ticonderoga, putting ashore late in the afternoon of the twentieth. St. Leger put his men to work repairing the barracks—he was prepared to spend the winter—and posted security. The German jaegers occupied the old French Lines, British light infantry took up positions near the lake opposite Mount Independence, and the loyalists proceeded to the landing, where they began the laborious process of transferring watercraft to Lake George. The colonel also posted lookouts on Mount Hope and Mount Defiance (still "Sugar Loaf" to the British).[18] St. Leger then turned to his political mission, putting Ticonderoga once again at the center of events in the northern war.

Across from the fort, Vermont's Brigadier General Roger Enos rushed militia to Mount Independence. One wonders about Enos. Originally from Connecticut, he was a veteran soldier with militia and Continental commissions at various periods. A veteran of Bunker Hill

Barrimore (Barry) Matthew St. Leger (1733-1793). Haldimand sent St. Leger to Ticonderoga in October 1781 on a largely political mission with hopes of encouraging Vermont's return to royal allegiance. The mission ended just under two weeks later when Vermont proved uninterested in British overtures and news of Cornwallis's surrender at Yorktown reached the northern theater. St. Leger was the last senior officer of any army to command at Ticonderoga. (*New York Public Library*)

and of Arnold's expedition against Quebec—from which he controversially withdrew before the rest of Arnold's men reached Canada (a court-martial acquitted him with honor)—he moved to Vermont in 1780. He became Ira Allen's father-in-law when Allen married Enos's daughter Jerusha. With a family connection to the Allens, it is unlikely he wasn't fully in the know about the nature of negotiations with the British. There were even rumors that he was willing to raise a Vermont regiment for the Crown in the event Vermont defected from the Revolution.[19] But we simply don't know for sure. We do know Enos reported St. Leger's arrival to the gathering legislators and awaited events. If there was a real effort to take Vermont back to the king, those responsible took no comfort from his report; the apparent British threat and the militia mobilization had excited a patriotic response. And, unlikely as it seems, Enos's next move suggests he may not have fully known what the Allens and others were up to, or that he may have disapproved, or that he was hedging his bets—for he reported what he knew of St. Leger to Continental Brigadier John Stark in Albany. If Enos was in on a secret, this was no way to keep it.

Enos wrote Stark on October 26. The report was brief, but it gave the Continental commander an overview of St. Leger's dispositions and the fact that British troops were mounting artillery and putting a new roof on the Ticonderoga barracks. They also had brought plenty of cattle—more evidence they intended a lengthy stay. Enos was sending out scouts and promised to keep Stark informed.[20] Stark in turn notified Schuyler, who saw no reason to doubt Enos's intelligence. "I conclude," the major general told Stark in reply, "the enemy intend a permanent post at Ticonderoga. Perhaps it may prove a cage in which we shall secure him." Schuyler failed to speculate on how the Americans might do that, for if they knew where St. Leger was, they as yet had no idea why he was there.

St. Leger made every effort to avoid any appearance of hostile intent. As Haldimand informed Clinton, the colonel was to show all signs of friendship toward the Grants. St. Leger was to employ no intimidation; in fact, he was to state plainly that the Crown wished to protect Vermont from a hostile New York.[21] Justus Sherwood, who remained with St. Leger at Ticonderoga, and George Smyth, who was back and forth between the old fort and St. John's, continued to exchange messages with Ira Allen, Fay, and others in Vermont. They gathered from these contacts that Vermont's leaders, angry with the rebel Congress, were generally sympathetic to a reunion with the Crown although worried about the timing and circumstances of any such rapprochement. But as September dragged into late October, the British negotiators stewed in quiet frustration at the lack of any really positive word from Vermont authorities.[22] Were the Vermonters negotiating seriously— or for some reason just stalling?

This frustration led to an unfortunate incident. According to historian Frederic Van de Water, on October 25, Sherwood, his patience exhausted, persuaded St. Leger to send a patrol to Mount Independence to bring back someone—even to the point of taking him prisoner—to carry an urgent message to the Allens or Chittenden. At the same time, Brigadier Enos, probably reacting to the presence of the

British patrol from Ticonderoga, had one of his subordinates (Lieutenant Colonel Samuel Robinson) dispatch a six-man scouting party
to investigate. The scouts unexpectedly ran into the British patrol, and
in a surprise exchange of fire, a musket ball killed Vermont Sergeant
Archelus Tupper. The British captured the five remaining scouts. It
was exactly the kind of thing St. Leger wanted to avoid. He quickly
sent a formal apology to Vermont authorities, released the prisoners,
returned Tupper's personal effects, and promised to give the unfortunate sergeant an honorable burial. He even invited Chittenden to
attend the funeral.[23]

When Enos sent word of the incident to his political masters, questions arose. Why would the British commander show such solicitude
over the death of a militia sergeant? Why would he invite Chittenden,
one of the chief political leaders of Vermont, to the funeral? The situation seemed to galvanize doubts about the real purpose of contacts
with the British—was this really just about prisoner exchanges?—
among the majority of Vermonters not privy to the sub rosa agenda
of the negotiators. In fact, the matter became a political tempest.

Continental officers were leery of St. Leger's conduct as well and
were asking similar questions about the death of the unfortunate Sergeant Tupper. In a pointed letter, Stark wrote Governor Chittenden
asking what was going on and informing the Vermont leader of his
intention of reporting on the affair to Congress. Stark wanted to see
the original copy of St. Leger's letter to Chittenden in order to fully
understand the situation. "The report, as brought to me," the
brigadier wrote, "is that, upon the [St. Leger] party's arrival at Ticonderoga, the British officer expressed great displeasure that the citizens
of Vermont had been disturbed" by the Tupper incident. Stark recounted his understanding of St. Leger's respectful treatment of the
sergeant's remains, his release of the rest of the captured scouting
party, and his letter of apology to Chittenden. But then Stark got to
the point: he insisted that if true, St. Leger's actions were more than
a token of respect for a dead soldier; rather, they indicated "a deep
stroke of policy on the part of the enemy, to raise a suspicion in the
minds of all Americans that the Vermonters are friendly to them or
that they have really some encouragement from some people in Vermont." Stark professed his belief in Vermont's fidelity to the Revolution, but "that like every other State," he supposed "it contains its

proportion of lurking traitors." In effect, he charged Chittenden with proving the would-be state's loyalty. "No exertion on my part shall be wanted to eradicate every suspicion injurious to the people of Vermont. Your compliance with my request will probably afford me one of the means; and I pray most earnestly your acquiescence, that I may detail the whole business in its true light." He closed with a reference to the recent surrender of Lord Cornwallis, "which has placed another British army in our power"—a none-too-subtle reminder of how the fortunes of war were running.[24] In a long follow-up letter to Washington, Stark recounted his perspective on events since St. Leger's arrival at Ticonderoga, and he concluded that, frankly, he did not trust what Vermont's leaders were up to and that they may well have been up to no good.[25]

Chittenden was in a tight spot, and he knew it. The St. Leger-Tupper incident had become an embarrassment and a political hot potato. Fully aware of Stark's apprehensions, the governor obviously felt the need to explain Vermont's (and his own) conduct to an authority higher than the brigadier, so he sent a long and rambling letter to Washington. Chittenden assured the commander in chief of Vermont's good intentions and loyalty to the Revolution. He recounted the history of Vermont's contributions to the struggle, including Ethan Allen's descent on Ticonderoga in 1775 and John Brown's 1777 raid "at the Landing near Ticonderoga." The governor did maintain his ground in one area in particular: he expressed genuine frustration at congressional refusal to recognize Vermont statehood, and he vented at New York and New Hampshire (although especially at New York) for their refusal to relinquish claims to territory within the would-be state. And feeling isolated from the rest of the states, Vermont felt compelled to talk with the British as a defensive ploy: "Vermont, being thus drove to Desparation by the injustice of those who should have been her Friends, was obliged to adopt Policy in the Room of Power." But Chittenden insisted that the various contacts with the British since 1780, including those with St. Leger, were solely negotiations to work out prisoner exchanges, and that the drawn-out discussions served to keep the British at bay. And as to the British with St. Leger? Vermont had seen them off. They had come in force to "Crown Point and Ticonderoga; but were manoeuvred out of their Expedition; and are returned into Winter Quarters in Canada, with great safety; that it might be fulfilled which was spoken by the prophet. 'I will put my Hook in their Nose, and turn them back by the way which they came, and they shall not come into this City (alias Vermont) saith the Lord.'" In much of this there was an air of "he doth protest too much"—but one must admire Chittenden's Old Testament flourish.[26]

In fact, Stark and Washington need not have worried about Vermont—or at least not about the self-proclaimed republic's return to the imperial fold. Amid the letter-writing campaign, the controversy over the Tupper affair stopped any notion of a Vermont rapprochement with the Crown dead in its tracks. The glare of public scrutiny was simply too much to allow any accommodation with Haldimand. The legislative session on which Haldimand, St. Leger, regional loyalists, and probably the Allens and their political friends had pinned their hopes did nothing to move Vermont toward Britain.

While St. Leger's political mission languished in unproductive talks and then died in the Vermont legislature, the colonel still had to manage military affairs. He intended no combat, but he was taking no chances; no doubt he recalled Brigadier Powell's unpleasant experience at the fort in 1777. His patrols from Ticonderoga and Crown Point (the British had men at both posts) were active on the western side of Lake Champlain, and detachments crossed to the eastern shore and revisited the ruins of Forts Ann and George. Gunboats on Lakes Champlain and George kept watch from the water. St. Leger sent a small party into the Mohawk Valley in an effort to contact Major Ross and notify him of St. Leger's whereabouts. And despite the peace overtures to Vermont, there was some mistrust of the republic's intentions. Two days after arriving at Ticonderoga, von Creutzburg—obviously not informed of the true political nature of St. Leger's mission—noted he would not be surprised if "the famous Ethan Allen and his Green Mountain Boys were to run against us here." Within a week, von Creutzburg also reported intelligence that "ill-disposed Green Mountain Boys" were planning an attempt against Mount Defiance. The attack never happened, but the report prompted increased security on Mounts Defiance and Hope, as well as on the road between Ticonderoga and Crown Point.[27] But there was no shooting. Except for the accidental death of Sergeant Tupper, the truce held with Vermont—but no one was dropping their guard.

Indeed, St. Leger actively sought intelligence on American strength and intentions to the south. On October 23, the colonel dispatched a scouting party south under New York loyalist Major Edward Jessup. This was a large detachment of some three hundred men, a good third of the colonel's total force. They were to gather intelligence on rebel strength and activities toward Albany. Jessup met no patriot forces as his command moved up Lake George. After camping for a night on Diamond Island—John Brown's nemesis—they landed at Fort George and soon after encountered a patriot hunting party.[28] An exchange of fire resulted in the deaths of two Americans. A third was wounded and escaped, while a fourth was captured and proved a wealth of information. The prisoner revealed that Brigadier General Stark, then rallying militia at a camp between Saratoga and Stillwater, knew the British were to his north and were "strong" but that "no one" among the rebels knew a large British party had come up as far as Lake George.[29]

In fact, the Americans would remain largely in the dark throughout Jessup's mission. Even when they determined that a British party had come up the lakes, and that a party had pushed south of Lake George, they completely misjudged what was happening. At first they didn't even know who they were facing or in what strength the enemy was coming; much less could they determine the direction of the main threat. On October 21, Schuyler, citing clearly erroneous intelligence, mistakenly notified the president of Congress that Riedesel had occupied Ticonderoga.[30] Wrong. In Albany, where Major General William Alexander (he preferred "Lord Stirling") commanded the Northern Department, news of the British incursion into the Mohawk Valley occasioned real alarm. At his camp north of Albany, Stark's reaction was similar. Indeed, confirmation of Ross's rampage through Warrensborough was a sensation. But the Continental generals had intelligence that St. Leger had come to Ticonderoga with two thousand men (or more) and that the British were headed toward Albany—Burgoyne redux. Wrong again. And between Ross and St. Leger, who posed the greater danger? Stark fully expected to be attacked south of Saratoga, and he and Stirling were so fixated on the supposed menace from

Ticonderoga that they refused to send reinforcements to patriot forces facing Ross—never knowing that Haldimand had hoped St. Leger's incursion would prompt just such an American response and divert pressure from the major's expedition. As late as October 30, patriots believed St. Leger had left only some four hundred to five hundred troops at Ticonderoga and had sent two thousand to three thousand men bearing down on Stark.[31] If this intelligence was wildly wrong, it certainly was scary. It virtually paralyzed the Continental generals. And thus, the reader will recall, it was New York Governor Clinton—not Stirling or Stark—who sent Marinus Willett to catch Ross at Johnstown and force his precipitous retreat. At the time, however, neither Stirling nor Stark knew that an invasion was never St. Leger's intention.

While the Americans tried to make sense of developments, the British tried to locate Major Ross. From Ticonderoga, St. Leger dispatched a follow-up patrol (his first scouting party having missed Ross) to the Mohawk Valley to search out the major. They also failed to find him.[32] Jessup, then based near the ruins of Fort George, determined to learn what was happening in the nearby Mohawk Valley and sent a small party of rangers to the Mohawk River to reconnoiter. They also missed Ross (who by this time was in full retreat west after the action at Johnstown), but they reported graphically on their understanding of Ross's progress. The redcoat major, they had gathered, "with his savages, were destroying many things, burning everything and escaping"; in their brutal work, Ross's troops had "behaved as trusty King's henchmen." Wounded American officers, the scouts continued, "could scarcely lament enough the number of their men killed and deserting."[33] Obviously, Jessup's rangers had turned back before learning of the action at Johnstown or the skirmish that killed Walter Butler five days later at Canada Creek. Thus, it was an optimistic report on Ross that Jessup's detachment brought back to St. Leger at Ticonderoga on November 1. By then, however, St. Leger had received news of greater import than the fate of Major John Ross.

On October 19, Charles, Lord Cornwallis, surrendered his army at Yorktown to the combined American and French armies of George

Washington and Jean-Baptiste Donatien de Vimeur, the comte de Rochambeau. By late October, unconfirmed reports of the event filtered north through various sources, and in Vermont the impact was immediate. Whatever plans anyone may have had for an agreement with the Crown were thrown into limbo—and then thrown out altogether as anti-British voices joined the Vermont legislature. Word of these sentiments quickly reached St. Leger, who wisely decided that issuing a proclamation from Haldimand offering terms to the republic was now pointless.[34] When confirmation of the developments at Yorktown arrived, the colonel knew his frustrating mission was over.

The rebels also knew as much. On November 1, Stirling added a punctuation mark: he sent a flag to Ticonderoga proposing a prisoner exchange and pointedly noted the British disaster in Virginia. St. Leger's response was a snarl of indignation; he refused to consider the proposal, denounced Stirling's character, and dismissed the American commander's flag as a "prostitution of Honour."[35] (Ensign John Enys shared St. Leger's dim view of Stirling. He claimed the American—who indeed was fond of the bottle—could have sent his flag three days earlier but for the fact he was "so intolerably drunk that he was not capable of dispatching the flag.")[36] With the return of Major Jessup's party to Ticonderoga on November 1, St. Leger ordered his small army to pack up, and the next day he began abandoning the old fort and setting course down Lake Champlain for Canada and winter quarters. On the Vermont side, Ira Allen put the best face on things that he could, painting his drawn-out and very questionable communications with the British as a crafty defensive exercise in buying time against a possible royal invasion. "Thus ended the campaign of 1781," he wrote in his later history of Vermont, "with the accidental loss of only one man [the unfortunate Sergeant Tupper] on the extensive frontiers of Vermont, exposed to an army of ten thousand"—true only if counting every soldier in all of Canada—"yet she did not incur any considerable debt. Such were the happy effects of these negotiations."[37]

Whatever Allen's motives for engaging with St. Leger may have been, the Vermont politico certainly was right about the campaign—it was over. Upon St. Leger's return to Canada, Haldimand conceded as much. Yorktown had effectively demolished any serious Vermont support for reconciliation with the Crown, making any further occu-

pation of Ticonderoga pointless. While the general praised the conduct of Ross and St. Leger, he also observed that, especially in Ross's
case, they had faced considerable hardship and increasingly effective
American opposition.[38] Backing away from his own policy of raiding
the New York frontiers, he warned Henry Clinton that excursions into
the rebel interior had become extremely dangerous. The governor
emphasized the same point in a message to Germain, telling the minister that had St. Leger remained at Ticonderoga, patriot forces would
have cut him off sometime in early 1782. Continental forces were not
really the problem, but the Americans had produced a war-wise "mul-
titude of militia men in arms" that had become a potent threat. (In
this regard, Haldimand may have had more respect for the rebel irregulars than many Continental officers.) It was time, he concluded,
to look to better means to defend Canada—means that did not em-
phasize carrying the war into the enemy's country, at least not into
New York or Vermont.[39]

American authorities couldn't quite believe the war in the North
had concluded. Certainly, Philip Schuyler didn't. On November 2, as
St. Leger was pulling out of Ticonderoga, he wrote a warning letter
to Washington advising against complacency after Yorktown. As far as
Schuyler knew—and as he wrote this he had not learned that St. Leger
was leaving—the British were remaining at Ticonderoga. They had repaired the barracks, were conducting highly suspicious talks with Vermont, and had not revealed their long-term plans. The war was not
over; it was no time for patriots to drop their guard. It was a message
he repeated in a follow-up letter (November 15) even after learning
of St. Leger's departure.[40] The commander in chief fully agreed. "My
great Fear," he responded, "is what you mention . . . all my Powers will
be exerted this Winter to prevent so great an Evil, and to stimulate
the States to vigorous Preparations for another Campaign."[41] And it
was a worthy sentiment. After all, the British had visited Ticonderoga
or its immediate environs three times since 1778—six times since
1775. Who knew what they really had in mind? Had Fort Ticonderoga
really seen the last of the war?

EPILOGUE
A Fort in the Wilderness

IN JUNE 1783, a year and a half after Yorktown and with the struggle for independence virtually over, Brigadier General Rufus Putnam—a distant cousin of the better-known Israel Putnam—took a few moments to write to the commander in chief. The long letter recommended one of Putnam's junior officers for a well-merited promotion before the army disbanded. But it was something more. The letter also afforded an opportunity for the brigadier to reflect on the war years. The Massachusetts Continental had seen a great deal. Indeed, as a younger man he had been present at the disastrous 1758 British assault on Fort Carillon, and he had served the Revolution capably as an engineer and infantry officer.[1] He remembered one episode, however, vividly: "Tis well known into what a panic and consternation the Country and even the whole Northern Army was thrown at the taking of Ticonderoga."[2] Even in victory, the shock from 1777 lingered.

But there would be no more shocks. When the disappointed Barry St. Leger sailed north, he took with him not only the Crown's dashed hopes for detaching Vermont from the Revolution but also the last troops to take station at Ticonderoga—and they had been there less than two weeks. The Americans saw no reason to send a garrison. Even as Washington and Schuyler questioned whether the war was really over after Yorktown, and as they warned fellow patriots of the dangers of complacency, they never seriously considered committing scarce rebel manpower to the fort. In the unlikely event the British did come back, patriots would react as they had previously: they would rush available Continentals to Albany and call out the militia. And while patriots were slow to realize it, the frustration of the Ross and St. Leger missions had left Governor Haldimand skeptical of any further major operations against the New York frontiers. It eventually dawned on the rebels that Ticonderoga was safe.

This is not to say that the old fort was out of mind. The Americans and the British toyed with new operations in the North, but such thoughts led to nothing. In December 1781, Haldimand considered sending Edward Jessup on a scouting mission to Ticonderoga and south to Saratoga. But if Jessup ever undertook the mission, it came to naught—and there is no record of the scout actually taking place. From New York City, Henry Clinton considered raiding Ticonderoga and Fort George—assuming the rebels had posted men in either location—from Canada if campaigning resumed in 1782. But by then Parliament had ordered a halt to offensive operations, and the point became moot.[3] Over spring 1782, Washington looked north as well. In correspondence with Brigadier General Moses Hazen—a Canadian who had thrown in with the Revolution—and in a long planning memorandum, the commander in chief considered the best means of advancing against Canada should a campaign of 1782 prove necessary. The general decided on the traditional Lake George-Lake Champlain route, in which case Ticonderoga would figure as a staging and supply base. But again, it was a moot point.[4] There remained the legalities between the warring nations to bring the conflict to a formal end— and American Indians would continue their struggle against white encroachments on the frontiers—but Ticonderoga's war was indeed over.

There were, of course, residual issues. How could there not be after eight years of struggle? After Burgoyne's capture of the fort, Congress had established a commission to examine claims of private citizens "for losses sustained . . . by the retreat of our Army from Tyconderoaga." But those claims were "so numerous"—involving lost livestock and crops, destroyed or impressed wagons, burned structures, and all manner of other missing property—that the commissioners warned of long delays for many settlements.[5] Years later there were still plenty of outstanding claims awaiting evaluation. Soldiers had claims as well. In 1779, still relatively early in the claims game, Lieutenant Colonel Udny Hay, a New York Continental, was involved in legal wrangling over crops he had contracted for on the army's behalf; but in the confusion of Burgoyne's invasion, the crops were never delivered (or even harvested), and thus not paid for. Hay was furious when the farmer sued him for payment anyway. As late as 1786, Giles Wolcott, a Massachusetts officer, begged relief from Congress for funds lost in the fort's evacuation. Wolcott had received $200 to recruit soldiers and $170 for other official expenses. But the funds were lost, along with official funds of Jeduthan Baldwin, when Wolcott's chest went missing somewhere in the confusion of St. Clair's retreat. Unsympathetic to his plight, army paymasters had stopped his pay for the full $370. Congress had reimbursed Baldwin, Wolcott pointed out; wouldn't it do the same for him?[6] Such tales of woe follow any war, and it didn't help that Congress and the later confederation governments were virtually broke.

There was even a curious British claim—this one, of course, to the royal Treasury. It was from Philip Wharton Skene, the founder of Skenesborough. He was a Scot in British service who had compiled an impressive combat record. He was wounded in Abercrombie's attack on Fort Carillon in 1758, and in 1759, under Jeffery Amherst, he had heroically tried to prevent the retreating French from detonating the fort's magazine. He founded his namesake village while still on active duty, and he developed it extensively when he settled permanently after the Seven Years' War. A committed loyalist, he had rendered all assistance in his power to Burgoyne in 1777. In fact, the general had used Skene's home as his headquarters during his long sojourn in Skenesborough. Patriots confiscated his property, for which the British government eventually granted him an annual pension and a generous lump-sum payment. But in 1784, Skene asked for something more. Just before the war, he had planned with Ethan Allen to carve out a new royal province from New York and the New Hampshire Grants, and in 1775, he had persuaded the Crown to name him lieutenant governor of Crown Point and Ticonderoga. Independence had blasted any such plans, but now Skene wanted almost ten years of back salary as lieutenant governor. The Treasury was not amused. Why had he waited so long to file a claim?[7] The Crown apparently saw no reason to pay for the nonservices of an empty title—a lieutenant governor of a province that never existed.

Then there were the many loyalists of far lesser means than Skene who passed through Ticonderoga on the way to Canada. Recall those who went north with Powell in 1777, the naval mission in 1778 to assist Tories trying to reach St. John's, and the loyalist parties escaping with St. Leger in 1781. Some had lived on or near the Ticonderoga peninsula for years; their numbers included veterans who had campaigned with Abercrombie and Amherst. Now, dispossessed and exiled, they could only hope a generous Crown would appreciate their loyalty and service. Fortunately, Britain would do well by many of them as they carved out new lives in (mostly) Canada, Great Britain, and elsewhere. Their many claims were part of the sad paper trail of war to which Ticonderoga contributed its share.

Washington also dealt with exiles. In particular, he was concerned that Congress do its best by Continental veterans who had enlisted from Canada and obviously could not go back. He read their various pleas knowing his hands were tied; he lacked the resources and the authority to take any concrete steps toward their relief. He could do little more than advocate for them with his political masters, knowing full well of the virtual insolvency of Congress. It was dispiriting, and the general admitted he needed a break. Thus, in July 1783, waiting at his headquarters at Newburgh, New York, for word of the definitive treaty of peace, he wrote to his friend Elias Boudinot, who also was the president of Congress. Washington announced that he was, in effect, going to take a brief vacation. "I have resolved to wear away a little Time," he told Boudinot, "in perform[in]g a Tour to the Northward, as far as Tyconderoga & Crown–point—and perhaps as far up the Mohawk River as Fort Schuyler—I shall leave this place on Friday next, & shall probably be gone about two Weeks, unless my Tour should be interrupted by some special recall."[8] And on July 18, the general was on his way.

Washington toured the battlefields and significant locations in the Northern Department he had never seen during the war. In company with Governor Clinton and Alexander Hamilton, the general visited Albany, Saratoga, Fort Edward, Lake George, Ticonderoga, and Crown Point; coming back he stopped in Ballston, Schenectady, Fort Stanwix, and various locations in the Mohawk River Valley. He was back in Newburgh on August 5 after traveling 750 miles in nineteen days. His horses, he noted, were "much fatigued."[9]

The general never recorded what he thought of the former Gibraltar of America. One wonders, however, at his reactions as he inspected the now-decrepit barracks, looked up from the glacis at Mounts Defiance and Independence, gazed out over Lake Champlain, and rode north over the road from Ticonderoga to Crown Point and back. These were place names that for years had meant so much and had caused him such anxiety. The fort had seen the passing of British and American armies, witnessed victory and defeat, served as a rendezvous and staging area for parties on both sides of the conflict, and played a role as a conduit north for loyalists fleeing erstwhile neighbors who had sided with the Revolution. Now, in effect, with the guns silent, Ticonderoga had become something of a tourist attraction. Indeed, Washington and his party had come and gone as sightseers.

Still, the Virginian was a soldier and had taken in everything with a soldier's eye. And he saw something that spelled the passing of an era: there appeared to be no reason for the new republic to restore the fort to operational status, much less to commit a garrison to its defense. To the extent the United States could spare manpower and resources, Washington looked west. He wanted roads and bridges west from the Mohawk Valley improved, bateaux positioned on appropriate water routes, and resources assembled preparatory to the quick occupation of posts the British were to evacuate under the terms of the peace treaty—places like Detroit, Oswego, and other locations on and near the Great Lakes and in Trans-Appalachia.[10] In fact, only days before leaving on his tour, Washington wrote Haldimand informing the governor that Major General Friedrich von Steuben would come to Quebec to discuss the transfer of these posts to American authorities. In August, Steuben would stop at Ticonderoga on his way north.[11] (It was a frustrating mission; the British refused to evacuate the posts until after the final approval of the Jay Treaty in 1796.) These were locations that would secure the West for American settlement, and this was a future in which Ticonderoga would play no role. With the coming of peace, the Lake Champlain-Hudson River corridor, once so crucial an avenue of communication, seemingly had lost its military significance, and the fort's importance had disappeared with it.

An episode in July added a benediction to Ticonderoga's life as a military installation. On the eighteenth, the very day Washington began his northern sojourn, a British delegation under loyalist officer Andrew Skene (son of Philip Skene, the loyalist founder of Skenesborough) met at the fort with American counterparts under a Rhode Island Continental, Ensign Ephraim Kirby. The British brought with them 196 rebel prisoners of war. The prisoners had fallen into British hands during various engagements and raids in places as far away as the Ohio River Valley, Kentucky (then part of Virginia), western Pennsylvania, and as nearby as the Mohawk Valley of New York, and Crown Point. Some had been prisoners since 1777, although most had been captives since the 1780s.[12] On July 18, 1783, the British released all of them to Ensign Kirby.

The prisoner release was a long time in the planning. As early as April, with the war all but over and offensive operations in the East (but not in the West) halted, Schuyler contacted Haldimand about a return of American prisoners. Haldimand agreed—at this point, why not?—with the exception of rebel prisoners who had enlisted with the British. He could not speak for them, and apparently he was not willing to force them to leave and face an uncertain future among the victorious Americans. Over June and early July, Haldimand's staff made arrangements to collect the captive rebels from various parts of Quebec province and have them sent to Ile aux Noix. From there, Skene had orders to escort them up Lake Champlain to American authorities at Crown Point or some other American advanced post—which turned out to be Ticonderoga. Skene was to have Kirby sign a copy of the prisoner list as a receipt.[13] The transaction came off without a hitch. And as the former captives made their ways south, one wonders if Washington didn't meet some of them as he rode north (if he did, he never mentioned it). In any event, Ticonderoga closed the war with a gesture of peace.

"Ruins of Fort Ticonderoga." Etching and engraving by Fenner, Sears & Co., 1831, after the painting by Thomas Cole of the Hudson River School. The abandoned fort simply fell apart over time. The timber and earthen works deteriorated and local inhabitants had used the stone as a quarry; cannon were hauled off and melted down. (*New York Public Library*)

War did come again to upper New York State and to Lake Champlain. The War of 1812 once more brought the misery of conflict to the state's borders with Canada, and American and British fleets fought a truly decisive naval battle on the lake in 1814 (in which the schooner *Ticonderoga* fought with distinction in the American victory). But none of this involved Fort Ticonderoga or any of its associated outposts. By the early nineteenth century, the fort's timber and earthen bastions were falling into rubble, local residents had helped themselves to the dressed stone of the barracks, and much of the fort's artillery, long out of use, disappeared to be melted down for iron. Inhabitants even broke up the gun carriages for firewood.[14] Nature had reclaimed most of the long-neglected works on Mounts Hope, Defiance, and Independence. Any ruins were relics of another time. Command of a critical location had determined the fort's original construction and maintenance for a generation. But that location no longer mattered. Fort Ticonderoga, once the Key to the Continent, was now an abandoned and picturesque landmark in a prosaic and tranquil landscape—and finally at peace.

NOTES

PREFACE

1. Edward Pierce Hamilton, *Fort Ticonderoga: Key to a Continent* (Boston: Little, Brown, 1964).
2. For example, Henry Beebe Carrington, *Battles of the American Revolution, 1775–1781, Historical and Military Criticism with Topographical Illustration* (New York: A. S. Barnes, 1876); Don Higginbotham, *The War of American Independence: Military Attitudes, Policies, and Practice, 1763–1789* (New York: Macmillan, 1971); Douglas R. Cubbison, *Burgoyne and the Saratoga Campaign: His Papers* (Norman: University of Oklahoma Press, 2012); Richard M. Ketchum, *Saratoga: Turning Point of America's Revolutionary War* (New York: Henry Holt, 1997); Christopher Ward, *The War of the Revolution*, 2 vols., ed. John Richard Alden (New York: Macmillan, 1952); Rupert Furneaux, *The Battle of Saratoga* (New York: Stein and Day, 1971); Max M. Minz, *The Generals of Saratoga: John Burgoyne and Horatio Gates* (New Haven: Yale University Press, 1992); *Gerald Howson, Burgoyne of Saratoga: A Biography* (New York: Times Books, 1979); Theodore Corbett, *No Turning Point: The Saratoga Campaign in Perspective* (Norman: University of Oklahoma Press, 2014).
3. Holly A. Mayer, *Belonging to the Army: Camp Followers and Community during the American Revolution* (Columbia: University of South Carolina Press, 1999).
4. For example, Alan Taylor's superb *The Divided Ground: Indians, Settlers, and the Northern Borderland of the American Revolution* (New York: Alfred A. Knopf, 2006), offers an inviting approach to a sociocultural ("borderlands") treatment of the Ticonderoga region.

CHAPTER ONE: A CROSSROADS OF WAR

1. Patricia O. Afable and Madison S. Beeler, "Place Names," in *Languages*, ed. Ives Goddard, vol. 17 of Handbook of North American Indians, ed. William C. Sturtevant, 20 vols. (Washington, DC: Smithsonian Institution, 1978–2008), 17:193.
2. Colin G. Calloway, *The Indian World of George Washington: The First President, the First Americans, and the Birth of the Nation* (New York: Oxford University Press, 2018), 30; William J. Miller, "The Adirondack Mountains," *New York State Museum Bulletin* 193 (1917): 74; Eliot A. Cohen, *Conquered into Liberty: Two Centuries of Battles along the Great Warpath that Made the American Way of War* (New York: Free Press, 2012), 1-16 passim.

3. David Hackett Fisher, *Champlain's Dream* (New York: Simon and Schuster, 2008), 1-3.

4. Jack Verney, *The Good Regiment: The Carignan-Salières Regiment in Canada, 1665–1668* (Montreal: McGill-Queen's University Press, 1991), 40-53, 71-84.

5. Michael O. Lugusz, *With Musket and Tomahawk: The Saratoga Campaign and the Wilderness War of 1777* (Philadelphia: Casemate, 2010); B. Sulte, "Le Régiment de Carignan," *Proceedings and Transactions of the Royal Society of Canada*, 2nd ser., 8 (1902): 77; Roger R. P. Dechame, "Why Carillon," *Bulletin of the Fort Ticonderoga Museum* 13, No. 6 (1980): 433, 444.

6. G. W. Schuyler, *Colonial New York; Philip Schuyler and His Family*, 2 vols. (New York: Charles Scribner's Sons, 1885), 1:305, 383-84; John H. G. Pell, "Schuyler, Peter," *Dictionary of Canadian Biography* 2 (1701–1740), accessed Sept. 28, 2021, http://www.biographi.ca/en/bio/schuyler_peter_1657_1723_24_2E.html.

7. Schuyler, *Colonial New York*, 2:150-51.

8. A convenient overview of these colonial conflicts is in Howard H. Peckham, *The Colonial Wars, 1689–1762* (Chicago: University of Chicago Press, 2001).

9. For an account of the Battle of Lake George and its implications, see Fred Anderson, *Crucible of War: The Seven Years' War and the Fate of Empire in British North America, 1754–1766* (London: Faber and Faber, 2000), 117-21.

10. J. W. Eccles, "Rigaud de Vaudreuil de Cavagnial, Pierre de, Marquis de Vaudreuil," *Dictionary of Canadian Biography* 4 (1771–1800), accessed Aug. 3, 2021, http://www.biographi.ca/en/bio/rigaud_de_vaudreuil_ de_cavagnial_pierre_de_4E.html. As Eccles explains, Vaudreuil began styling himself "marquis" sometime after the death of his father (1725) who also was the marquis de Vaudreuil and also governor general of New France.

11. Another story of the name suggested an origin from the sound of the rapids on the La Chute, which supposedly reminded listeners of a carillon's bells. The best evidence, however, is in favor of Carrion. See Dechame, "Why Carillon," 444.

12. On the construction of the fort, see J. E. Kaufmann and Tomasz Idzikowski, *Fortress America: The Forts that Defended America, 1600 to the Present* (Cambridge, MA: Da Capo, 2004), 75-76; Hamilton, *Fort Ticonderoga*, 39-49; Carroll Vincent Lonergan, *Ticonderoga: Historic Portage* (Ticonderoga, NY: Fort Mount Hope Society Press, 1959), 17, 19-25, 26; Stephen Pell, *Fort Ticonderoga: A Short History* (Ticonderoga, NY: Fort Ticonderoga Museum, 1966), 19-26; William R. Nester, *The Epic Battles for Ticonderoga, 1758* (Albany: State University of New York Press, 2008), 111.

13. Accounts of French numbers at Carillon vary appreciably, from 400 to some 1,500. It really didn't matter, as Amherst had more than enough men to take the fort.

14. Hamilton, *Fort Ticonderoga*, 102-103.

15. Mark Puls, *Henry Knox: Visionary General of the American Revolution* (New York: Palgrave Macmillan, 2008), 43-45; North Callahan, *Henry Knox: General Washington's General* (New York: Rinehart, 1958), 46-50; Noah Brooks, *Henry Knox, A Soldier of the Revolution: Major-general in the Continental Army, Washington's Chief of Artillery, First Secretary of War under the Constitution, Founder of the Society of the Cincinnati; 1750–1806* (New York: G. P. Putnam's Sons, 1900), 43-45.

16. G. P. Browne, "Carleton, Guy, 1st Baron Dorchester," *Dictionary of Canadian Biography* 5 (1801–1820), accessed Nov. 16, 2018, http://www.biographi.ca/en/bio/carleton_guy_5E.html.

17. Paul David Nelson, *General Horatio Gates: A Biography* (Baton Rouge: Louisiana State University Press, 1976), 67-70.

18. The best account and assessment of Valcour Island is in James Kirby Martin, *Benedict Arnold, Revolutionary Hero: An American Warrior Reconsidered* (New York: New York University Press, 1997), 269-90.

19. Ibid., 288-89; William Maxwell to William Livingston, Oct. 20, 1776, *American Archives*, 5th ser., 2:1143.

20. James M. Hadden, *Hadden's Journal and Orderly Books: A Journal Kept in Canada and upon Burgoyne's Campaign in 1776 and 1777*, ed. Horatio Rogers (Albany: Joel Munsell's Sons, 1884), 24-25.

21. Ibid., 33-34.

CHAPTER TWO: WINTER TO SPRING 1776–1777

1. Nelson, *Horatio Gates*, 74-75.

2. Anthony Wayne to Benjamin Franklin, July 31, 1776, *Papers of Benjamin Franklin*, ed. Leonard W. Labaree, William B. Willcox, et al., 43 vols. (New Haven, CT: Yale University Press, 1959–), 22:539–42.

3. "Wayne, Anthony," *Encyclopedia of the American Revolution*, 2nd ed., 2 vols., ed. Harold E. Selesky (Detroit: Thomson Gale, 2006), 2:1246-47; Mary Stockwell, *Unlikely General: "Mad" Anthony Wayne and the Battle for America* (New Haven, CT: Yale University Press, 2018), 58-63.

4. On Schuyler's career, see Don R. Gerlach, *Proud Patriot: Philip Schuyler and the War of Independence, 1775–1783* (Syracuse, NY: Syracuse University Press, 1964), and Selesky, ed., *Encyclopedia*, 2:1043-45.

5. Robert K. Wright Jr., *The Continental Army* (Washington, DC: Center of Military History, US Army, 1983), 84, 431.

6. Nelson, *Horatio Gates*, 58-61.

7. Wayne quoted in Hamilton, *Fort Ticonderoga*, 142-43.

8. Anthony Wayne to Abraham Robinson, Apr. 1, 1777, "Original Letters from Gen. Wayne," *Historical Magazine* 5 (Feb. 1861): 58.

9. David R. Starbuck, "The General Hospital on Mount Independence: 18th-Century Health Care at a Revolutionary War Cantonment," *Northeast Historical Archaeology* 19 (1990): 56.

10. Philip Schuyler to George Washington (hereafter GW), Feb. 27, 1777, *Papers of George Washington Digital Edition* (hereafter *PGWde*), Revolutionary War Series (hereafter RWS), 8:459-60.

11. Francis B. Heitman, *Historical Register of Officers of the Continental Army during the War of the Revolution, April 1775, to December 1783* (Washington, DC: Rare Book Shop Publishing, 1914), 404.

12. John Trumbull, *Autobiography, Reminiscences and Letters of John Trumbull, from 1756 to 1841* (New York: Wiley and Putnam, 1841), 31-34; James Thacher, *Military Journal of the American Revolution: Comprising a Detailed Account of the Principal Events and Battles of the Revolution, with Their Exact Dates, and a Biographical Sketch of the Most Prominent Generals* (Gansevoort, NY: Corner House Historical Publications, 1998 [orig. publ. 1823]), 80-81.

13. Cubbison, *Burgoyne*, 56.

14. *Maryland Gazette* (Annapolis), Dec. 19, 1776, 2 [Wayne], Wayne Orderly Book, Ticonderoga, Folder 35, entry of Feb. 7, 1777, uncataloged MSS, Fort Ticonderoga Museum Collection (hereafter FTMC); entry of Dec. 12, 1776 [Wayne], Northern Army Orderly Book, 117, FTMC.

15. Feb. 27 and Feb. 8, 1777, Wayne Orderly Book, Ticonderoga, Folder 35, uncataloged MSS, FTMC.

16. Ibid., Apr. 19, 1777.

17. Philip Schuyler to GW, Jan. 15, 1777, *PGWde*, RWS, 8:77-78; Philip Schuyler to GW, Feb. 1, 1777, *PGWde*, RWS, 8:219-20; GW to the Massachusetts General Court, Feb. 8, 1777, ibid., RWS, 8:275-76.

18. Philip Schuyler to GW, Jan. 30, 1777, ibid., RWS, 8:192-94; Philip Schuyler to GW, Mar. 4, 1777, ibid., RWS, 8:514.

19. Jonathan Trumbull Jr. to Jonathan Trumbull Sr., Dec. 16, 1776, *American Archives*, 5th ser., 3:1250.

20. Anthony Wayne to Horatio Gates, Nov. 20, 1776, ibid., 5th ser., 3:785.

21. These supply concerns are noted variously in Thomas Egleston, *The Life of John Paterson, Major General in the Revolutionary Army* (New York: G. P. Putnam's Sons, 1894), 73; George Measam to Horatio Gates, Dec. 15, 1776, *American Archives*, 5th ser., 3:1237-38; Massachusetts Council to GW, Mar. 20, 1777, *PGWde*, RWS, 8:604; Philip Schuyler to John Hancock, Dec. 30, 1776, *Am Arch.*, 5th ser. 3:1795. As late as June 1777, New Hampshire authorities were pleading for clothing, noting that their Continentals were "ragged" and without uniforms. John Langdon to GW, June 16, 1777, *PGWde*, RWS, 10:51. See a good summary of these issues in "By Taylors of Their Respective Companies," Fort Ticonderoga, Oct. 17, 2014, accessed Dec. 9, 2018, https:/fortti-conderoga.org/blog/by-taylors-of-their-respective-companies/.

22. "Historic Average: Ticonderoga, NY," intellicast: The Authority in Expert Weather, accessed Oct. 1, 2021, http://www.intellicast.com/Local/History.aspx?month=12.

23. [Anthony Wayne], *Orderly Book of the Northern Army, at Ticonderoga and Mount Independence from October 17th, 1776, to January 1777, with Biographical and Explanatory Notes and an Appendix* (Albany, NY: J. Munsell, 1859), 135.

24. Thacher, *Military Journal*, 73; Philip Schuyler to GW, Feb. 27, 1777, *PGWde*, RWS, 8:460; Philip Schuyler to GW, Feb. 27, 1777, ibid., RWS, 8:514.

25. Jeduthan Baldwin, *The Revolutionary Journal of Col. Jeduthan Baldwin*, ed. Thomas Williams Baldwin (Bangor, ME: Printed for the De Burians, 1906), 94-100.

26. Elisha Avery, Return of Provisions in the Northern Department, Jan. 23, 1777, Papers of the Continental Congress (hereafter PCC), Record Group (hereafter RG) 360; Letters from Gen. Philip Schuyler, 1775–85 (hereafter Schuyler Letters), 3:86, https://www.fold3.com/image/246/390441.

27. Asa Douglas to Ye Honble Genll Court of the Massachusetts State or to the Honble Council, 19 May 1777, in Egleston, *Life of John Paterson*, 73-74; entry of Feb. 3, 1777, [Wayne] Orderly Book, Ticonderoga, Feb. 2 1777–April 28, 1777, Folder 35, uncataloged MSS, FTMC.

28. Richard L. Blanco, *Physician of the American Revolution: Jonathan Potts* (New York: Garland STPM Press, 1979), 94.

29. Nelson, *Horatio Gates*, 64-65. See Blanco, *Physician*, 94-106, for an informed discussion of the medical efforts at Ticonderoga and Fort George. Horatio Gates to GW, Aug. 28, 1776, *PGWde*, RWS, 6:146.

30. Wayne quoted in Hamilton, *Fort Ticonderoga*, 165.

31. Entry of Feb. 2, 1777, Orderly Book, Ticonderoga, Feb. 2, 1777–April 28, 1777, FTMC, Folder 35, uncataloged MSS.

32. Philip Schuyler to John Hancock, Feb. 15, 1777, PCC, Schuyler Letters, 3:92-94, https://www.fold3.com/image/246/390548.

33. William Heath to GW, Apr. 9, 1777, *PGWde*, RWS, 9:99-100; GW to Joseph Spencer, Mar. 3, 1777, ibid., RWS, 8:505.

34. Lewis Beebe, "Journal of a Physician on the Expedition against Canada, 1776," ed. Frederick R. Kirkland, *Pennsylvania Magazine of History and Biography* 59 (1935): 327; Blanco, *Physician*, 100-101,105-6.

35. Thacher, *Military Journal*, 66, 78.

36. Report of the Committee Sent to the Northern Department, Nov. 27, 1776, *American Archives*, 5th ser., 3:1584; President of Congress to Philip Schuyler, Dec. 30, 1776, ibid., 5th ser., 1478.3.

37. Horatio Gates, "List of the Wants of the Northern Army," [Nov. 1776], PCC, RG 360, Reports on the Army, 1775–85, 82, https://www.fold3.com/image/246/457558.

38. Blanco, *Physician*, 107; Anthony Wayne to Jonathan Potts, Mar. 7, 1777, No. 2134, FTMC; Anthony Wayne to Jonathan Potts, Apr. 14, 1777, No. 2132, FTMC; Philip Schuyler to Jonathan Potts, June 21, 1777, No. 2122, FTMC.

39. Gates, "List of the Wants of the Northern Army," [Nov. 1776], PCC, RG 360, 85, 81, https://www.fold3.com/image/246/457553.

40. Philip Schuyler to GW, Jan. 30, 1777, *PGWde*, RWS, 8:192-94.

41. Charles H. Lesser, ed., *The Sinews of Independence: Monthly Strength Reports of the Continental Army* (Chicago: University of Chicago Press, 1976), 41. Lesser cites a return of 16 Nov. 1776 for his authority. For slightly different numbers, see "State of Troops at Ticonderoga, 17 November 1776," *American Archives*, 5th ser., 3:743. This listing has a total of 2,902, with only 1,339 effectives.

42. Wayne's return of 1 Feb. was included with Philip Schuyler to GW, 4-5 Feb.1777, *PGWde*, RWS, 8:244n1.

43. William Heath to GW, May 5, 1777, *PGWde*, RWS, 9:251.

44. Anthony Wayne to James Bowdoin, Feb. 3, 1777, "Original Letters from Gen. Wayne," *Historical Magazine* 5 (Feb. 1861): 58.

45. Anthony Wayne to the President of Congress, Feb. 2, 1777, *The St. Clair Papers: The Life and Public Services of Arthur St. Clair, Soldier of the Revolutionary War; President of the Continental Congress; and Governor of the North-Western Territory; with His Correspondence and Other Papers*, ed. William Henry Smith, 2 vols. (Cincinnati: Robert Clarke, 1882), 1:384-85.

46. Anthony Wayne to Horatio Gates, Feb. 4, 1777, ibid., 1:385-86.

47. Hamilton, *Fort Ticonderoga*, 169.

48. Joseph Bloomfield, *Citizen Soldier: The Revolutionary War Journal of Joseph Bloomfield*, ed. Mark Edward Lender and James Kirby Martin (Yardley, PA: Westholme, 2018), 111.

49. Ibid., 114-15, 124.

50. Entry of Feb. 2, 1777, Orderly Book, Feb. 2 to April 28, 1777, Folder 35, uncataloged MSS, FTMC.

51. Hamilton, *Fort Ticonderoga*, 169.

52. For example, Ebenezer Cox to Whom It May Concern, 10 Mar. 1777, No. 2093, FTMC; Jabez Colton to Stephen Williams, June 19, 1777, No. 1998, FTMC.

53. Philip Schuyler to the New York Committee of Safety, 16 Dec. 1776, *American Archives*, 5th ser., 3:1249; Philip Schuyler to Jonathan Trumbull Sr., Dec. 19, 1776, ibid., 3:1301.

54. Schuyler's correspondence with the states is detailed in a lengthy note to George Washington, Feb. 1, 1777, *PGWde*, RWS, 8:219-20, n2. Philip Schuyler to GW, Feb. 4–5, 1777, *PGWde*, RWS, 8:243-44.

55. Philip Schuyler to GW, Mar. 25, 1777, *PGWde*, RWS, 8:633.

56. Dec. 7, 1776, *Journals of the Continental Congress* (hereafter *JCC*), 6:1009.

57. For example, GW to the Massachusetts General Court, Feb. 8, 1777, *PGWde*, RWS, 8:275-76; GW to Joseph Spencer, Mar. 3, 1777, ibid., 8:505; William Heath to GW, Apr. 9, 1777, ibid., 9:99-100.

58. Massachusetts Council to GW, Feb. 13, 1777, *PGWde*, RWS, 8:325; New Hampshire Committee of Safety to GW, Feb. 21, 1777, ibid., 8:399.

59. GW to Philip Schuyler, Mar. 12, 1777, *PGWde*, RWS, 8:560-62; GW to William Heath, Mar. 13 , 1777, ibid., 9:564-65.

60. Philip Schuyler to GW, Mar. 25, 1777, ibid., 8:632-33.

61. "Memorandum of sundry articles that may be necessary to carry on the works in the Northern Army in the year 1777," *Am Arch.*, 5th ser. 3:1585; Jeduthan Baldwin, "Memorandum of works to be done near Ticonderoga next spring," [Feb. 1777?], ibid., 3:1585.

62. "Memorandum of sundry articles that may be necessary to carry on the works in the Northern Army in the year 1777," *Am Arch.*, 5th ser. 3:1585.

63. Ebenezer Stevens, "A calculation of Ordnance and Ordnance Stores wanted for the Army of the Northern department, made by order of General Schuyler," Nov. 30, 1776, ibid., 3:1590.

64. Jeremiah Powell to Philip Schuyler, Mar. 13, 1777, PCC, RG 360, Schuyler Letters, 3:118, https://www.fold3.com/image/246/390866.

65. William Heath to GW, May 5, 1777, *PGWde*, RWS, 9:351-52; Philip Schuyler to GW, Jan. 30, 1777, ibid., 8:193-94.

66. "Extract of a letter from Albany, Feb. 25, 1777," *Maryland Gazette* (Annapolis), Mar. 13, 1777, 2; *Maryland Gazette* (Annapolis), Apr. 3, 1777, 1.

67. Jan. 1, 1777, Northern Army Orderly Book, 134; Philip Schuyler, Jan. 14, 1777, *American Archives*, 5th ser., 3:1495-96.

68. Horatio Gates to GW, May 24, 1777, *PGWde*, RWS, 9:515.

69. William Heath to GW, Apr. 30, 1777, ibid., 9:307; GW to William Heath, May 10, 1777, ibid., 9:376-77.

70. Entry of Feb. 7, 1777, Wayne, Ticonderoga Orderly Book, Folder 35, uncataloged MSS, FTMC.

71. Peter Force and M. St. Clair, eds., *American Archives: Consisting of a Collection of Authentick Records, State Papers, Debates, and Letters and Other Notices of Publick Affairs, the Whole Forming a Documentary History of the Origin and Progress of the North American Colonies*, 9 vols. (Washington, DC: M. St. Clair Clarke and Peter Force, 1837–1853), 3:529.

72. Baldwin, *Revolutionary Journal*, xxi, xxviii-xxx, 93; Heitman, *Historical Register*, 72.

73. Baldwin, *Revolutionary Journal*, 95, 104 passim.

74. [Anthony Wayne], *Orderly Book of the Northern Army, at Ticonderoga and Mt. Independence from October 17th, 1776, to January 1777, with Biographical and Explanatory Notes and an Appendix* (Albany, NY: J. Munsell, 1859), 116.

75. Philip Schuyler to John Hancock, Feb. 8, 1777, PCC, Schuyler Letters, 3:114, https://www.fold3.com/image/246/390658. This letter may have mangled the Frenchman's name, as the standard references on French officers serving with the Continental army list no "Marquisie"—or any name even close.

76. Baldwin, *Revolutionary Journal*, 93.

77. George Measam to Horatio Gates, Dec. 15, 1776, *American Archives*, 5th ser., 3:1238.

78. Hamilton, *Fort Ticonderoga*, 170.

79. Baldwin, *Revolutionary Journal*, 94; entries of Mar. 5, 8, 9, 1777, Wayne Orderly Book, Ticonderoga, Folder 35, uncataloged MSS, FTMC.

80. Thacher, *Military Journal*, 67.

81. Dec. 12, 1776, Northern Army Orderly Book, 121; Bloomfield, *Journal*, 118-19.

82. Philip Schuyler to GW, Jan. 30, 1777, *PGWde*, RWS, 8:192-94; Thacher, *Military Journal*, 66-71.

83. Entries from Mar. 15 to Mar. 23, 1777, Wayne Orderly Book, Ticonderoga, Folder 35, uncataloged MSS, FTMC.

84. [Wayne], Nov. 20, 1776, *Orderly Book of the Northern Army*, 9; Anthony Wayne to Horatio Gates, Nov. 20, 1777, *Am Arch.*, 5th ser., 3:375; Heitman, *Historical Register*, 410, 430.

85. For example, "Return of the Forces of the United States of America which compose the garrisons of Ticonderoga and Mount Independence, under command of Colonel Anthony Wayne," [c. Dec. 1776], *American Archives*, 5th ser., 3:1589. The return noted 1,109 effectives of a total of 2,451 men, with only 3 deserters.

86. Wayne's orderly book entry of 13 Mar. 1777, spelled Van Alstine as "Van Allston." Wayne Orderly Book, Ticonderoga, Folder 35, uncataloged MSS, FTMC; Frederic G. Mather, ed., *New York in the Revolution as a Colony and State: A Collection of Documents and Records from the Office of the State Comptroller,* 2nd ed., 2 vols. (Albany, NY: J. B. Lyon, printers, 1904), 1:178; Van Alstine, Nicholas, S. 23,982, RG 15, M804, Revolutionary War Pension and Bounty-Land Warrant Application Files, National Archives and Records Administration, accessed Dec. 7, 2018, https://www.fold3.com/document/20401975/.

87. For an excellent overview of these differing sectional outlooks on relationships between enlisted and commissioned ranks and on military discipline generally, see "Too Opposite Characters," Fort Ticonderoga Museum, Aug. 22, 2014, accessed Dec. 7, 2020, https://www.fortticonderoga.org/blog/too-opposite-characters/.

88. Thacher, *Military Journal*, 60; Philip Schuyler to GW, Jan. 30, 1777, *PGWde*, RWS, 8:192-94.

89. Thacher, *Military Journal*, 68-69.

90. Daniel Whiting to Philip Schuyler, Jan. 3, 1777, PCC, RG 360, Letters from Philip Schuyler, 3:83-84, https://www.fold3.com/image/246/390422; Thacher, *Military Journal*, 69.

91. Daniel Whiting to Philip Schuyler, Jan. 3, 1777, PCC, RG 360, Letters from Philip Schuyler, 3:83-84, https://www.fold3.com/image/246/390422; Thomas Craig to Philip Schuyler, 28 Jan. 1777, Philip Schuyler Papers, Letters Received, Manuscripts and Archives Division, New York Public Library Digital Collections, , accessed Dec. 7, 2020, https://digital collections.nypl.org/items/75063950-6334-0134-eea2-00505 686a51c; Ebenezer Elmer, "Journal Kept during an Expedition to Canada in 1776," *Proceedings of the New Jersey Historical Society* 3 (1848): 51; Thacher, *Military Journal*, 69.

92. Thomas Craig to Philip Schuyler, Jan. 28, 1777, Philip Schuyler Papers, Letters Received, Manuscripts and Archives Division, New York Public Library Digital Collections, accessed Dec. 7, 2020, https://digital collections.nypl.org/items/75063950-6334-0134-eea2-00505686a51c.

93. Thacher, *Military Journal*, 69; Heitman, *Historical Register*, 139, 431.

94. Anthony Wayne to Horatio Gates. Feb. 4, 1777, in Smith, ed., *St. Clair Papers*, 1:385-86; Philip Schuyler to GW, Jan. 25, 1777, *PGWde*, RWS, 8:155.

95. Hamilton, *Fort Ticonderoga*, 168.

96. Baldwin, *Revolutionary Journal*, 99.

97. Anthony Wayne to the Massachusetts Council, Mar. 25, 1777, *PGWde*, RWS, 9:38-39n2.

CHAPTER THREE: COMMANDERS AND CONTROVERSIES

1. Mar. 15, 1777, *JCC*, 7:180-81.

2. Mar. 25 and 31, 1777, *JCC*, 7:202, 211. For the politics behind these resolutions, see Benson J. Lossing, *The Life and Times of Philip Schuyler*, 2 vols. (New York: Sheldon, 1872–73), 2:164-67.

3. For example, journal entries from Apr. 23, 1777, to May 15, 1777, *JCC*, 7:294-362; Lossing, *Life and Times*, 2:168-71.

4. Michael Bellesiles, "Schuyler, Philip," Selesky, ed., *Encyclopedia*, 2:1044; Lossing, *Life and Times*, 2:171-72; Philip Schuyler to GW, Apr. 30, 1777, *PGWde*, RWS, 9:311-12; Philip Schuyler to GW, May 3, 1777, ibid., 9:339.

5. On Gates's arrival in Albany, see Nelson, *Horatio Gates*, 80-82; 12 Mar. 1777, *JCC*, 7:171.

6. Horatio Gates to GW, Apr. 19, 1777, *PGWde*, RWS, 9:208-9; GW to Horatio Gates, Apr. 28, 1777, ibid., RWS, 9:292.

7. Arthur St. Clair, "The Trial of Major General St. Clair, August, 1778," *Collections of the New-York Historical Society, 1880* (New York: Printed for the Society, 1881), 49-50. Gates later added that if he had known Burgoyne was coming with over ten thousand men, he would have asked for even more Continentals.

8. Horatio Gates to John Hancock, Apr. 22, 1777, PCC, Letters from Maj. Gen. Horatio Gates, 1775-81, item 171, p. 78, accessed Dec. 16, 2018, https://www.fold3.com/image/251522.

9. GW to Horatio Gates, May 15, 1777, *PGWde*, RWS, 9:429.

10. Horatio Gates to GW, May13, 1777, ibid., RWS, 9:410-11.

11. GW to Horatio Gates, May 15,1777, *PGWde*, RWS, 9:429.

12. GW to Horatio Gates, May 19, 1777, ibid., RWS, 9:471-72.

13. Horatio Gates to GW, May 24, 1777, ibid., RWS, 9:514.

14. On the full story of the Washington-Gates quarrel and the course of the cabal, see Mark Edward Lender, *Cabal!: The Plot against General Washington* (Yardley, PA: Westholme, 2019).

15. Anthony Wayne to the Massachusetts Council, Mar. 25, 1777, in *PGWde*, RWS, 9:37-39n2.

16. Richard Varick to Philip Schuyler, Apr. 21, 1777, Philip Schuyler Papers, Papers Concerning the Affairs at Ticonderoga, 1775–1781 (Colonial North America at Harvard University, MS Sparks 60), Houghton Library, Harvard University.

17. Isaac Smith Sr. to John Adams, Apr. 25, 1777, *Adams Family Correspondence: December 1761–March 1778* (hereafter *AFC*), ed. L. H. Butterfield et al., 2 vols. (Cambridge, MA: Harvard University Press,1963), 2:222; John Adams to unknown, Apr. 28, 1777, *Papers of John Adams* (hereafter *PJA*), ed. Robert J. Taylor et al., 17 vols. (Cambridge, MA: Harvard University Press, 1977–2014), 5:167-68.

18. Apr. 29, 1777, *JCC*, 7:307; Nathanael Greene to John Adams, May 2, 1777, *PJA*, 5:171-73; Labaree, Willcox, *Papers of Benjamin Franklin*, 24:15.

19. For example, Nathanael Greene to John Adams, Apr. 5, 1777, *PJA*, 5:142.

20. On Washington's thinking in this regard, see GW to Philip Schuyler, Mar. 12, 1777,

PGWde, RWS, 8:560-61; GW to William Heath, Mar. 13, 1777, ibid., RWS, 8:564-65. On similar sentiments in Congress and among other senior patriots in the late spring, see Smith, *St. Clair Papers*, 1:54, and James Wilkinson, *Memoirs of My Own Times*, 3 vols. (Philadelphia: Printed by Abraham Small, 1816), 1:168-69; St. Clair, "Trial of Major General St. Clair, August, 1778," 135-36.

21. Charles Carroll of Carrollton to Charles Carroll Sr., May 10, 1777, *LDC*, 7:60; Richard Henry Lee to Patrick Henry, May 13, 1777, ibid., 7:76.

22. John Adams to Abigail Adams, May 6, 1777, *LDC*, 7:28; John Adams to James Warren, June 19, 1777, ibid., 7:220.

23. Horatio Gates to John Hancock, May 11, 1777, PCC, Letters from Maj. Gen. Horatio Gates, RG 360, item 171, pp. 89-90, accessed Dec. 16, 2020, https://www.fold3.com/image/251526, https://www.fold3.com/image/251567.

24. GW to Philip Schuyler, June 20, 1777, *PGWde*, RWS, 10:90.

25. Egleston, *Life of John Paterson*, 2-72; Harold E. Selesky, "Paterson, John," Selesky, ed., *Encyclopedia*, 2:875-76.

26. Wilkinson, *Memoirs*, 1:164.

27. "Horatio Gates' Notes for a Speech to Congress" [June 18, 1777], *LDC*, 7:214-15.

28. John Paterson to the President of the Massachusetts Council, May 2, 1777, in Egleston, *Life of John Paterson*, 72-73.

29. Baldwin, *Journal*, 101.

30. Alex Storozynski, *The Peasant Prince: Thaddeus Kosciuszko and the Age of Revolution* (New York: St. Martin's, 2009), 25.

31. Ibid., *Peasant Prince*, 26; Baldwin, *Journal*, 104.

32. *Storozynski, Peasant Prince*, 26-27.

33. Livingston's testimony in St. Clair, "Trial of Major General St. Clair," 116.

34. James Wilkinson to Horatio Gates, May 26, 1777, in Wilkinson, *Memoirs*, 1:165-66.

35. Wilkinson, *Memoirs*, 1:171; Armstrong quoted in Storozynski, *Peasant Prince*, 24, 26-27; Nelson, *Horatio Gates*, 91-92.

36. May 22, 1777, *JCC*, 8:375; Jonathan Trumbull to Horatio Gates, May 24, 1777, Horatio Gates Papers, New-York Historical Society; Lossing, *Life and Times*, 2:178; Nelson, *Horatio Gates*, 85-86.

37. Smith, *St. Clair Papers*, 1:53.

38. "Horatio Gates' Notes for a Speech to Congress" [June 18, 1777], *LDC*, 7:213-16.

39. William Duer to Philip Schuyler, June 19, 1777, *LDC*, 7:228-31.

40. Baldwin, *Journal*, 105; Apr. 1, 1777, *JCC*, 7:217.

41. John Sullivan to GW, Mar. 9, 1777, *PGWde*, RWS, 8:547.

42. GW to John Sullivan, Mar. 15, 1777, *PGWde*, RWS, 8:580-81; Charles Whittemore, *A General of the Revolution: John Sullivan of New Hampshire* (New York: Columbia University Press, 1961), 51-52.

43. St. Clair lacks a modern biography that deals fully with his career during the Revolution. This sketch was based on Smith, *St. Clair Papers*, 1:2-11, and Michael Bellesiles, "St. Clair, Arthur," in Selesky, ed., *Encyclopedia*, 2:1015-16.

44. Heitman, *Historical Register*, 380; Smith, *St. Clair Papers*, 1:12-44.

45. James Wilkinson to Horatio Gates, June 10, 1777, in Wilkinson, *Memoirs*, 172; Richard Varick to Philip Schuyler, June 12, 1777, Schuyler Papers, Affairs at Ticonderoga, 1775–1781.

46. Frank C. Mevers, "Poor, Enoch," Selesky, ed., *Encyclopedia*, 2:922; Baldwin, *Journal*, 102.

47. Mary Theresa Leiter, *Biographical Sketches of the Generals of the Continental Army of the Revolution* (Cambridge, MA: John Wilson and Son, 1889), 97-98; GW to Philip Schuyler, July 27, 1777, *PGWde*, RWS, 10:443; André Lasseray, *Les Fran ais sous les Treize Étoiles, 1775–1783* (Paris: Macon, 1935), 267-68.

48. The various Ticonderoga-Mount Independence defensive works as of July 6, 1777 are clearly noted on a British map, "Plan of Ticonderoga and Mount Independence, including Mount Hope, and shewing the rebel works & batteries, as they were when His Majesty's troops took possession of them on 6th July 1777," c. 1780, John Carter Brown Map Collection, Acc. No. 31267, John Carter Brown Library, Brown University, Providence, RI, https://jcb.lunaimaging.com/luna/servlet/workspace/ handleMediaPlayer?lunaMediaId= JCBMAPS~1~1~2703~101233, accessed Dec. 28, 2018.

49. Storozynski, *Peasant Prince*, 27.

50. Smith, *St. Clair Papers*, 1:56.

51. Richard Varick to Philip Schuyler, June 12, 1777, Schuyler Papers, Affairs at Ticonderoga, 1775–1781; "Council of General Officers, Held at Ticonderoga, on Friday, the 20th of June, 1777," in Smith, *St Clair Papers*, 1:404; Arthur St. Clair to Philip Schuyler, June 28, 1777, ibid., 1: 411.

52. Arthur St. Clair to Philip Schuyler, June 28, 1777, in Smith, *St. Clair Papers*, 1:411; St. Clair, "Trial of Major General St. Clair, August, 1778," 110.

53. Jabez Colton to Stephen Williams, 19 June 1777, MS 1998, FTMC.

54. See two letters from Arthur St. Clair to Philip Schuyler, June 24 and 25, 1777, in Smith, *St. Clair Papers*, 1:406-7, 409-10.

55. Arthur St. Clair to Philip Schuyler, June 26, 1777, in Smith, *St. Clair Papers*, 1:410.

56. St. Clair quoted in Smith, *St. Clair Papers*, 1:54; "Council of General Officers, Held at Ticonderoga, on Friday, the 20th of June, 1777," in ibid., 1:404-405; Arthur St. Clair to James Wilson, June 18, 1777, in ibid., 1:403-4.

57. Wilkinson, *Memoirs*, 174; Smith, *St. Clair Papers*, 1:59.

58. Arthur St. Clair to Philip Schuyler, June 28, 1777, in Smith, *St Clair Papers*, 1:411.

59. Jabez Colton to Stephen Williams, June 19, 1777, MS 1998, FTMC. Ketchum, *Saratoga*, 157, thinks the death was an accident, but the circumstances clearly point to suicide.

60. Arthur St. Clair to James Wilson, June 18, 1777, in Smith, *St. Clair Papers*, 1:404.

61. Arthur St. Clair to Philip Schuyler, June 26, 1777, in ibid., 1:410.

62. Arthur St. Clair to Philip Schuyler, June 28, 1777, in ibid., 1:411; Arthur St. Clair to Philip Schuyler, June 30, 1777, in ibid., 1:414. This optimistic letter of June 30 has been misinterpreted, leading some authors to charge St. Clair with issuing a falsely confident picture of affairs at Ticonderoga. In fact, the major general was referring only to Seth Warner's activities, not to operations near Ticonderoga proper or Mount Independence.

63. Ketchum, *Saratoga*, 158; Wilkinson, in his *Memoirs*, 1:173, has Schuyler arriving on 17 June.

64. Council of General Officers, Held at Ticonderoga, on Friday, the 20th of June, 1777, in Smith, ed., *St. Clair Papers*, 1:404-5.

CHAPTER FOUR: THE THREAT

1. Hadden, *Hadden's Journal*, 35-36, 54; Joshua Pell, "Diary of Joshua Pell: An Officer of the British Army in America, 1776–1777," ed. James L. Onderonk, *Magazine of American History, with Notes and Queries* 2 (1878): 107.

2. Julius Friedrich von Hille [?], *The American Revolution: Garrison Life in French Canada and New York: Journal of an Officer in the Prinz Friedrich Regiment,* trans. Helger Doblin, ed. Mary C. Lynn (Westport, CT: Greenwood Press, 1993), 73-74; Hadden, *Hadden's Journal,* 35-38, 54.

3. Hadden, *Hadden's Journal,* 35, 39-42.

4. The best available compilation of Revolutionary War engagements, Howard H. Peckham's *The Toll of Independence: Engagements and Battle Casualties of the American Revolution* (Chicago: University of Chicago Press, 1974), 24-32, lists no fighting in the Ticonderoga vicinity between October 14, 1776, and late March 1777. (The listing for early March is an obvious error, a duplication of the McKay raid of later in the month.)

5. Bloomfield, *Citizen Soldier,* 117; for example, entry of Feb. 14, 1777, Anthony Wayne Orderly Book at Fort Ticonderoga, Feb. 2, 1777 –Apr. 28, 1777, Uncatalogued MSS, Folder 35, FTMC.

6. On McKay, see the lengthy editor's note in *Hadden's Journal,* 39-43; Worthington Chauncey Ford, comp., *British Officers Serving in America, 1754–1774* (Boston: David Clapp & Son, 1894), 64.

7. Hadden, *Hadden's Journal,* 39-40; Philip Schuyler to GW, Mar. 25, 1777, *PGWde,* RWS, 8:633.

8. Hadden, *Hadden's Journal,* 42-43, ed. note.

9. On the origins of the new plan, see Ira D. Gruber, *The Howe Brothers and the American Revolution* (New York: Norton, 1972); Troyer Steele Anderson, *Command of the Howe Brothers during the American Revolution* (New York: Oxford University Press, 1936); Andrew Jackson O'Shaughnessy, *The Men Who Lost America: British Leadership, the American Revolution, and the Fate of the Empire* (New Haven, CT: Yale University Press, 2013).

10. John Burgoyne has a literature all his own. Unless noted otherwise, this biographical sketch is based on Mintz, *Generals of Saratoga;* Howson, *Burgoyne of Saratoga;* and Richard Hargrove, *General John Burgoyne* (Newark: University of Delaware Press, 1983).

11. This biographical sketch is drawn from James Stokesbury, "Burgoyne, John," *Dictionary of Canadian Biography* 4 (1771–1800), accessed Sept. 30, 2021, http://www.biographi.ca/en/bio.php?id_nbr=1782.

12. Tony Jacques, *Dictionary of Battles and Sieges* (Westport, CT: Greenwood Press, 2007), 1075.

13. Burgoyne's persona gave rise to the sobriquet of "Gentleman Johnny" among nineteenth-century authors. No one (that we know of) called him that during his lifetime.

14. Henry Clinton, *The American Rebellion: Sir Henry Clinton's Narrative of His Campaigns, 1775–1782, with an Appendix of Original Documents,* ed. William B. Willcox (New Haven, CT: Yale University Press, 1954), 60-61; Clinton quoted in Cubbison, *Burgoyne,* 32.

15. Hadden, *Hadden's Journal,* 43.

16. Richard Tomczak, "French Canadian Laborers in the 1777 Northern Campaign," *Bulletin of the Fort Ticonderoga Museum* 17, no. 1 (2016):50.

17. Cubbison, *Burgoyne,* 48, 51.

18. John Luzader, *Decision on the Hudson: The Battle of Saratoga* (Fort Washington, PA: Eastern National, 2002), 19.

19. John Burgoyne to Lord George Germain, July 11, 1777, in Cubbison, *Burgoyne,* 265-66.

20. Barbara Graymont, *The Iroquois in the American Revolution* (Syracuse, NY: Syracuse University Press, 1972), 150.

21. *Maryland Gazette* (Annapolis), Dec. 26, 1776; for Phillips's service in Canada before the Saratoga campaign, see Robert P. Davis, *Where a Man Can Go: Major General William Phillips, British Royal Artillery, 1731–1781* (Westport, CT: Greenwood Press, 1999), 39-54.

22. Hadden, *Hadden's Journal*, 468-69.

23. Worthington Chauncey Ford, comp., *British Officers Serving in the American Revolution, 1774–1783* (Brooklyn, NY: Historical Printing Club, 1897), 146; Philip R. N. Katcher, *Encyclopedia of British, Provincial, and German Army Units, 1775–1783* (Harrisburg, PA: Stackpole Books, 1973), 59-60; Hadden, *Hadden's Journal*, 464-67.

24. In 1758, James Abercrombie's assault came to grief well outside the fort on Montcalm's hastily constructed French Lines; the British never reached the fort itself.

25. "Barrimore Matthew ST LEGER," *ACAD: A Cambridge Alumni Database*, University of Cambridge, accessed Jan. 9, 2019, http://venn.lib.cam.ac.uk/Documents/acad/intro.html; Graymont, *Iroquois in the Revolution*, 130, 135-36, 144-46; John C. Fredriksen, *America's Military Adversaries: From Colonial Times to the Present* (Santa Barbara, CA: ABC-CLIO, 2002), 484-85.

26. Friedrich Adolf Riedesel, *Memoirs, and Letters and Journals, of Major General Riedesel during His Residence in America*, ed. Max von Eelking, trans. William L. Stone, 2 vols. (Albany, NY: J. Munsell, 1868), 1:1-29.

27. Johann Friedrich Specht, *The Specht Journal: A Military Journal of the Burgoyne Campaign*, trans. Helga Doblin, ed. Mary C. Lynn (Westport, CT: Greenwood Press, 1995), *116-17*; "Skeffington Lutwidge," *The Royal Navy, 1776–1815: A Biographical History and Chronicle*, accessed Jan. 9, 2019, https://morethannelson.com/officer/skeffington-lutwidge/; Cubbison, *Burgoyne*, 268n133; Pell, "Diary," 107.

28. Riedesel, *Memoirs*, 1:106.

29. "Substance of the Speech of Lieut. Genl. Burgoyne to the Indians in Congress at the Camp upon the River Boquet, June 21, 1777. And of Their Answer," in Cubbison, *Burgoyne*, 198-201.

30. "Copy of Manifesto Issued by Lieut. Genl. Burgoyne," June 24, 1777, ibid., 201-3.

31. A New Jersey Man [William Livingston], "Parody on Burgoyne's Proclamation," Aug. 26, 1777, *PWL*, 2:41-46.

32. Burke quoted in Cubbison, *Burgoyne*, 47.

33. Graymont, *Iroquois in the Revolution*, 151; Philip Schuyler to GW, July 9, 1777, *PGWde*, RWS, 10:234.

34. Henry Brockholst Livingston to William Livingston, July 12, 1777, *PWL*, 2:19.

35. Hadden, *Hadden's Journal*, 53, 82.

36. August Wilhelm Du Roi, *Journal of Du Roi the Elder: Lieutenant and Adjutant, in the Service of the Duke of Brunswick, 1776–1778*, trans. Charlotte S. J. Epping (Philadelphia: University of Pennsylvania, D. Appleton & Co., agents, 1911), 87-88, 90.

CHAPTER FIVE: INVASION

1. "Genl Orders Crown Point June 30th 1777," in Cubbison, *Burgoyne*, 203-4.

2. Riedesel, *Memoirs*, 1:110-12; Cubbison, *Burgoyne*, 52-53.

3. James Wilkinson to Horatio Gates, June 25, 1777, in Smith, *St. Clair Papers*, 1:408.

4. Arthur St. Clair to Philip Schulyer, July 1, 1777, ibid., 1:415.

5. Ibid., 1:416.

6. Arthur St. Clair to Udney Hay, July 1, 1777, ibid., 1:414-15.

7. Samuel Brewer to William Heath, July 3, 1777, in William Heath, *The Heath Papers*, 3 vols. (Boston: Massachusetts Historical Society, 1878–1905), 2:116.

8. Gregory J. W. Urwin, "From Parade Ground to Battlefield: How the British Army Adapted to War in North America, 1775–1783," presented at the 2019 International Conference on the American Revolution, Museum of the American Revolution, Oct. 4, 2019, Philadelphia, 21.

9. This action is described similarly in Wilkinson, *Memoirs*, 1:282-83; Ketchum, *Saratoga*, 165-66; and Cubbison, *Burgoyne Papers*, 58-59. Unless noted otherwise, what follows on the events of July 2 is drawn from these sources.

10. Wilkinson, *Memoirs*, 1:283; Riedesel, *Memoirs*, 1:112, put British losses in killed and wounded at "one officer and a few men"; American losses he estimated at "one officer, and about twenty men." Burgoyne reported a similar estimate of British losses. Cubbison, *Burgoyne Papers*, 58; Henry Brockholst Livingston to William Livingston, July 3, 1777, *PWL*, 2:9. Ketchum, *Saratoga*, 166, cites seemingly reliable sources reporting seven American dead and eleven wounded. See also Thomas Blake, "Lieutenant Thomas Blake's Journal," in Frederick Kidder, *History of the First New Hampshire Regiment in the War of the Revolution* (Albany, NY: Joel Munsell, 1868), 27.

11. Henry Brockholst Livingston to William Livingston, July 3, 1777, *PWL*, 2:9-10.

12. Wilkinson, *Memoirs*, 1:283; Arthur St. Clair to Philip Schuyler, July 3, 1777, in Smith, *St. Clair Papers*, 1:419.

13. "Asa Douglas," Douglas Archives, accessed Jan. 18, 2019, http://www.douglashistory.co.uk/history/asadouglas.htm.

14. Christian Julius Prätorius, "Journal of Lt. Colonel Christian Julius Prätorius, 2 June 1777–19 July 1777," trans. Helga Doblin, *Bulletin of the Fort Ticonderoga Museum* 15, no. 3 (1991): 64.

15. There are different recollections of Phillips's remark, and if he didn't say exactly this he likely said something close to it. On July 11, 1777, Major General William Heath, commenting on the fall of Ticonderoga, recognized the significance of Mount Defiance. He credited a Phillips-like observation to Frederick William I of Prussia (father of Frederick the Great): "but they should have recollected what had been said by the late King of Prussia, as to such positions that 'where a goat can go, a man may go; and where a man can go, artillery may be drawn up.'" Phillips loved his guns, and he would have appreciated such a line. So perhaps Phillips was quoting Frederick William? See William Heath, *Memoirs of Major-General Heath* (Boston: I. Thomas and E. T. Andrews, 1798), 111; and Davis, *Where a Man Can Go*, 65.

16. Davis, *William Phillips*, 65; Michael Bellesiles, "Ticonderoga, New York, British Capture of," in Selesky, ed., *Encyclopedia*, 2:1154-55.

17. Arthur St. Clair to Philip Schuyler, July 5, 1777, in Smith, *St. Clair Papers*, 1:420.

18. Ebenezer Fletcher, *A Narrative of the Captivity and Suffering of Ebenezer Fletcher of New Ipswich* (Windsor, VT: Printed by Charles Kendall, 1813), [1].

19. Henry Brockholst Livingston to William Livingston, July 12, 1777, *PWL*, 2:18.

20. Blake, "*Blake's Journal*," 28.

21. Kidder, *History of the First New Hampshire*, 96-97. The same tale is in Caleb Stark, *Memoir and Official Correspondence of Gen. John Stark, with Notices of Several Other Officers of the Revolution. Also, a Biography of Capt. Phinehas Stevens and of Col. Robert Rogers, with an Account of His Services in America during the "Seven Years' War"* (Concord, NH: Parker Lyon, 1860), 337.

22. Thacher, *Military Journal*, 82-83.

23. Thomas Anburey, "The Taking of Ticonderoga," *Bulletin of the Fort Ticonderoga Museum* 2, no. 1 (1930): 22-23; Bellesiles, "Ticonderoga," 2:1155.

24. Bruce M. Venter, *The Battle of Hubbardton: The Rear Guard Action That Saved America* (Charleston, SC: History Press, 2015), 36.

25. Thacher, *Military Journal*, 83.

26. The best account of Hubbardton is Venter, *Battle of Hubbardton*.

27. Du Roi, *Journal*, 93. The rebel flag may not have been the Stars and Stripes; it may have been just a banner with stripes. See Stephen Stach, "A New Look at the Regimental Colors of the Second New Hampshire Regiment 1777," *Military Collector and Historian* 37, no. 3 (1985).

28. Cubbison, *Burgoyne Papers*, 65.

29. Bellesiles, "Ticonderoga," 2:1155.

30. John Burgoyne to George Germain, July 11 1777, in Cubbison, *Burgoyne Papers*, 265, 274.

31. The quote is attributed to George III in Horace Walpole, *Journal of the Reign of King George the Third, from the Year 1771 to 1783*, ed. Dr. [John] Doran, 2 vols. (London: Richard Bentley, 1859), 2:131. One can ask how Walpole, a well-informed British politico and wag, was well-informed *enough* to know what the king actually said in the bed chamber of the queen. With the publication of Walpole's *Journal*, however, the king's alleged quote became a standard part of the Ticonderoga-Saratoga narrative. American historians from the nineteenth century on have accepted the veracity of Walpole's report, albeit a bit too uncritically. For examples, see William L. Stone, *The Campaign of Lieut. Gen. John Burgoyne, and the Expedition of Lieut. Col. Barry St. Leger* (Albany, NY: Joel Munsell, 1877), 19; James Fiske, *The American Revolution*, 2 vols. (Boston: Houghton Mifflin, 1891), 1:271; and even early school books—for example, Alfred F. Blaisdell, *The Story of American History: For Elementary School* (N.p.: Forgotten Books, 2016; orig. publ. 1902), 84. Patriotic nineteenth-century fiction used Walpole as well; for example, Mark Lee Luther, "The Livery of Honor," *Lippincott's Monthly Magazine* 64 (Nov. 1899): 692. Most modern historians also have accepted the phrase as coming from George III; see, for example, John S. Pancake's excellent *1777: The Year of the Hangman* (Tuscaloosa: University of Alabama Press, 1977), 124. The king's words properly belong in the file of things that, if not true, *ought* to be true. It's too good a line not to use.

32. GW to John Hancock, July 5, 1777, *PGWde*, RWS, 10:195-96; GW to Edward Rutledge, July 5, 1777, ibid., RWS, 10:198-99; GW to James Bowdoin, Nickolas Cooke, and the New Hampshire Convention, July 7, 1777, ibid., RWS, 10:214-15; GW to Jonathan Trumbull, July 7, 1777, ibid., RWS, 10:222-23. On this point, see also GW's detailed letter to Hancock, July 2, 1777, ibid., RWS, 10:168-70.

33. GW to John Sullivan, July 8, 1777, *PGWde*, RWS, 10:230; William Heath to GW, July 7, 1777, ibid., RWS, 10:216-17.

34. See four letters from Schuyler to GW of July 7 (two letters), July 9 and July 10, 1777, *PGWde*, RWS, 10:219, 220, 234, 244.

35. GW to Philip Schuyler, July 10, 1777, *PGWde*, RWS, 10:244.

36. John Adams to James Warren, July 7, 1777, *LDC*, 7:308; George Frost to Josiah Bartlett, July 7, 1777, ibid., 7:314; John Hancock to the New York Council of Safety, July 8, 1777, ibid., 7:323; July 7, 1777, *JCC*, 8:537; Board of War to GW, July 8, 1777, *LDC*, 7:319.

37. July 11, 1777, *JCC*, 8:546.

38. George Frost to Josiah Bartlett, July 12, 1777, *LDC*, 7:338.

39. John Adams to Abigail Adams, July 13, 1777, *LDC*, 7:339; John Adams to Abigail

Adams, July 16, 1777, ibid., 7:347; James Lovell to Joseph Trumbull, 15 July 1777, ibid., 7:347.

40. Mark Bird to Jonathan Potts, July 16, 1777, No. 1995, FTMC.

41. GW to John Hancock, July 12, 1777, *PGWde*, RWS, 10:252-54.

42. GW to Jonathan Trumbull, July 31, 1777, ibid., RWS, 10:471; GW to the New York Council of Safety, Aug. 4, 1777, ibid., RWS, 10:502-503.

43. Smith, *St. Clair Papers*, 78, 440.

44. Jonathan Trumbull to Baron J. D. Vander Capellan, Aug. 31, 1779, *Collections of the Massachusetts Historical Society*, ser. 1, 6 (1799): 170.

45. John Adams to Abigail Adams, July 18, 1777, *LDC*, 7:350-51.

46. Adams quoted in Ketchum, *Saratoga*, 335; John Adams to James Warren, Aug. 12, 1777, *LDC*, 7:460.

47. Samuel Adams to James Lovell, Mar. 27, 1778, *The Writings of Samuel Adams*, ed. Harry Alonzo Cushing, 4 vols. (New York: G. P. Putnam's Sons, 1907), 4:17.

48. William Gordon to GW, Jan. 12, 1778, *PGWde*, RWS, 13:205-6.

49. GW to William Heath, July 27, 1777, *PGWde*, RWS, 10:438; GW to the New York Council of Safety, Aug. 4, 1777, ibid., RWS, 10:502; Smith, *St. Clair Papers*, 1:72.

50. July 30 and Aug. 1, 1777, *JCC*, 8:590, 596; GW to John Hancock, Aug. 9, 1777, *PGWde*, RWS, 10:564-65.

51. St. Clair, "Trial of Major General St. Clair, August, 1778," 52; Philip Schuyler, "The Trial of Major General Schuyler, October, 1778," *New-York Historical Society Collections*, vol. 12 (New York: New-York Historical Society, 1880).

52. Lasseray, *Les Fran ais sous les Treize Étoiles*, 267-68. La Rochefermoy's officers never were happy under his command, repeatedly complaining that the brigadier couldn't speak English and that they couldn't understand his commands. Philip Schuyler to GW, Aug. 4, 1777, *PGWde*, 10:505-6.

53. Samuel Adams to Samuel Cooper, July 15, 1777, *LDC*, 7:343; Samuel Adams to Richard Henry Lee, July 15, 1777, ibid., 7:344.

54. On Gates's appointment, see Aug. 4, 1777, *JCC*, 8:604; Nelson, *Horatio Gates*, 106-109.

CHAPTER SIX: COUNTERATTACK

1. "Genl Orders Crown Point June 30th 1777," in Cubbison, *Burgoyne Papers*, 203-4.

2. Cubbison, ibid., 78-79, has convincingly shown that rebel efforts to obstruct Burgoyne's march were not nearly as effective as most previous writers have assumed. The British needed about a week to clear the road been Skenesborough and Fort Ann, and after that, rebel obstructions were little "more than a passing hindrance" on the road to Fort Edward. British officers did not report real difficulties in clearing felled trees, large rocks, and other impediments; and loyalists with the army were as good with axes as patriots. Burgoyne's real problem was logistical: the challenge of the timely movement of tons of provisions, fodder, materiel, and artillery. An army so burdened did not move quickly.

3. Clinton, *American Rebellion*, 80n, 83.

4. GW to Horatio Gates, Aug. 20, 1777, *PGWde*, 11:12; Gates to GW, Aug. 23, 1777, ibid., 11:52.

5. Benjamin Lincoln to the Council of Massachusetts, Aug. 25, 1777, in Jared Sparks, ed., *Correspondence of the American Revolution*, 4 vols. (Boston: Little Brown, 1853), 2:520.

6. Benjamin Lincoln to John Laurens, Feb. 5, 1781, in ibid., 2:533-34.

7. David B. Mattern, *Benjamin Lincoln and the American Revolution* (Columbia: University of South Carolina Press, 1995), 22-40.

8. Ibid., 42, 44-45.

9. Josiah Gilbert Holland, *History of Western Massachusetts: The Counties of Hampden, Hampshire, Franklin, and Berkshire,* 2 vols. (Springfield, MA: Samuel Bowles, 1855), 2:274.

10. John Brown has no modern biography; for background see Archibald Murray Howe, *Colonel John Brown, of Pittsfield, Massachusetts, the Brave Accuser of Benedict Arnold* (Boston: W. B. Clarke, 1908), 1-6, and Garret L. Roof, *Colonel John Brown: His Services in the Revolutionary War, Battle of Stone Arabia* (Utica, NY: Ellis H. Roberts, 1884), 3-12.

11. James Kirby Martin, *Benedict Arnold, Revolutionary Hero: An American Warrior Reconsidered* (New York: New York University Press, 1997), 164; Howe, *Colonel John Brown,* 10-11; Heitman, *Historical Register,* 102.

12. Edward A. Hoyt, "The Pawlet Expedition, September 1777," *Vermont History* 75, no. 2 (2007): 90; Heitman, *Historical Register,* 418, 430.

13. Hoyt, "Pawlet Expedition," 86-87.

14. Benjamin Lincoln to John Brown, Sept. 12, 1777, in Sparks, ed., *Correspondence of the American Revolution,* 2:525; John Brown to Benjamin Lincoln, Sept. 14, 1777, "Colonel John Brown's Expedition against Ticonderoga and Diamond Island, 1777," *New England Historical and Genealogical Register* 74 (Oct. 1920): 284-85; John Brown to Benjamin Lincoln, Dec. 13, 1777, ibid., 286.

15. Benjamin Lincoln to Horatio Gates, Sept. 14, 1777, in Sparks, ed., *Correspondence of the Revolution,* 2:526.

16. Du Roi, *Journal,* 100.

17. For this paragraph, see Hamilton's various general orders between July 19 and Aug. 9, 1777, in Willard M. Wallace, ed., "The British Occupation of Fort Ticonderoga, 1777," *Bulletin of the Fort Ticonderoga Museum* 8, No. 7 (1951): 308, 310-12, 317; Du Roi, *Journal,* 101; Ronald F. Kingsley, ed., and Helga Doblin, trans., "A German Perspective on the American Attempt to Recapture the British Forts at Ticonderoga and Mount Independence on September 18, 1777," *Vermont History* 67, nos. 1 and 2 (1999): 7.

18. William Digby, *The British Invasion from the North: The Campaigns of Generals Carleton and Burgoyne, from Canada, 1776–1777, with the Journal of Lieut. William Digby, of the 53d, Or Shropshire Regiment of Foot,* ed. James Finney Baxter (Albany, NY: Joel Munsell's Sons, 1887), 240; Du Roi, *Journal,* 101.

19. "General Orders," July 24, 1777, in Wallace, ed., "British Occupation," 311; Kingsley, ed., "German Perspective," 7.

20. [von Hille?], *American Revolution,* 74; Digby, *Journal,* 240.

21. John Starke, "Manuscript Map of John's Brown's Attack on Fort Ticonderoga in the Fall of 1777," T-1.63M, FTMC. Ford, *British Officers in America,* 58, shows Davis as an ensign in 1776—but he was the only Davis in the 53rd, so we can assume he was the Davis noted on Starke's map.

22. Hamilton, *Fort Ticonderoga,* 215-16; 2:523; Robert B. Roberts, *New York's Forts in the Revolution* (Rutherford, NJ: Fairleigh Dickinson University Press, 1980), 182; Du Roi, *Journal,* 101; Ernst Christian Schroeder to Friedrich Adoph von Riedesel, Sept. 26, 1777, in Kingsley, ed., "German Perspective," 13; Friedrich Wilhelm von Hille to Eckert Heinrich von Stammer, Sept. 23, 1777, in ibid., 14.

23. John Starke, "His Account of John Brown's Attack on Ticonderoga in September, 1777," No. 2126, FTMC.

24. [von Hille?], *American Revolution*, 78. Von Hille may have picked up hints of rebel activity simply from talk among officers, and there was at least one piece of intelligence that became common knowledge. In mid-July, the garrison learned that Continental Colonel Seth Warner was near Manchester, New Hampshire, and was gathering militia. Did von Hille have Warner in mind? We simply don't know. See Riedesel, *Memoirs*, 120.

25. John Burgoyne to George Germain, Oct. 20, 1777, in Cubbison, *Burgoyne Papers*, 331.

26. Robert T. Pell, "John Brown and the Dash for Ticonderoga," *Bulletin of the Fort Ticonderoga Museum* 2, no. 1 (1930): 33.

27. Lemuel Roberts, *Memoirs of Captain Lemuel Roberts: Containing Adventures in Youth, Vicissitudes Experienced as a Continental Soldier, His Sufferings as a Prisoner and Escape from Captivity, with Suitable Reflections on the Changes of Life* (Bennington, VT: Printed by Anthony Haswell, for the author, 1809), 54.

28. John Brown to unknown general officer, Oct. 4, 1777, in "Col. John Brown's Expedition," 292-93.

29. Pell, "John Brown," 33; Starke, "His Account."

30. R. K. Clark, "History of the Town of South Hero," *Gazetteer of Vermont*, Hayward, 1849, accessed May 20, 2019, http://sites.rootsweb.com/~vermont/GrandIsleSouth-Hero.html; Willard Sterne Randall, *Ethan Allen: His Life and Times* (New York: W. W. Norton, 2012), 261.

31. Accounts differ on how many British were on Mount Defiance and how much of a fight they put up in the face of Captain Allen's assault. Hamilton, *Fort Ticonderoga*, 218, thinks Allen caught them "soundly asleep," while Ketchum, *Saratoga*, 378, and Starke, "Account of John Brown's Attack," FTMC, believe they offered a brief but stiff resistance. The fact that some British were killed and wounded and that some managed to escape would seem to support Ketchum's history and Starke's contemporary account.

32. Hamilton, *Fort Ticonderoga*, 218; Pell, "John Brown," 33-36.

33. Roberts, *Memoirs*, 55, 59.

34. Starke, "Manuscript Map of John's Brown's Attack," FTMC; Ford, *British Officers in America*, 112.

35. The cannon, as some historians have suggested, may have been from the captured sloop. But Starke, in "Manuscript Map of John's Brown's Attack," FTMC, discounts this, claiming the patriots found guns much closer to the fort. This is probable, as removing six-pounders from naval mountings and dragging them well over a mile from the Lake George landing over a rough road would have taken considerable time—and it appears the rebels opened fire soon after reaching the French Lines. See also Hamilton, *Fort Ticonderoga*, 219.

36. John Brown to Samuel Johnson, Sept. 18, 1777, in "Col. John Brown's Expedition," 285; John Brown to Benjamin Lincoln, Sept. 19, 1777, in ibid., 286-87; Hamilton, *Fort Ticonderoga*, 219; Ketchum, *Saratoga*, 378-79; Michael Bellesiles, "Ticonderoga Raid," in Selesky, ed., *Encyclopedia*, 2:115-56.

37. Henry Watson Powell to John Brown, Sept. 18, 1777, in Ketchum, *Saratoga*, 379; Friedrich Wilhelm von Hille to Eckert Heinrich von Stammer, Sept. 23, 1777, in Kingsley, ed., "German Perspective," 15.

38. Powell quoted in Ketchum, *Saratoga*, 379.

39. Jonathan Warner to "the Commanding Officer at Mount Independence," Sept. 19, 1777, in Pell, "John Brown," 37; Friedrich Wilhelm von Hille to Eckert Heinrich von Stammer, Sept. 23, 1777, in Kingsley, ed., "German Perspective," 11, 16.

40. Hamilton, *Fort Ticonderoga*, 222.

41. On the eighteenth-century aristocratic honor code within the British officer corps, and officers as "gentlemen," see Arthur N. Gilbert, "Law and Honour among Eighteenth-Century British Army Officers," *The Historical Journal* 19, No. 1 (1976): 75-87; Armstrong Starkey, "War and Culture, A Case Study: The Enlightenment and the Conduct of the British Army in America, 1755–1781," *War and Society* 8 (1990): 1-28; Stephen Conway, "To Subdue America: British Army Officers and the Conduct of the Revolutionary War," *William and Mary Quarterly*, 3rd ser., 43 (1986): 381-407.

42. Unless noted otherwise, this account is based on Brown's letters to Johnson and Lincoln: John Brown to Samuel Johnson, Sept. 18, 1777, in "Col. John Brown's Expedition," 285; John Brown to Benjamin Lincoln, Sept. 19, 1777, in ibid., 286-87 (both 18 Sept.); and a third letter, John Brown to an unknown general officer, Oct. 4, 1777, in ibid., 292-93. On the death of the unfortunate Lieutenant Volckmar, see von Hille, *Journal*, 78-79; Friedrich Wilhelm von Hille to Eckert Heinrich von Stammer, Sept. 23, 1777, in Kingsley, ed., "German Perspective," 11, 16; Du Roi, *Journal*, 101. Douglas R. Cubbison, in *The Artillery Never Gained More Honour: The British Artillery in the 1776 Valcour Island and 1777 Saratoga Campaigns* (Fleischmanns, NY: Purple Mountain Press, 2007), 130, clarifies what happened to Volckmar. While the German accounts state that a "ton" of powder caught fire, Cubbison makes clear that the reference was to a single cask.

43. Roberts, *Memoirs*, 61.

44. Friedrich Wilhelm von Hille to Eckert Heinrich von Stammer, Sept. 23, 1777, in Kingsley, ed., "German Perspective," 16-17.

45. Starke, "Account of John Brown's Attack," FTMC.

46. Starke, "Manuscript Map of John's Brown's Attack," FTMC.

47. Starke, "Account of John Brown's Attack," FTMC.

48. Friedrich Wilhelm von Hille to Eckert Heinrich von Stammer, Sept. 23, 1777, in Kingsley, ed., "German Perspective," 16-17; Du Roi, *Journal*, 101.

49. Friedrich Wilhelm von Hille to Eckert Heinrich von Stammer, Sept. 23, 1777, in Kingsley, ed., "German Perspective," 18.

50. Unless noted otherwise, this account of the Diamond Island operation is based on John Brown to Benjamin Lincoln, Sept. 26, 1777, in "Col. John Brown's Expedition," 289-90; Bruce Venter, "The Forgotten Battle of Diamond Island on Lake George," *Adirondack Almanac*, June 17, 2015, accessed Apr. 16, 2019, https://www.adirondackalmanack.com/2015/06/forgotten-battle-diamond-island-lake-george.html; and B. F. DeCosta, *The Fight at Diamond Island, Lake George* (New York: J. Sabin & Sons, 1872).

51. Pell, "John Brown," 39.

52. John Brown to Benjamin Lincoln, Sept. 26, 1777, in "Col. John Brown's Expedition," 289-90; Roberts, *Memoirs*, 63.

53. Ketchum, *Saratoga*, 379.

54. John Mawney to Dr. Stimson, Sept. 30, 1777, Sol Feinstone Collection, No. 925, David Library of the American Revolution, Washington Crossing, PA.

55. James Wilkinson to Arthur St. Clair, Sept. 21, 1777, in Smith, ed., *St. Clair Papers*, 1:443.

56. Digby, *Journal*, 276-77.

57. Copy of John Burgoyne to Henry Watson Powell, Sept. 20, 1777, Emmet Collection, MSS Division, New York Public Library, https://picryl.com/media/letter-to-gen-henry-watson-powell-ticonderoga-28a4b6; John Burgoyne to Henry Watson Powell, Sept. 21, 1777, Emmet Collection, ibid., https://picryl.com/media/letter-to-gen-henry-watson-powell-ticonderoga-77ff0c.

58. Ward, *War of the Revolution*, 2:524; Bellesiles, "Ticonderoga Raid," 2:1156; Riedesel, *Memoirs*, 157.

59. General Orders, Sept. 28, 1777, *PGWde*, RWS, 11:337.

60. GW to William Heath, Sept. 30, 1777, ibid., RWS, 11:351.

61. Benjamin Lincoln to John Laurens, Feb. 5, 1781, in Sparks, ed., *Correspondence of the Revolution*, 2:533-34; Benjamin Lincoln to John Brown, Sept. 21, 1777, in "Col. John Brown's Expedition," 288-89.

62. Mattern, *Benjamin Lincoln*, 48-49.

63. Benjamin Lincoln to John Brown, Sept. 30, 1777, in "Col. John Brown's Expedition," 290.

64. Digby, *Journal*, 285-86, 292, 300-302.

65. Nelson, *Horatio Gates*, 147; GW to Alexander Hamilton, Oct. 30, 1777, *PGWde*, RWS, 12:61; Alexander Hamilton to GW, Nov. 6, 1777, ibid., RWS, 12:141; Alexander Hamilton to GW, Nov. 12, 1777, ibid., RWS, 12:226.

66. G. F. G. Stanley, "Maclean, Allan," *Dictionary of Canadian Biography*, accessed May 2, 2019, http://www.biographi. ca/en/bio/maclean_allan_4E.html; Guy Carleton to Hector Theophilus Cramahé, Sept. 21, 1777, in "Register of Letters from Sir Guy Carleton, 1776 to 1778," in *Report on Canadian Archives, 1885*, vol. 2, ed. Douglas Brymner (Ottawa: Printed by Maclean, Roger, 1886), 268; Guy Carleton to Allan Maclean, Sept. 23, 1777, in ibid., 268.

67. Guy Carleton to Allan Maclean, Sept. 28, 1777, in ibid., 269; Guy Carleton to Henry Watson Powell, Sept. 29, 1777, in ibid., 269.

68. Extract of Allan Maclean to Guy Carleton, Sept 30, 1777, *Bulletin of the Fort Ticonderoga Museum* 7, no. 2 (1945): 35-36.

69. A good account of the British evacuation is in von Hille, *Journal*, xxiii, 82, 86.

70. There is some debate over the evacuation of Crown Point, with some sources insisting the British never relinquished the post. But Roberts, *New York's Forts*, 182, is certainly correct in having the Crown Point outpost follow Powell north. The British would be back to Crown Point in 1780, but they would not have remained in the aftermath of Burgoyne's debacle without the protection of the larger garrison at Ticonderoga.

71. Thomas Chittenden to Horatio Gates, Nov. 22, 1777, in Sparks, ed., *Correspondence of the Revolution*, 2:531; Cubbison, *Artillery*, 140; John J. Duffy, Samuel B. Hand, and Ralph H. Orth, eds., "Green Mountain Continental Rangers," *Vermont Encyclopedia* (Hanover, NH: University Press of New England, 2003), 144-45.

72. Ebenezer Allen "to whom it may concern," July 26, 1780, in *Collections of the Vermont Historical Society*, 2 vols. (Montpelier, VT: Printed for the Society, 1870–71), 1:249.

CHAPTER SEVEN: A WAR CONTINUED

1. Gavin K. Watt, *Fire & Desolation: The Revolutionary War's 1778 Campaign as Waged from Quebec and Niagara against the American Frontiers* (Toronto: Dundurn Press, 2017), 18-19. Peckham's compilation of revolutionary engagements shows no significant mil-

itary activity in the Lake Champlain-Lake George region through June, although the frontiers west of Albany and in Pennsylvania saw some serious fighting. *Toll of Independence*, 48-51.

2. Philip Schuyler to GW, Apr. 26, 1778, *PGWde*, RWS, 14:655.

3. John Williams to George Clinton, Apr. 25, 1778, in George Clinton, *Public Papers of George Clinton, First Governor of New York: 1777–1795—1801–1804*, ed. Hugh Hastings and J. A. Holden, 10 vols. (Albany, NY: James B. Lyon, State Printer, 1899–1914), 3:213-14.

4. Watt, *Fire & Desolation*, 25-26, 28-29, 31.

5. *Quebec Gazette*, June 4, 1778, no. 666, 3.

6. Stuart R. J. Sutherland, Pierre Tousignant, and Madeleine Dionne-Tousignant, "Haldimand, Sir Frederick," in *Dictionary of Canadian Biography* 5 (1801–1820), University of Toronto/Université Laval, 2003–, accessed Apr. 23, 2019, http://www.biographi.ca/en/bio/haldimand_frederick_5E.html.

7. Henry Steele Wardner, "The Haldimand Negotiations," *Proceedings of the Vermont Historical Society* 2, no. 1 (1931): 3-29; Thomas Albert Chadsey, "General Haldimand and the Vermont Negotiations, 1780–1783" (master's thesis, University of Ottawa, 1953), 39-61.

8. Jean N. McIlwraith, *Sir Frederick Haldimand* (London, ON: T. C. & E. C. Jack, 1905), 126, 132-34; Frederick Haldimand to Henry Clinton, Aug. 4, 1778, in "Haldimand Collection," *Report on Canadian Archives, 1886*, ed. Douglas Brymner (Ottawa: Printed by Maclean, Roger, 1887), 394; William Twiss to Frederick Haldimand, Jan. 15, 1778, Haldimand Papers: Correspondence with Officers of the Engineers, 1777–1783, H-1651, image 6, accessed Apr. 23, 2019, *Heritage Canadiana*, http://heritage.canadiana.ca/view/ oocihm.lac_reel_h1651/6?r=0&s=1.

9. Frederick Haldimand to George Germain, Oct. 15, 1778, in McIlwraith, *Sir Frederick Haldimand*, 137-38; Watt, *Fire & Desolation*, 55-59.

10. McIlwraith, *Sir Frederick Haldimand*, 137-38.

11. Allan Maclean to Frederick Haldimand, Oct. 16, 1778, "Haldimand Collection," *Report on Canadian Archives, 1888*, ed. Douglas Brymner (Ottawa: Printed for the Queen's Printer and Controller of Stationary, 1889), 634.

12. Ida H. Washington and Paul A. Washington, *Carleton's Raid* (Weybridge, VT: Cherry Tree Books, 1977), 17.

13. "Private Letter from Canada Which Arrived in Lower Saxony Aug. 1st 1777," in William L. Stone, trans., *Letters of Brunswick and Hessian Officers during the American Revolution* (Albany, NY: Joel Munsell's Sons, 1891), 64.

14. Washington and Washington, *Carleton's Raid*, 33-62; Watt, *Fire & Desolation*, 65-66, 70-72.

15. GW to Philip Schuyler, Dec. 25, 1779, *PGWde*, RWS, 23:722.

16. George Clinton to the Officers of the Militia at Castleton, May 29, 1780, in Clinton, *Public Papers*, 5:770; George Clinton to New York Delegates in Congress, June 14, 1780, ibid., 5:822.

17. Because Haldimand's plan bore a superficial resemblance to the Burgoyne-St. Leger operations of 1777, at least one author has suggested Haldimand also wanted to cut off New England from the states to the south in a grand effort to defeat the rebellion. See E. M. [Eleanor M. Murray], "The Invasion of Northern New York, 1780," *Bulletin of the Fort Ticonderoga Museum* 7, no. 4 (1946): 3. However, Haldimand lacked the strength or intention to undertake any such effort. Murray also suggested that

Haldimand's plan was coordinated with Benedict Arnold's October scheme to betray West Point to the British, although no primary sources support such a conjecture. Ibid., 3.

18. Frederick Haldimand to George Germain, Oct. 25, 1780, in "Extracts from a Letter from General Haldimand, Governor and Commander in Chief of his Majesty's Forces in the Province of Quebec to Lord George Germain, One of His Majesty's Principal Secretaries of State," *Bulletin of the Fort Ticonderoga Museum* 7, no. 4 (1946): 31. The entire 1780 campaign is the subject of Gavin K. Watt's *The Burning of the Valleys: Daring Raids from Canada against the New York Frontier in the Fall of 1780* (Toronto: Dundurn Press, 1997).

19. Peckham, ed., *Toll of Independence*, 76; Watt, *Burning of the Valleys*, 18, 137-56.

20. John Enys, *The American Journals of Lt. John Enys*, ed. Elizabeth Cometti (Syracuse, NY: Syracuse University Press, 1976), 35, lists a total roster of 875; a careful count by Watt in *Burning of the Valleys*, 94, found a total of 971. It really made little difference, given the paltry number of rebels they would face, but in either case, Carleton had a considerable force.

21. Enys, *American Journals*, 37.

22. Murray, "Invasion of Northern New York," 12; Enys, *American Journals*, 40.

23. Murray, "Invasion of Northern New York," 45.

24. Watt, *Burning of the Valleys*, 100; Enys, *American Journals*, 52; "Return of the Killed and Wounded of the Detachment under the Command of Major Carleton, the 11th of October 1780," *Bulletin of the Fort Ticonderoga Museum* 7, no. 4 (July 1776): 25.

25. Enys, *American Journals*, 47, 280n47.

26. James Scott, Melinda Walker, and Aaron Nash, "The Raid on Ballston, 1780," *Bulletin of the Fort Ticonderoga Museum* 7, no. 4 (July 1946): 12-24; Michael Aikey, "Ballston Raid of 1780: Military Operation or a Time to Settle Old Scores," *Journal of the American Revolution*, Dec. 6, 2017, accessed May 7, 2019, https://allthingsliberty.com/2017/12/ballston-raid-1780-military-operation-time-settle-old-scores/.

27. Enys, *American Journals*, 50-51.

28. GW to Samuel Huntington, Nov. 7, 1780, *Founders Online*, National Archives, accessed May 23, 2019, https://founders.archives.gov/documents/Washington/99-01-02-03851.

29. Enys, *American Journals*, 50-51.

30. Frederick Haldimand to George Germain, Oct. 25, 1780, in "Extracts from a Letter from General Haldimand," 29.

31. George Clinton to GW, Oct. 14, 1780, *Founders Online*, National Archives, accessed May 23, 2019, https://founders.archives.gov/documents/Washington/99-01-02-03573.

32. Casualty estimates are from Peckham, *Toll of Independence*, 76-77, and "Return of the Killed and Wounded," 25. Other damages are reported in George Clinton to GW, Oct. 30, 1780, *Founders Online*, National Archives, accessed Apr. 26, 2019, https://founders.archives.gov/documents/Washington/99-01-02-03743.

CHAPTER EIGHT: A WAR NOT ENDED

1. Richard Cannon, *Historical Record of the Thirty-First, or, the Huntingdonshire Regiment of Foot: Containing an Account of the Formation of the Regiment in 1702, and of Its Subsequent Services to 1850* (London: Parker, Furnivall & Parker, 1850), 41.

2. For a concise account of Vermont in the Revolution and its relations with Congress,

New York, and the British, see Michael Bellesiles, "Vermont, Mobilization in," Selesky, ed., *Encyclopedia*, 2:1195-99.

3. On this point, see "Haldimand Negotiations," in Duffy, Hand, and Orth, eds., *Vermont Encyclopedia*, 148-49.

4. Chadsey, "General Haldimand," 103-106, 121.

5. Ibid., 67.

6. Ibid., 70-71; Frederick Haldimand to George Germain, Mar. 3, 1779, Frederick Haldimand, "The Haldimand Papers, with Contemporaneous History," *Collections of the Vermont Historical Society* (hereafter *CVHS*) (Montpelier, VT: J. & M. Polard, printer, 1871), 2:59; Frederick Haldimand to Thomas Chittenden, Oct. 22, 1780, ibid., 2:70-71; Ethan Allen to Christian Carleton, Oct. [29], 1780, ibid., 2:71; Ethan Allen to Colonel Webster, Oct. 31, 1780, ibid., 2:72; editor's notes, ibid., 2:73.

7. On the concerns about Ethan Allen, see the communications between Schuyler and GW over late October and mid-November 1780, as well as editorial comments, in ibid., 2:76-78; Stephen Lush to George Clinton, Nov. 7, 1780, ibid., 2:78; George Clinton to Stephen Lush, Nov. 9, 1780, ibid., 2:78.

8. Beverley Robinson to Ethan Allen, Feb. 2, 1781, ibid., 2:92.

9. Duffy, Hand, and Orth, eds., "Haldimand Negotiations," 148.

10. "Fay, Joseph," in ibid., 122.

11. See the various letters of Smyth and Sherwood between Sept. 11, 1781, and Nov. 2, 1781—documenting their use of Ticonderoga as their headquarters—to Haldimand and other royal officials in Brymner, ed., "Haldimand Collection," *Report on the Canadian Archives, 1888*, 785-853.

12. Frederick Haldimand to Henry Clinton, Sept. 27, 1781, "Haldimand Papers," *CVHS* 2:176-77.

13. Carl Adolf Christoph von Creutzburg, "Relation of the secret expedition under the command of Colonel St. Leger on September ninth, 1781," Hanau Jaeger Journal [Sept. 9-Nov. 2,1781], Lidgerwood Collection, Morristown National Historical Park, 36.

14. John Ross to Frederick Haldimand, Nov. 7, 1781 [misdated 7 Oct.], Haldimand Papers, B-127:266-74, H-1452, images 850-58, *Heritage Canadiana*, accessed Apr. 23, 2019, http://heritage.canadiana.ca/view/oocihm.lac_reel_h1452/850?r=0&s=1; Barrimore St. Leger to Frederick Haldimand, "Minutes and Journal of Proceedings on the Expedition—1781," c. Nov. 16, 1781, Haldimand Papers, B-134:179-206, H-1453, images 852-879, http://heritage.canadiana.ca/view/oocihm. lac_reel_h1453/852?r=0&s=1; Frederick Haldimand to George Germain, Nov. 23, 1781, B-55:125-28, H 1436, images 386-89, accessed June 5, 2019, http://heritage.canadiana.ca/view/oocihm.lac_reel_h1436/386?r=0&s=1.

15. Clinton, *American Rebellion*, 574-76. Clinton did want Haldimand's cooperation in the West. He wanted an expedition out of Canada toward Fort Pitt and the Ohio Valley to support Indian operations against rebel forces. See Clinton, *American Rebellion*, 292, 574-76. Around this time, Clinton was thinking about potential operations in the Chesapeake and even against Philadelphia, Boston, or any joint venture with Haldimand in New England.

16. Peckham, *Toll of Independence*, 92; Ward, *War of the Revolution*, 2:651-52. I use the word "stop" rather than "defeat" because American and Canadian sources differ as to who won or lost at Johnstown. Compare Ward with Richard A. Preston, "Ross, John," *Dictionary of Canadian Biography* (Toronto: University of Toronto/Université Laval, 1979), IV (1771–1800), accessed May 29, 2919, www.biographi.ca/en/bio/ross_john_1762_89_4E.html.

17. Frederick Haldimand to Henry Clinton, Sept. 27, 1781, "Haldimand Papers," *CVHS* 2:176-77.

18. According to von Creutzburg, the lights were from the 29th, 31st, and 44th Foot; the additional redcoats were from the 34th. The assembling of this small army and its dispatch to Ticonderoga is tracked in von Creutzburg, "Relation of the secret expedition under Colonel St. Leger," 33.34, 35-41. But according to Major H. Everard, the historian of the 29th, in his *History of Thos Farrington's Regiment: Subsequently Designated the 29th (Worcestershire) Foot, 1694–1891* (Worcester: Littlebury, 1891), 96, the expedition's lights were from the 29th, 31st, 34th, and 44th Regiments, with additional redcoats from the line companies of the 29th and 34th.

19. Gavin K. Watt, *I am heartily ashamed: The Revolutionary War's Final Campaign as Waged from Canada in 1782* (Toronto: Dundurn Press, 2010), 2:346.

20. Roger Enos to John Stark, Oct. 26, 1778, in Stark, *Memoir*, 282.

21. Frederick Haldimand to Henry Clinton, Oct. 1, 1781, "Haldimand Papers," 2:179-80.

22. For example, Ira Allen and Joseph Fay to George Smyth and Justus Sherwood, Sept. 16, 1781, in Brymner, ed., "Haldimand Collection," *Report on the Canadian Archives, 1888*, 785; Justus Sherwood to Captain Mathews, Sept. 30, 1781, in ibid., 786; Ira Allen to Justus Sherwood, Oct. 20, 1781, in ibid., 787.

23. Frederic F. Van de Water, *The Reluctant Republic: Vermont, 1724–1791* (New York: John Day, 1941), 283-87; editorial comments, "Haldimand Papers," *CVHS*, 2:193; "Petition of Lt. Col. Saml Robinson," Feb. 13, 1782, in Joseph E. Goodrich, comp. and ed., *The State of Vermont: Rolls of the Soldiers in the Revolutionary War, 1775 to 1783* (Rutland, VT: Tuttle, 1904), 795.

24. John Stark to Thomas Chittenden, Nov. 6, 1781, in Stark, *Memoir*, 285-86.

25. John Stark to GW, Dec. 27, 1781, *Founders Online*, National Archives, https://founders.archives.gov/documents/Washington/99-01-02-07597.

26. Thomas Chittenden to GW, Nov. 14, 1781, *Founders Online*, National Archives, https://founders.archives.gov/documents/Washington/99-01-02-07403.

27. Von Creutzburg, "Relation of the secret expedition under St. Leger," 36, 38.

28. Everard, *History of Thos Farrington's Regiment*, 96.

29. Von Creutzburg, "Relation of the secret expedition under St. Leger," 37, 39-40.

30. Philip Schuyler to Thomas McKean, Oct. 21, 1781, PCC, RG 360, 3:584, https://www.fold3.com/image/392669.

31. "Haldimand Papers," Extracts of Letters, Oct. 27-Oct. 30, 1781, *CVHS*, 2:192-93; Frederick Haldimand to George Germain, Nov. 23 , 1781, B-55:125, H-1436, image 386, accessed May 21, 2019, http://heritage.canadiana.ca/view/oocihm.lac_reel_h1436/386?r=0&s=1; Paul David Nelson, *The Life of William Alexander, Lord Stirling* (Tuscaloosa: University of Alabama Press, 1987), 164-66; Roger Enos to John Stark, Oct. 30, 1781, *CVHS*, 2:193.

32. Barrimore St. Leger, "Minutes and Journal of Proceedings on the Expedition—1781," Haldimand Papers, B-134:183, 186, Reel H-1453, images 856, 859, accessed May 21 , 2019, http://heritage.canadiana.ca/view/oocihm.lac_reel_h1453/852?r=0&s=2.

33. Von Creutzburg, "Relation of the secret expedition under St. Leger," 40.

34. St. Leger, "Minutes and Journal," reel H-1453, images 866-67, B-134:193-95, accessed May 21, 2019, http://heritage.canadiana.ca/view/oocihm.lac_reel_h1453/866?r=0&s=2.

35. St. Leger quoted in Nelson, *Life of William Alexander*, 166.

36. Enys, *Journal*, 53.

37. Ira Allen, *The Natural and Political History of the State of Vermont, One of the United States of America* (London: Printed by J. W. Myers, 1798), 193.

38. Frederick Haldimand to George Germain, Nov. 23, 1781, Haldimand Papers, B-55:128, H-1436, image 389, accessed June 6 , 2019, http://heritage.canadiana.ca/view /oocihm.lac_reel_h1436/389?r=0&s=1.

39. Frederick Haldimand to Henry Clinton, Apr. 28, 1782, *CVHS*, 2:266.

40. Philip Schuyler to GW, Nov. 1781, FTMC; Schuyler to GW, Nov. 15, 1781, John C. Fitzpatrick, ed., *Calendar of the Correspondence, of George Washington: Commander in Chief of the Continental Army, with the Officers*, 4 vols. (Washington, DC: Government Printing Office, 1915), 3:1994.

41. GW to Philip Schuyler, Nov. 25, 1781, John C. Fitzpatrick, ed., *The Writings of George Washington from the Original Manuscript Sources, 1745–1799*. 39 vols. (Washington, DC: Government Printing Office, 1931–1944), 23:361.

EPILOGUE: A FORT IN THE WILDERNESS

1. Rufus Putnam, *The Memoirs of Rufus Putnam and Certain Official Papers and Correspondence*, ed. Rowena Buell (Boston: Houghton, Mifflin, 1905), 22-25, 54-99; Heitman, *Historical Register*, 338.

2. Rufus Putnam to GW, June 3, 1783, Letters and Reports from Maj. Gen. Benjamin Lincoln, Secretary at War, 1781-83, PCC, 3:214, accessed June 19, 2019, https://www. fold3.com/image/428557.

3. Frederick Haldimand to Edward Jessup, Dec. 8, 1781, in Brymner, ed., "Haldimand Collection," *Report on Canadian Archives, 1886*, 544; Clinton, *American Rebellion*, 576.

4. GW to Moses Hazen, Apr. 10, 1782, Fitzpatrick, ed., *Writings of George Washington*, 24:108; Memorandum, May 1, 1781, ibid., 24:194-214.

5. John Wells, "Report of Claims Commissioners," May 28, 1778, PCC, RG 360, 2:331, accessed June 21, 2019, https://www.fold3.com/image/224418.

6. Udny Hay to GW, Jan. 5, 1779, *PGWde*, RWS, 18:572-73; Giles Wolcott to Congress, Feb. 7, 1786, Petitions to Congress, PCC, RG 360, 8:342-43, accessed June 21, 2019, https://www.fold3.com/image/425183.

7. "Skene, Philip," in Selesky, ed., *Encyclopedia*, 2:1062; Thomas Steele to Philip Skene, Feb. 11, 1784, MS 3041, FTMC.

8. GW to Elias Boudinot, July 16, 1783, Papers of George Washington, *Founders Online*, National Archives, https://founders.archives.gov/documents/Washington/99-01-02-11601.

9. William S. Baker, *Itinerary of General Washington from June 15, 1775, to December 23, 1783* (Philadelphia: J. B. Lippincott, 1892), 302; Roberts, *New York's Forts*, 183; GW to Elias Boudinot, Aug. 6, 1783, *Founders Online*, National Archives, https://founders. archives.gov/ documents/Washington/99-01-02-11652.

10. GW to Marinus Willet, Aug. 6, 1783, *Founders Online*, National Archives, https://founders.archives.gov/ documents/99-01-01-11651; GW to Elias Boudinot, Aug. 6, 1783, *Founders Online*, National Archives, https://founders.archives.gov/ documents/Washington/99-01-02-11653; GW to Robert Morris, Aug. 6, 1783, *Founders Online*, National Archives, https://founders.archives.gov/ documents/Washington/99-01-02-11655.

11. GW to Haldimand, July 12, 1783, "Haldimand Papers," *Heritage Canada*, http://

heritage.canadiana.ca/view/oocihm.lac_reel_h1736/219?r=0&s=4, H-1736, image 219, B-175, 221-212. Steuben's mission was fruitless, as Haldimand demurred, citing a lack of instructions from London on the matter. For the various intricacies of the Steuben mission, see Steuben to Haldimand, Aug. 3, 1783, Haldimand to Steuben, Aug. 6, 1783, Steuben to Haldimand, Aug. 11, 1783, Haldimand to Washington, Aug. 11, 1783, and Haldimand to Steuben, Aug. 12, 1783, all ibid., http://heritage.canadiana.ca/view/oocihm. lac_reel_h1736/226?r=0&s=3, images 226-235, B-175, 218-226.

12. Philip Schuyler to Haldimand, Apr. 17, 1783, ibid., B-175, 191-92, H-1736, http://heritage.canadiana.ca/view/oocihm.lac_reel_h1736/199?r=0&s=4, images 199-200; Haldimand to Philip Schuyler, June 30, 1783, ibid., B-175, 207-9, http://heritage.canadiana.ca/view/oocihm.lac_reel_ h1736/215?r=0&s=4, H-1736, images 215-17; "Return of the American Prisoners forwarded from Ticonderoga to their representative states, July 18th 1783 by order of His Excellency General Haldimand," ibid., B-183, 279-279G, http://heritage.canadiana.ca/view/oocihm.lac_ reel_h1738/427?r=0&s=3, H-1738, images 427-33.

13. My thanks to Matt Keagle, curator at the Fort Ticonderoga Museum, for bringing this prisoner release and its related documents to my attention. He is now completing a full study of the episode. The most pertinent staff correspondence dealing with the negotiations and implementation of the release is found in R. B. Lernoult to St. Leger, June 30, 1783, ibid., B-82, 29-30, http://heritage.canadiana.ca/view/ oocihm.lac _reel_h1442/903?r=0&s=5, H-1442, images 903-4; R. B. Lernoult to Generals Commanding Districts, June 30, 1783, B-82, 32, http://heritage.canadiana.ca/view/oocihm.lac_reel_h1442/906?r=0&s=5, H-1442, image 906; R. B. Lernoult to [Andrew] Skene, "Instructions to Captain Skene Major of Brigade for Assembling Such Prisoners of War As Are Still Remaining in the District of Montreal," July 1, 1783, ibid., B-82, 32-33, http://heritage.canadiana.ca/view/oocihm.lac_reel_h1442/906?r=0&s=5, H-1442, images 906-7. The receipt for the POWs signed by Ensign Ephraim Kirby is on the last page of "Return of the American Prisoners," ibid., B-183, 279G, http://heritage.canadiana.ca/view/oocihm.lac_reel_h1738/433?r=0&s=3, H-1738, image 433. On Kirby, see Heitman, *Historical Register*, 334.

14. Roberts, *New York's Forts*, 183.

SELECTED BIBLIOGRAPHY

WITH SEVERAL EXCEPTIONS, I have confined the sources in this bibliography to those cited in notes. Sources included but not cited in the notes are works I relied on frequently in writing *Fort Ticonderoga, The Last Campaigns* and should be of interest to anyone looking further into Ticonderoga's role in the northern war. During my research, I consulted a range of contemporary American, British (including Tory), and Canadian newspapers. They are cited in the notes and do not have a separate listing below.

MANUSCRIPT SOURCES

Fort Ticonderoga Numbered Manuscripts. Fort Ticonderoga Museum Collection, Ticonderoga, NY.

Fort Ticonderoga Uncatalogued Manuscripts. Fort Ticonderoga Museum Collection, Ticonderoga, NY.

Gates, Horatio. Papers. Manuscripts and Archives Division, New York Public Library.

————. Papers. New-York Historical Society, New York.

Gates, Maj. Gen. Horatio. Transcripts of Letters. Papers of the Continental Congress. Library of Congress, Washington, DC.

Gilder Lehrman Collection. Gilder Lehrman Institute, New York.

Lidgerwood Collection, Morristown National Historical Park, Morristown, New Jersey.

Schuyler, Philip. Papers, Letters Received. Manuscripts and Archives Division. New York Public Library Digital Collections.

————. Philip Schuyler Papers, Papers Concerning the Affairs at Ticonderoga, 1775–1781. Colonial North America at Harvard University, MS Sparks 60. Houghton Library, Harvard University.

————. Transcripts of Letters. Papers of the Continental Congress. Library of Congress, Washington, DC.

Society Collection. Historical Society of Pennsylvania, Philadelphia.

Sol Feinstone Collection. American Philosophical Society, Philadelphia.

Wayne, Anthony. Letters. Special Collections and Archives. West Chester University of Pennsylvania, West Chester, PA.

————. Papers. Historical Society of Pennsylvania, Philadelphia.

William A. Oldridge Collection of George Washington's Headquarters Staff Writings. Library of Congress, Washington, DC.

MEMOIRS AND PUBLISHED PAPERS

Adams Family Correspondence: December 1761-March 1778. Edited by L. H. Butterfield et al. 2 vols. Cambridge, MA: Harvard University Press, 1963.

Adams, John. *Diary and Autobiography of John Adams.* 4 vols. Edited by L. H. Butterfield et al. New York: Atheneum, 1964.

————. *Papers of John Adams.* 17 vols. Edited by Robert J. Taylor et al. Cambridge, MA: Harvard University Press, 1977–2014.

Adams, Samuel. *The Writings of Samuel Adams,* 4 vols. Edited by Harry Alonzo Cushing. New York: G. P. Putnam's Sons, 1907.

Allen, Ebenezer. "To whom it may concern." *Collections of the Vermont Historical Society.* 2 vols. Montpelier, VT: Printed for the Society, 1870–71, 1: 249.

Anburey, Thomas. "The Taking of Ticonderoga." *Bulletin of the Fort Ticonderoga Museum* 2, no. 1 (1930): 15-23.

Baldwin, Jeduthan. *The Revolutionary Journal of Col. Jeduthan Baldwin.* Edited by Thomas Williams Baldwin. Bangor, ME: Printed for the De Burians, 1906.

Beebe, Lewis. "Journal of a Physician on the Expedition against Canada, 1776." Edited by Frederick R. Kirkland. *Pennsylvania Magazine of History and Biography* 59 (1935): 321-61.

Blake, Thomas. "Lieutenant Thomas Blake's Journal." In Frederick Kidder, *History of the First New Hampshire Regiment in the War of the Revolution.* Albany, NY: Joel Munsell, 1868.

Bloomfield, Joseph. *Citizen Soldier: The Revolutionary War Journal of Joseph Bloomfield.* 2nd ed. Edited by Mark Edward Lender and James Kirby Martin. Yardley, PA: Westholme, 2018.

Boudinot, Elias. *Journal of Historical Recollections of American Events during the Revolutionary War.* Philadelphia: F. Bourquin, 1894.

Brymner, Douglas, ed. *Report on Canadian Archives, 1885.* Ottawa: Printed by Maclean, Roger, 1886.

———. *Report on Canadian Archives, 1886.* Ottawa: Printed by Maclean, Roger, 1887.

———. *Report on Canadian Archives, 1888.* Ottawa: Printed for the Queen's Printer and Controller of Stationary, 1889.

Clinton, George. *Public Papers of George Clinton, First Governor of New York: 1777-1795—1801-1804.* Edited by Hugh Hastings and J. A. Holden, 10 vols. Albany, NY: James B. Lyon, State Printer, 1899–1914.

Clinton, Henry. *The American Rebellion: Sir Henry Clinton's Narrative of His Campaigns, 1775–1782, with an Appendix of Original Documents.* Edited by William B. Willcox. New Haven, CT: Yale University Press, 1954.

"Colonel John Brown's Expedition against Ticonderoga and Diamond Island, 1777." *New England Historical and Genealogical Register* 74 (Oct. 1920).

Continental Congress. *Journals of the Continental Congress, 1774–1789.* 34 vols. Edited by Worthington C. Ford et al. Washington, DC: Government Printing Office, 1904–1937.

Digby, William. *The British Invasion from the North: The Campaigns of Generals Carleton and Burgoyne, from Canada, 1776–1777, with the Journal of Lieut. William Digby, of the 53d, Or Shropshire Regiment of Foot.* Edited by James Finney Baxter. Albany, NY: Joel Munsell's Sons, 1887.

Du Roi, August Wilhelm. *Journal of Du Roi the Elder: Lieutenant and Adjutant, in the Service of the Duke of Brunswick, 1776–1778.* Translated by Charlotte S. J. Epping. Philadelphia: University of Pennsylvania, D. Appleton & Co., agents, 1911.

Elmer, Ebenezer. "Journal Kept during an Expedition to Canada in 1776." *Proceedings of the New Jersey Historical Society* 3 (1848): 21-56, 90-102.

Enys, John. *The American Journals of Lt. John Enys.* Edited by Elizabeth Cometti. Syracuse, NY: Syracuse University Press, 1976.

"Extracts from a Letter from General Haldimand, Governor and Commander in Chief of His Majesty's Forces in the Province of Quebec to Lord George Germain, One of His Majesty's Secretaries of State." *Bulletin of the Fort Ticonderoga Museum* 7, no. 4 (1946): 29-31.

Fletcher, Ebenezer. *A Narrative of the Captivity and Suffering of Ebenezer Fletcher of New Ipswich.* Windsor, VT: Printed by Charles Kendall, 1813.

Force, Peter, and M. St. Clair, eds. *American Archives: Consisting of a Collection of Authentick Records, State Papers, Debates, and Letters and Other Notices of Publick Affairs, the Whole Forming a Documentary History of the Origin and Progress of the North American Colonies.* 9 vols. Washington, DC: M. St. Clair Clarke and Peter Force, 1837–1853.

Franklin, Benjamin. *Papers of Benjamin Franklin.* Edited by Leonard W. Labaree, William B. Willcox, et al. 43 vols. New Haven, CT: Yale University Press, 1959–.

Goodrich, Joseph E., comp. and ed. *The State of Vermont: Rolls of the Soldiers in the Revolutionary War, 1775 to 1783.* Rutland, VT: Tuttle, 1904.

Hadden, James M. *Hadden's Journal and Orderly Books: A Journal Kept in Canada and upon Burgoyne's Campaign in 1776 and 1777.* Edited by Horatio Rogers. Albany: Joel Munsell's Sons, 1884.

Haldimand, Frederick. "The Haldimand Papers, with Contemporaneous History." *Collections of the Vermont Historical Society.* 2 vols. Montpelier, VT: J. & M. Pollard, printer, 1870–71, 2:59-366.

Hamilton, Alexander. *The Papers of Alexander Hamilton.* Edited by Harold C. Syrett and Jacob E. Cooke. 27 vols. New York: Columbia University Press, 1961–87.

Heath, William. The Heath Papers. *Collections of the Massachusetts Historical Society,* 5th ser., vol. 4 (1878), 7th ser., vols. 4 and 5 (1904-1905). Boston: Massachusetts Historical Society, 1878–1905.

———. *Memoirs of Major-General Heath.* Boston: I. Thomas and E. T. Andrews, 1798.

Kingsley, Ronald F., ed., and Helga Doblin, trans. "A German Perspective on the American Attempt to Recapture the British Forts at Ticonderoga and Mount Independence on September 18, 1777." *Vermont History* 67, nos. 1 and 2 (1999): 5-26.

Livingston, William. *The Papers of William Livingston.* Edited by Carl E. Prince and Dennis P. Ryan. 5 vols. Trenton, NJ: New Jersey Historical Commission, 1979–1988.

Mather, Frederic G., ed. *New York in the Revolution as a Colony and State: A Collection of Documents and Records from the Office of the State Comptroller.* 2nd ed. 2 vols. Albany, NY: J. B. Lyon, printers, 1904.

Pell, Joshua. "Diary of Joshua Pell: An Officer of the British Army in America,1776–1777." Edited by James L. Onderonk. *Magazine of American History, with Notes and Queries* 2 (1878): 43-47, 107-112.

Prätorius, Christian Julius. "Journal of Lt. Colonel Christian Julius Prätorius, 2 June 1777–19 July 1777." Translated by Helga Doblin. *Bulletin of the Fort Ticonderoga Museum* 15, no. 3 (1991): 57-68.

Putnam, Rufus. *The Memoirs of Rufus Putnam and Certain Official Papers and Correspondence.* Edited by Rowena Buell. Boston: Houghton, Mifflin, 1905.

Riedesel, Friederike Charlotte Luise. *Letters and Journals Relating to the War of the American Revolution, and the Capture of the German Troops at Saratoga.* Translated by William L. Stone. Albany, NY: J. Munsell, 1867.

Riedesel, Friedrich Adolf. *Memoirs, and Letters and Journals, of Major General Riedesel during His Residence in America.* Edited by Max von Eelking, translated by William L. Stone. 2 vols. Albany, NY: J. Munsell, 1868.

Roberts, Lemuel. *Memoirs of Captain Lemuel Roberts: Containing Adventures in Youth, Vicissitudes Experienced as a Continental Soldier, His Sufferings as a Prisoner and Escape from Captivity, with Suitable Reflections on the Changes of Life.* Bennington, VT: Printed by Anthony Haswell, for the author, 1809.

Schuyler, Philip. "The Trial of Major General Schuyler, October, 1778." *New-York Historical Society Collections.* Vol. 12. New York: New-York Historical Society, 1880.

Smith, Paul H., and Ronald M. Gephart, eds. *Letters of Delegates to Congress, 1774–1789.* 26 vols. Washington, DC: Library of Congress, 1976–2000.

Sparks, Jared, ed. *Correspondence of the American Revolution.* 4 vols. Boston: Little Brown, 1853.

Specht, Johann Friedrich. *The Specht Journal: A Military Journal of the Burgoyne Campaign.* Translated by Helga Doblin. Edited by Mary C. Lynn. Westport, CT: Greenwood Press, 1995.

Starke, John. "His Account of John Brown's Attack on Ticonderoga in September, 1777." No. 2126, Fort Ticonderoga Museum Collection.

————. "Manuscript Map of John's Brown's Attack on Fort Ticonderoga in the Fall of 1777." T-1.63M, Fort Ticonderoga Museum Collection.

St. Clair, Arthur. *The St. Clair Papers: The Life and Public Services of Arthur St. Clair, Soldier of the Revolutionary War; President of the Continental Congress; and Governor of the North-Western Territory, with His Correspondence and Other Papers.* Edited by William Henry Smith. 2 vols. Cincinnati: Robert Clarke, 1882.

————. "The Trial of Major General St. Clair, August, 1778." *New-York Historical Society Collections.* Vol. 13. New York, 1881.

Thacher, James. *Military Journal of the American Revolution: Comprising a Detailed Account of the Principal Events and Battles of the Revolution, with Their Exact Dates, and a Biographical Sketch of the Most Prominent Generals.* Gansevoort, NY: Corner House Historical Publications, 1998 [orig. 1823].

Trumbull, John. *Autobiography, Reminiscences and Letters of John Trumbull, from 1756 to 1841.* New York: Wiley and Putnam, 1841.

————. "Letter from His Late Excellency Jonathan Trumbull, Esq. to Baron J. D. Vander Capellan." *Collections of the Massachusetts Historical Society,* ser.1, 6 (1799): 154-86.

von Hille, Julius Friedrich [?]. *The American Revolution: Garrison Life in French Canada and New York: Journal of an Officer in the Prinz Friedrich Regiment.* Translated by Helger Doblin, edited by Mary C. Lynn. Westport, CT: Greenwood Press, 1993.

Wallace, Willard M., ed. "The British Occupation of Fort Ticonderoga, 1777." *Bulletin of the Fort Ticonderoga Museum* 8, no. 7 (1951).

Walpole, Horace. *Journal of the Reign of King George the Third, from the Year 1771 to 1783.* Edited by Dr. [John] Doran. 2 vols. London: Richard Bentley, 1859.

Washington, George. *The Papers of George Washington.* Edited by W. W. Abbot et al. Charlottesville: University of Virginia Press, 1987–.

————. *The Papers of George Washington Digital Edition.* Edited by Theodore J. Crackel et al. Charlottesville: University of Virginia Press, Rotunda, 2007.

————. *The Writings of George Washington from the Original Manuscript Sources, 1745–1799.* 39 vols. Edited by John. C. Fitzpatrick. Washington, DC: Government Printing Office, 1931–1944.

————. *The Writings of George Washington: Being the Correspondence,*

Addresses, Messages, and Other Papers, Official and Private, Selected and Published from the Original Manuscripts. 12 vols. Edited by Jared Sparks. Boston: Russell, Odiorne, and Metcalf, and Hilliard, Gray, 1833–1839.

[Wayne, Anthony]. *Orderly Book of the Northern Army, at Ticonderoga and Mount Independence from October 17th, 1776, to January 1777, with Biographical and Explanatory Notes and an Appendix.* Albany, NY: J. Munsell, 1859.

———. "Original Letters from Gen. Wayne," *Historical Magazine* 5 (Feb. 1861).

Wilkinson, James. *Memoirs of My Own Times.* 3 vols. Philadelphia: Printed by Abraham Small, 1816.

SECONDARY SOURCES

Afable, Patricia O., and Madison S. Beeler. "Place Names." In *Languages.* Edited by Ives Goddard. Vol. 17 of Handbook of North American Indians. Edited by William C. Sturtevant, 20 vols. Washington, DC: Smithsonian Institution, 1978–2008.

Allen, Ira. *The Natural and Political History of the State of Vermont, One of the United States of America.* London: Printed by J. W. Myers, 1798.

Anderson, Fred. *Crucible of War: The Seven Years' War and the Fate of Empire in British North America, 1754–1766.* London: Faber and Faber, 2000.

Anderson, Troyer Steele. *Command of the Howe Brothers during the American Revolution.* New York: Oxford University Press, 1936.

Baker, William S. *Itinerary of General Washington from June 15, 1775, to December 23, 1783.* Philadelphia: J. B. Lippincott, 1892.

Blaisdell, Alfred F. *The Story of American History: For Elementary School* N.p.: Forgotten Books, 2016. Originally published 1902.

Blanco, Richard L. *Physician of the American Revolution: Jonathan Potts.* New York: Garland STPM Press, 1979.

Brooks, Noah. *Henry Knox, a Soldier of the Revolution: Major-general in the Continental Army, Washington's Chief of Artillery, First Secretary of War under the Constitution, Founder of the Society of the Cincinnati; 1750–1806.* New York: G. P. Putnam's Sons, 1900.

Bush, Martin R. *Revolutionary Enigma: A Reappraisal of General Philip Schuyler of New York.* Empire State Historical Publications Series, no. 80. Port Washington, NY: Ira J. Friedman, 1969.

Callahan, North. *Henry Knox: George Washington's General.* New York: Rinehart, 1958.

Calloway, Colin G. *The Indian World of George Washington: The First President, the First Americans, and the Birth of the Nation.* New York: Oxford University Press, 2018.

Cannon, Richard. *Historical Record of the Thirty-First, or, the Huntingdonshire Regiment of Foot: Containing an Account of the Formation of the Regiment in 1702, and of Its Subsequent Services to 1850.* London: Parker, Furnivall & Parker, 1850.

Carrington, Henry Beebe. *Battles of the American Revolution, 1775-1781: Historical and Military Criticism with Topographical Illustration.* New York: A. S. Barnes, 1876.

Clement, Justin, and Douglas R. Cubbison. "'The Artillery Never Gained More Honour': The British and Hesse-Hanau Artillery Gun Boats at the Battle of Valcour Island." *Journal of the Society for Army Historical Research* 85, no. 343 (2007): 247-55.

Cohen, Eliot A. *Conquered into Liberty: Two Centuries of Battles along the Great Warpath that Made the American Way of War.* New York: Free Press, 2012.

Corbett, Theodore. *No Turning Point: The Saratoga Campaign in Perspective.* Norman: University of Oklahoma Press, 2014.

Cubbison, Douglas R. *The Artillery Never Gained More Honour: The British Artillery in the 1776 Valcour Island and 1777 Saratoga Campaigns.* Fleischmanns, NY: Purple Mountain Press, 2007.

———. *Burgoyne and the Saratoga Campaign: His Papers.* Norman: University of Oklahoma Press, 2012.

Davis, Robert P. *Where a Man Can Go: Major General William Phillips, British Royal Artillery, 1731–1781.* Westport, CT: Greenwood Press, 1999.

Dechame, Roger R. P. "Why Carillon." *Bulletin of the Fort Ticonderoga Museum* 13, No. 6 (1980): 432-46.

DeCosta, B. F. *The Fight at Diamond Island, Lake George.* New York: J. Sabin & Sons, 1872.

Duffy, John J., Samuel B. Hand, and Ralph H. Orth, eds. "Green Mountain Continental Rangers." *Vermont Encyclopedia.* Hanover, NH: University Press of New England, 2003.

Egleston, Thomas. *The Life of John Paterson, Major General in the Revolutionary Army.* New York: G. P. Putnam's Sons, 1894.

E. M. [Eleanor M. Murray]. "The Invasion of Northern New York, 1780." *Bulletin of the Fort Ticonderoga Museum* 7, no. 4 (1946): 3-12.

Everard, H. *History of Thos Farrington's Regiment: Subsequently Designated the 29th (Worcestershire) Foot, 1694–1891.* Worcester: Littlebury, 1891.

Everest, Alan S. *Moses Hazen and the Canadian Refugees in the American Revolution.* Syracuse, NY: Syracuse University Press, 1976.

Fisher, David Hackett. *Champlain's Dream.* New York: Simon and Schuster, 2008.

Fiske, James. *The American Revolution.* 2 vols. Boston: Houghton Mifflin, 1891.

Fitzpatrick, John C., ed. *Calendar of the Correspondence, of George Washington: Commander in Chief of the Continental Army, with the Officers.* 4 vols. Washington, DC: Government Printing Office, 1915.

Ford, Worthington Chauncey, comp. *British Officers Serving in America, 1754–1774.* Boston: David Clapp & Son, 1894.

———. *British Officers Serving in the American Revolution, 1774–1783.* Brooklyn, NY: Historical Printing Club, 1897.

Fredriksen, John C. *America's Military Adversaries: From Colonial Times to the Present.* Santa Barbara, CA: ABC-CLIO, 2002.

Furneaux, Rupert. *The Battle of Saratoga.* New York: Stein and Day, 1971.

Gerlach, Don R. *Proud Patriot: Philip Schuyler and the War of Independence, 1775–1783.* Syracuse, NY: Syracuse University Press, 1964.

Gordon, William. *The History of the Rise, Progress, and Establishment of the Independence of the United States of America; Including an Account of the late War; and of the Thirteen Colonies, from their Origin to that Period.* 4 vols. London: Printed for the author, 1788.

Graymont, Barbara. *The Iroquois in the American Revolution.* Syracuse, NY: Syracuse University Press, 1972.

Gruber, Ira D. *The Howe Brothers and the American Revolution.* New York: W. W. Norton, 1972.

Hamilton, Edward Pierce. *Fort Ticonderoga: Key to a Continent.* Boston: Little, Brown, 1964.

Hargrove, Richard. *General John Burgoyne.* Newark: University of Delaware Press, 1983.

Heitman, Francis B. *Historical Register of Officers of the Continental Army during the War of the Revolution, April 1775, to December 1783.* Washington, DC: Rare Book Shop Publishing, 1914.

Hoffman, Elliot W. "The Germans against Ticonderoga." *Bulletin of the Fort Ticonderoga Museum* 14, no. 1 (1981): 32-39.

Holland, Josiah Gilbert. *History of Western Massachusetts: The Counties of Hampden, Hampshire, Franklin, and Berkshire,* 2 vols. Springfield, MA: Samuel Bowles, 1855.

Howe, Archibald M. *Colonel John Brown of Pittsfield, Massachusetts: The Brave Accuser of Benedict Arnold.* Boston: W. B. Clark, 1908.

Howson, Gerald. *Burgoyne of Saratoga: A Biography.* New York: Times Books, 1979.

Hoyt, Edward A. "The Pawlet Expedition, September 1777." *Vermont History* 75, no. 2 (2007).

Jaques, Tony. *Dictionary of Battles and Sieges.* Westport, CT: Greenwood Press, 2007.

Katcher, Philip R. N. *Encyclopedia of British, Provincial, and German Army Units, 1775-1783.* Harrisburg, PA: Stackpole Books, 1973.

Kaufmann, J. E., and Tomasz Idzikowski. *Fortress America: The Forts that Defended America, 1600 to the Present.* Cambridge, MA: Da Capo, 2004.

Ketchum, Richard M. *Saratoga: Turning Point of America's Revolutionary War.* New York: Henry Holt, 1997.

Lasseray, André. *Les Fran ais sous les Treize Étoiles, 1775-1783.* Paris: Macon, 1935.

Leiter, Mary Theresa. *Biographical Sketches of the Generals of the Continental Army of the Revolution.* Cambridge, MA: John Wilson and Son, 1889.

Lender, Mark Edward. *Cabal!: The Plot against General Washington.* Yardley, PA: Westholme, 2019.

———. *The War for American Independence.* Santa Barbara, CA: ABC-CLIO, 2016.

Lesser, Charles H., ed. *The Sinews of Independence: Monthly Strength Reports of the Continental Army.* Chicago: University of Chicago Press, 1976.

Lonergan, Carroll Vincent. *Ticonderoga: Historic Portage.* Ticonderoga, NY: Fort Mount Hope Society Press, 1959.

Lossing, Benson John, ed. *The American Historical Record, and Repository of Notes and Queries.* Philadelphia: John E. Potter, 1874.

———. *The Life and Times of Philip Schuyler.* 2 vols. New York: Sheldon, 1872-73.

————. *The Pictorial Field-Book of the American Revolution: Or, Illustrations, by Pen and Pencil, of the History, Biography, Scenery, Relics, and Traditions of the War for Independence.* 2 vols. New York: Harper & Brothers, 1852.

Lugusz, Michael O. *With Musket and Tomahawk: The Saratoga Campaign and the Wilderness War of 1777.* Philadelphia: Casemate, 2010.

Luzader, John. *Decision on the Hudson: The Battle of Saratoga.* Fort Washington, PA: Eastern National, 2002.

Martin, James Kirby. *Benedict Arnold, Revolutionary Hero: An American Warrior Reconsidered.* New York: New York University Press, 1997.

Martin, James Kirby, and Mark Edward Lender. *A Respectable Army: The Military Origins of the Republic, 1763–1789.* 3rd ed. Malden, MA: Wiley Blackwell, 2015.

Mattern, David B. *Benjamin Lincoln and the American Revolution.* Columbia: University of South Carolina Press, 1995.

McIlwraith, Jean N. *Sir Frederick Haldimand.* London, ON: T. C. & E. C. Jack, 1905.

Miller, William J. "The Adirondack Mountains." *New York State Museum Bulletin* 193 (1917): 1-164.

Minz, Max M. *The Generals of Saratoga: John Burgoyne and Horatio Gates.* New Haven, CT: Yale University Press, 1992.

Nelson, Paul David. *Anthony Wayne: Soldier of the Early Republic.* Bloomington: Indiana University Press, 1985.

————. *General Horatio Gates: A Biography.* Baton Rouge: Louisiana State University Press, 1976.

————. *The Life of William Alexander, Lord Stirling.* Tuscaloosa, AL: University of Alabama Press, 1987.

Nester, William R. *The Epic Battles for Ticonderoga, 1758.* Albany: State University of New York Press, 2008.

O'Shaughnessy, Andrew Jackson. *The Men Who Lost America: British Leadership, the American Revolution, and the Fate of the Empire.* New Haven, CT: Yale University Press, 2013.

Paine, Lauran. *Gentleman Johnny: The Life of General John Burgoyne.* London: Hale, 1973.

Pancake, John S. *1777: The Year of the Hangman.* Tuscaloosa: University of Alabama Press, 1977.

Peckham, Howard H. *The Colonial Wars, 1689–1762.* Chicago: University of Chicago Press, 2001.

————, ed. *The Toll of Independence: Engagements and Battle Casualties of the American Revolution.* Chicago: University of Chicago Press, 1974.

Pell, John H. G. "Schuyler, Peter." *Dictionary of Canadian Biography* 2 (1701-1740). Accessed Oct. 7, 2018. http://www.biographi.ca/en/bio/schuyler_peter_1657_1723_24_2E.html.

Pell, Robert T. "John Brown and the Dash for Ticonderoga." *Bulletin of the Fort Ticonderoga Museum* 2, no. 1 (1930): 23-39.

Pell, Stephen. *Fort Ticonderoga: A Short History.* Ticonderoga, NY: Fort Ticonderoga Museum, 1966.

Puls, Mark. *Henry Knox: Visionary General of the American Revolution.* New York: Palgrave Macmillan, 2008.

Ramsay, David. *The History of the American Revolution.* Philadelphia: Printed by R. Aitken & son, 1789.

Randall, Willard Sterne. *Ethan Allen: His Life and Times.* New York: W. W. Norton, 2012.

"Return of the Killed and Wounded of the Detachment under the Command of Major Carleton, the 11th of October 1780." *Bulletin of the Fort Ticonderoga Museum* 7, no. 4 (July 1776): 25.

Roberts, Robert B. *New York's Forts in the Revolution.* Rutherford, NJ: Fairleigh Dickinson University Press, 1980.

Schuyler, G. W. *Colonial New York; Philip Schuyler and His Family.* 2 vols. New York: Charles Scribner's Sons, 1885.

Scott, James, Melinda Walker, and Aaron Nash. "The Raid on Ballston, 1780." *Bulletin of the Fort Ticonderoga Museum* 7, no. 4 (July 1946): 12-24.

Selesky, Harold E., ed. *Encyclopedia of the American Revolution.* 2nd ed., 2 vols. Detroit: Thomson Gale, 2006.

Stach, Stephen. "A New Look at the Regimental Colors of the Second New Hampshire Regiment 1777." *Military Collector and Historian* 37, no. 3 (1985).

Starbuck, David R. "The General Hospital on Mount Independence: 18th-Century Health Care at a Revolutionary War Cantonment." *Northeast Historical Archaeology* 19 (1990): 50-67.

Stark, Caleb. *Memoir and Official Correspondence of Gen. John Stark, with Notices of Several Other Officers of the Revolution. Also, a Biography of Capt. Phinehas Stevens and of Col. Robert Rogers, with an Account of His Services in America during the "Seven Years' War."* Concord, NH: Parker Lyon, 1860.

Stille, Charles J. *Major-General Anthony Wayne and the Pennsylvania Line in the Continental Army.* Philadelphia: J. B. Lipincott, 1893.

Stockwell, Mary. *Unlikely General: "Mad" Anthony Wayne and the Battle for America.* New Haven, CT: Yale University Press, 2018.

Stone, William L., ed. *Ballads and Poems Relating to the Burgoyne Campaign.* Albany, NY: Joel Munsell's Sons, 1893.

———. *The Campaign of Lieut. Gen. John Burgoyne, and the Expedition of Lieut. Col. Barry St. Leger.* Albany, NY: Joel Munsell, 1877.

———, trans. *Letters of Brunswick and Hessian Officers during the American Revolution.* Albany, NY: Joel Munsell's Sons, 1891.

Storozynski, Alex. *The Peasant Prince: Thaddeus Kosciuszko and the Age of Revolution.* New York: St. Martin's, 2009.

Stryker, William S., comp. *Official Register of the Officers and Men of New Jersey in the Revolutionary War.* Trenton, NJ: Wm. T. Nicholson, 1872.

Sulte, B. "Le Régiment de Carignan," *Proceedings and Transactions of the Royal Society of Canada,* 2nd ser., sec. 1, 8 (1902): 25-95.

Swiggett, Howard. *War out of Niagara: Walter Butler and the Tory Rangers.* New York: Columbia University Press, 1933.

Taylor, Alan. *The Divided Ground: Indians, Settlers, and the Northern Borderland of the American Revolution.* New York: Alfred A. Knopf, 2006.

Tomczak, Richard. "French Canadian Laborers in the 1777 Northern Campaign." *Bulletin of the Fort Ticonderoga Museum* 17, no. 1 (2016): 46-56.

Van de Water, Frederic F. *The Reluctant Republic: Vermont, 1724–1791.* New York: John Day, 1941.

Venter, Bruce M. *The Battle of Hubbardton: The Rear Guard Action That Saved America.* Charleston, SC: History Press, 2015.

———. "Behind Enemy Lines: Americans Attack Burgoyne's Supply Line." *Patriots of the American Revolution Magazine* (2011): 12-18.

Verney, Jack. *The Good Regiment: The Carignan-Salières Regiment in Canada, 1665–1668.* Montreal: McGill-Queen's University Press, 1991.

Ward, Christopher. *The War of the Revolution.* 2 vols. Edited by John Richard Alden. New York: Macmillan, 1952.

Wardner, Henry Steele. "The Haldimand Negotiations." *Proceedings of the Vermont Historical Society* 2, no. 1 (1931): 3-29.

Warren, Mercy [Otis]. *History of the Rise, Progress and Termination of the American Revolution. Interspersed with Biographical, Political and Moral Observations.* 3 vols. Boston: Manning and Loring, 1805.

Washington, Ida H., and Paul A. Washington. *Carleton's Raid.* Weybridge, VT: Cherry Tree Books, 1977.

Watt, Gavin K. *The Burning of the Valleys: Daring Raids from Canada against the New York Frontier in the Fall of 1780.* Toronto: Dundurn Press, 1997.

———. *Fire & Desolation: The Revolutionary War's 1778 Campaign as Waged from Quebec and Niagara against the American Frontiers.* Toronto: Dundurn Press, 2017.

———. *I am heartily ashamed: The Revolutionary War's Final Campaign as Waged from Canada in 1782.* Toronto: Dundurn Press, 2010.

Whittemore, Charles. *A General of the Revolution: John Sullivan of New Hampshire.* New York: Columbia University Press, 1961.

Wright, Robert K., Jr. *The Continental Army.* Washington, DC: Center of Military History, US Army, 1983.

THESES AND UNPUBLISHED STUDIES

Chadsey, Thomas Albert. "General Haldimand and the Vermont Negotiations, 1780–1783." Master's thesis, University of Ottawa, 1953.

Lenig, Wayne. "The Ross Expedition: The Battle of Johnstown and the Death of Walter Butler." Historical Methods Paper, University of Buffalo, 1973.

Urwin, Gregory J. W. "From Parade Ground to Battlefield: How the British Army Adapted to War in North America, 1775–1783." Presented at the 2019 International Conference on the American Revolution, Museum of the American Revolution, Oct. 4, 2019, Philadelphia.

INTERNET SOURCES

ACAD: A Cambridge Alumni Database. University of Cambridge. Accessed Jan. 9, 2019. http://venn.lib.cam.ac.uk/Documents/acad/intro.html.

Aikey, Michael. "Ballston Raid of 1780: Military Operation or a Time to Settle Old Scores." *Journal of the American Revolution*, Dec. 6, 2017. Accessed May 7, 2019. https://allthingsliberty.com/2017/12/ballston-raid-1780-military-operation-time-settle-old-scores/.

Browne, G. P. "Carleton, Guy, 1st Baron Dorchester." *Dictionary of Canadian Biography* 5 (1801–1820). Accessed Nov. 16, 2018. http:// www.biographi.ca/en/bio/carleton_guy_5E.html.

"By Taylors of Their Respective Companies." Oct. 17, 2014. Fort Ticonderoga. Accessed Dec. 9, 2018. https:/fortticonderoga.org/blog/by-taylors-of-their-respective-companies/.

Clark, R. L. "History of the Town of South Hero." *Gazetteer of Vermont.* Hayward, 1849. Accessed May 20, 2019. http://sites.rootsweb.com/ ~vermont/GrandIsleSouthHero.html.

Dictionary of Canadian Biography. http://www.biographi.ca/en/.

Douglas Archives. http://www.douglashistory.co.uk/history/asadou glas.htm.

Eccles, J. W. "Rigaud de Vaudreuil de Cavagnial, Pierre de, Marquis de Vaudreuil." *Dictionary of Canadian Biography* 4 (1771–1800). Accessed Aug. 3, 2021. http://www.biographi.ca/en/bio/rigaud_ de_vaudreuil_ de_cavagnial_pierre_de_4E.html.

Founders Online. National Archives. https://founders.archives.gov/.

Haldimand Papers. *Heritage Canadiana.* http://heritage.canadiana.ca.

"Historic Average: Ticonderoga, NY." intellicast: The Authority in Expert Weather. Accessed Oct. 1, 2021. http://www.intellicast.com /Local/History.aspx?month=12.

"Skeffington Lutwidge." *The Royal Navy, 1776–1815: A Biographical History and Chronicle.* Accessed Jan. 9, 2019. https://morethan nelson.com/officer/skeffington-lutwidge/.

Stokesbury, James. "Burgoyne, John." *Dictionary of Canadian Biography* 4 (1771–1800). Accessed Sept. 30, 2021. http://www.biographi.ca/ en/bio.php?id_nbr=1782.

Sutherland, Stuart R. J., Pierre Tousignant, and Madeleine Dionne-Tousignant. "Haldimand, Sir Frederick." In *Dictionary of Canadian Biography* 5 (1801–1820). University of Toronto/Université Laval, 2003–. Accessed Apr. 23, 2019. http://www.biographi.ca/en/ bio/haldimand_frederick_5E.html.

"Too Opposite Characters." Fort Ticonderoga Museum. Aug. 22, 2014. Accessed Dec. 7, 2020. https://www.fortticonderoga.org/blog/too-opposite-characters/.

Venter, Bruce. "The Forgotten Battle of Diamond Island on Lake George." *Adirondack Almanac,* June 17, 2015. Accessed Apr. 16, 2019. https://www.adirondackalmanack.com/2015/06/forgotten-battle-diamond-island-lake-george.html.

ACKNOWLEDGMENTS

MY FIRST CONTACT with Fort Ticonderoga came as part of a family vacation in the Adirondack Mountains. I was thirteen years old, and while touring the fort I wandered away from my parents and brothers. On my own for the better part of two hours, I scoured every part of the fort and got into some areas I'm sure I was not supposed to go (security is better today). I was hooked, and the history bug has never left me. When the Fort Ticonderoga Museum proposed a trilogy on the fort, and when Westholme Publishing agreed to publish the three volumes, I was delighted to accept an invitation to write one of them. In fact, it's been a project I've particularly enjoyed—a reminder of how and why I've pursued a career in history.

Fort Ticonderoga is blessed with a talented and dedicated staff, and I relied heavily on them during my research and writing. My thanks go to Beth Hill, Fort Ticonderoga's President and CEO, for her support of the project and making me welcome during my visits to the fort. Miranda L. Peters, Director of Collections, and Tabitha Hubbard, Assistant Registrar, at various times guided me through the library's wonderful print and manuscript collections. Curator Matthew B. P. Keagle's assistance was indispensable. An established scholar himself, he carefully read my chapters and made innumerable suggestions, prevented many a slip, located key manuscripts, and helped me navigate the transcript and on-line versions of the invaluable Frederick

Haldimand Papers. He shared his time and expertise freely in person, via e-mail, and over the telephone. Many thanks, Matt.

I also owe considerable thanks to Bruce Venter, Bill Welsch, Steven Elliott, and David Ward—fine historians all—who reviewed sections of my manuscript. Their suggestions led to many improvements, and I learned from all of them. At the Fort Plain Museum, Brian Mack kindly read Chapter Six and invited me to present on Col. John Brown's raid on Ticonderoga at the annual Mohawk Valley Conference on the American Revolution. At Westholme, Bruce H. Franklin was enthusiastic about the Ticonderoga trilogy from the start. Once more, I've appreciated his advice and the fact that in his hands, Westholme produces such high-quality volumes and makes publishing such a pleasurable experience. Ron Silverman brought his sharp copyeditor's eye to my manuscript, for which I am grateful. *Fort Ticonderogay, The Last Campaigns* is the third book I've written at Sugar & Twine, Richmond's best coffee shop and bakery. I still swear by the cinnamon rolls, but consider the almond puffs.

As always, Penny Booth Page read everything with her practiced editorial eye. Nothing goes to other readers without her blessing, and her efforts make Bruce Franklin's easier. She really is the best.

All errors, of course, are mine.

INDEX